WILD
MEDICINAL
PLANTS

Anny Schneider

Photographs: Ulysse Charette

WILD MEDICINAL PLANTS

What to look for
When to harvest
How to use

Translated by Linda Hilpold

STACKPOLE BOOKS

Printed in Canada
10 9 8 7 6 5 4 3 2 1

First edition

Cover design: Peter Maher
Electronic formatting: Jean Lightfoot Peters

Library of Congress Cataloging-in-Publication Data

Schneider, Anny.
    [Plantes sauvages mèdicinales. English]
    Wild medicinal plants: know them, gather them, use them / Anny Schneider; photographs by Ulysse Charette.—1st ed.
       p. cm.
    "First published in English in Canada by Key Porter Books Ltd., Toronto, Canada, 2002"— T.p. verso.
    Includes bibliographical references and index.
    ISBN 0-8117-2987-7
    1. Medicinal plants—North America. 2. Materia medica, Vegetable—North America. I. Title.

RS171 .S3613 2002
615'.321—dc21
                                 2001055148

Table of Contents

To medicinal plants,
To the true friends of medicinal plants
And to their Creator.
Blessed are they
For their many graces!

To Ulysse Charette for his dedication, his patience and his perseverance.

To Danièle Laberge for having opened her magnificent garden and her heart, and for sharing her vast wealth of knowledge.

To the Miel Brothers for having lent me their beautiful home for all these years.

To Lise Côté for her open mind.

Anny Schneider

WARNING

*T*his guide on the use of wild medicinal plants discusses, among other things, traditional methods of treatment according to recipes proven over the centuries by herbalists, apothecaries and physicians, past and present.

None of the directions for use exclude obtaining in advance a precise diagnosis from a medical practitioner certified by the official health care system, especially in the case of a chronic illness.

I am nothing but an imperfect interpreter of this marvelous curative art, and in my short life I have not yet been able to check all the details of what I am passing on. But for me, my family and for all those I have advised and cared for over the past 20 years, curative plants, when chosen carefully and used properly, and with the grace of God, will cure almost all ailments.

Introduction

The study of plants is for those willing to abandon themselves to an unending source of innocent, sweet pleasures, and whose moral bearing is delicate, pure and sacred.
—L.F. Jéhan

Since the beginning of civilization, the plant world has contributed to the survival of the human race, not only as a source of food and oxygen, but also as a source of natural remedies. Currently in the West, we are witnessing a veritable tidal wave of information, with books and magazines proclaiming the merits and medicinal effectiveness of plants. Unfortunately, the process of extracting, standardizing, and marketing these simple curative herbs has made them unusually expensive and increasingly less effective. Common sense and experience have shown that plants freshly picked, which involve a minimum amount of processing, are better able to retain their active principles and therapeutic value.

In this book, I present my gentle green friends, the wild medicinal plants. Nature offers them to us for free, but it is important to harvest them mindful of the need to leave enough of them to ensure their survival, both for the good of the species and for that of our descendants.

I am a woman of the forests and the fields, an ordinary girl, a daughter of the Earth, who is proud of her ancestral heritage. I became interested in wildflowers as a child growing up in rural Alsace. What fascinating discoveries! Later, thanks to my studies in phytotherapy (plant-based therapy), I was able to name the medicinal plants and discover their characteristics and virtues. I have faithfully visited them for some 20 years now. One does not become an herbalist in a few months. Despite this long apprenticeship, I still cannot claim to know all the plants or, for that matter, all their qualities, for nature is too generous and prolific. Nonetheless, this fascinating world remains within reach of all those with an open mind.

I deliberately chose to describe the wild plants and trees that are widely found throughout the northern hemisphere. I am not a specialist in plant biology, nor a botanist or a plant pharmacologist, but rather an herbalist at the service of both people and nature. I have attempted to render a popular science as old as the world more comprehensible, and to propose a treatment and survival tool accessible to all children of the Earth. My only goal is to convey to you, dear reader, that nature is a beautiful, bountiful garden filled with good things for those who know how to unlock its secrets and who respect it.

This illustrated guide offers a little of this immense plant diversity which is, unfortunately, threatened in Canada as in Europe. I sincerely hope that these living treasures bring you happiness and good health for a long time to come.

Editor's Note: Comparing metric measurement equivalents can be confusing. For example, while 20 grams of crushed figwort equals 3 tablespoons, 20 grams of slippery elm equals 1 1/4 tablespoons—because of the different weights of the measured material. The standard measurements in this book are followed by their metric volume or liquid measurement equivalents, shown in parentheses, which are estimated as accurately as possible.

CHAPTER 1

The History of Phytotherapy

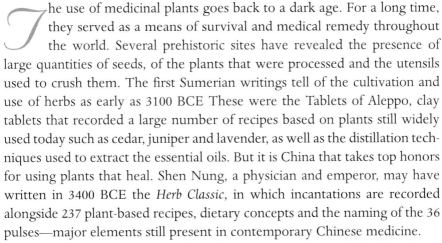

*It is time to return to a simple and natural
medicine, one that made generations of people strong,
and old age long and peaceful.*

—DR. MADEUF
Health for Everyone

The use of medicinal plants goes back to a dark age. For a long time, they served as a means of survival and medical remedy throughout the world. Several prehistoric sites have revealed the presence of large quantities of seeds, of the plants that were processed and the utensils used to crush them. The first Sumerian writings tell of the cultivation and use of herbs as early as 3100 BCE These were the Tablets of Aleppo, clay tablets that recorded a large number of recipes based on plants still widely used today such as cedar, juniper and lavender, as well as the distillation techniques used to extract the essential oils. But it is China that takes top honors for using plants that heal. Shen Nung, a physician and emperor, may have written in 3400 BCE the *Herb Classic*, in which incantations are recorded alongside 237 plant-based recipes, dietary concepts and the naming of the 36 pulses—major elements still present in contemporary Chinese medicine.

As early as 2500 BCE, in India, physicians noted in the Veda "the physician is the priest to whom God has entrusted the guarding of the human temple." In addition to prayers and dietary advice, they often recommended the use of aromatic herbs such as cinnamon, citronella, sandalwood or vervain.

The Bible often mentions medicinal plants. The Old Testament contains a detailed recipe for holy oil (Ex. 30, 22–25) that calls for precious spices and refers to the Queen of Sheba who brought back to Salomon huge quantities of myrrh from the region of Aromata. This was used during religious ceremonies, and for sterilizing homes and wounds. Salomon, the greatest king and sage of Israel, declared: "God causes the earth to produce its own remedies and a sensible man does not disdain them."

The Egyptians were highly qualified in the art of using plants. They were obsessed with cleanliness and practiced daily fumigations using myrrh, olibanum (purifying aromatic resins) and thyme, washed with kaolin, senna and olive oil, and chewed propolis. They believed—not incorrectly—that unpleasant odors were the source of illness and that constant purification was essential. They also worshiped garlic and onion, believed to keep misfortune and evil spirits away; they even fed their slaves with these substances to strengthen them and to care for them. The Ebers Papyrus (1600 B.C.) is a 20m-long scroll cataloging more than 700 plants used in Egypt, most of which are still used in the same way today.

Greece continued to use Egyptian knowledge, but it was Hippocrates, the ancient "father of medicine," born on the island of Kos, who conceived the basics of medical practice. He asserted, for example, that at least 72 factors needed to be considered to determine the cause of an illness. To return to good health, he advised rest, a healthy diet, hydrotherapy and massage, not to mention the possible use of 300 plants.

In his treatise on the natural sciences entitled *Physics*, the great philosopher Aristotle (384–322 B.C.) attributed a soul to plants. In 300 B.C., his disciple, the philosopher and naturalist Theophrastus (372–395), wrote the *History of Plants*, a medical treatise documenting 455 plants and their use. Much later, during the first century, Pedanius Dioscorides, a Greek physician in the service of the emperor Nero, described in detail the shape of more than 600 plants and how to use them in his famous *De Materia Medica* (*On Medical Matters*). Galen (A.D. 129–ca. 199), a Greek physician, called the "father of pharmacy," knew about anatomy and chemistry. He discovered several very complex remedies such as a cure-all that contained no fewer than 84 plants. This remedy was copied and sold even to this day.

Much later, the Arab physician Avicenna (980–1037), or ibn Sina, wrote, in Latin, a very interesting summary of previous medicines, published in his *Canon medicina* (*Canon of Medicine*). He added African remedies such as camphor or nux vomica (poison nut).

During the first centuries of Christianity, the West saw several wars, famines and epidemics. In the event of illness, only the local healer, who received her knowledge from a relative or a master, cared for the ill. Women healers were more numerous than their male counterparts for different reasons. First, eligible men left to fight in the wars and were therefore not available to engage in the healing arts. Second, the Druidic therapeutic approach was to choose mostly women, called *vates*, or women healers who worshiped the Mother goddess personified by the earth. Finally, it was believed that woman who, by her nature, gives and perpetuates life, is closer to the secrets of nature, of the earth, and of the harvests it so tirelessly offers.

Saint Hildegard, the abbess of Bingen in Germany at the beginning of the 11th century, established a bridge between 2 great therapeutic approaches that would mark the second millennium: she created a link between physical health and that of the soul, thanks to faith and a knowledge of the nature of both the human body and plants. It was the Nestorians, Syrian monks exiled in India towards the 6th century—and to the Benedictines who recopied them century after century—that we owe all the manuscripts concerning phytotherapy including those of Hildegard of Bingen. If she had lived 2 centuries later, she would have been burned at the stake as a witch, as had thousands of other women in Europe between the 13th and 17th centuries, under the Inquisition, a purge organized by the devout followers of the Catholic Church.

The Salerno medical school, created in the 11th century in Italy, and that of Montpellier in France, in 1220, trained the first recognized physicians. Their training was based on knowledge of the plant world. Today, it is still possible to find numerous writings relating to their teachings, as well as gardens of simples (plants harvested for their medicinal properties) that resemble the medicinal plants of old from the East and West.

The Renaissance, a time when reason was supposed to replace superstition, curiously marks the beginning of alchemy, which arose from the Church, with Albertus Magnus (1200–1280) and his treatises on magic and

Roger Bacon and his strange experiments recorded in his *Opus*. Nicknamed the "father of chemistry," Paracelsus, a physician and alchemist born in 1493 in Switzerland, and whose real name was Theophrastus Philippus Aureolus Bombastus von Hohenheim, was the first to question the theories of Hippocrates and Galen. He announced his theory of signatures, according to which there exists a link between the appearance of a plant and its intrinsic properties, therefore, between its form and its function. This theory is justified. For example, consider the similarity between a peony, its virtues and its blood-red color, or celandine juice and bile, or the softness and shape of lamb's ear and the human ear. Although we owe a more effective medicine to Paracelsus, the premature death of many patients can also be attributed to him. It was he who concentrated the active principles of the poppy in laudanum and those of mercury in calomel, a powerful purgative. These two medications were extremely dangerous.

Englishman John Gerard wrote the first bestseller of the Renaissance, *The Herball*, in 1597.

In 1652, Nicholas Culpeper published his book *The Complete Herball*. It was reprinted roughly 100 times, but discredited because its author was a Protestant, moreover, one who constantly referred to astrology.

With the conquest of the New World, new remedies appeared such as coca, quinine, cascara, buckthorn, goldenseal, Indian tobacco and sarsaparilla. Many settlers survived in North America thanks to the Indians and their knowledge of medicinal plants.

The English settler Samuel Thompson (1760–1843) is a typical example of the link between tradition and modernity in North America. He studied the power of plants with the aboriginals and women healers of his area, and created a school called the Reformed Medical Society to train naturopathic physicians. He was officially opposed to the Regulars, who mostly practiced purging and bleeding. From this rebel branch were born the Eclectics, who taught thousands of herbalists until 1939, and the Physiomedicalists, who influenced English medicine. English medicine continues to use many North American plants.

At the beginning of the 19th century, the first experiments involving the synthesis of active principles drawn from plants took place: digitalin for the heart is derived from foxglove, while heroin, morphine and calming alkaloids are produced from poppies, and salicylic acid (used in the preparation of aspirin) is made from white willow. Gradually, the use of medicinal plants is evolving. Since the beginning of the 20th century, herbalists and phytotherapists in Europe and in North America have been fined, imprisoned and banned from practicing. Despite this, plant medicine has undergone a resurgence in popularity, and there is hope, as we begin the new millennium, that the trend will continue.

In France, Drs. Yves Gattefossé, Henri Leclerc, Jean-Marie Pelt and Jean Valnet, as well as Fabrice Bardeau, Maurice Mésségué, Jean Palaiseul and Yves Rocher, all contributed to restore to medicinal plants their status as "true healers." In North America, the stars of phytotherapy, both living and deceased, are many. Some of the more famous men include John Christopher, John Lust, Jethro Kloss, Michael Castleman, Michael Tierra, Varro Tyler and Fritz Weiss. Women are once again distinguishing themselves in this area. Rosemary Gladstar, Alma Hutchens and Susun Weed in the United States, as well as Danièle Laberge and Marie Provost in Quebec, represent some of the many female faces of modern phytotherapy. Today, herbs still make up 80% of all remedies used around the world and represent 40% of the basic ingredients used in allopathic (treatment of disease by conventional means) remedies. Paradoxically, the biggest laboratories on the planet are seeking new therapeutic molecules which copy those of previously unknown plants, or which are the subjects of renewed chemical research. Rather than relying on tradition and the know-how of herbalists, we prefer to ignore them and to standardize plant life for purely lucrative reasons. Indeed, the pharmaceutical industry constitutes the primary source of global capital.

Despite all this, things are changing and there is a gradual return to common sense. People are becoming more conscious of nature's generosity and of their responsibility for their own health and the health of their children. We are witnessing a new understanding of vital emotional and psychic needs, and those who now pick plants to treat their ailments at little cost are increasingly following the advice of naturopaths.

In North America and in Europe (Spain, Germany and England), herbalists are setting up corporations. They are joining forces, acting and defining their goals based on reciprocity and openness. Nearly half of all American universities offer courses on alternative therapies. As in France, plants are increasingly regaining their place in pharmacies, natural food stores and even grocery stores. I am pleased to see this, as I consciously participate in this movement through teaching and promoting the merits of medicinal plants and their immeasurable qualities.

Cultivation and harvesting of medicinal plants in the Middle Ages (anonymous).

REMARKABLE FIGURES IN THE HISTORY OF PHYTOTHERAPY

A physician has no need of eloquence or literary knowledge, but a deep understanding of nature and its benefits.

PARACELSUS

LABYRINTHIS MEDICORUM

Antiquity

- **Hippocrates** (460–377 B.C.) nicknamed the "father of medicine" or the "Master of Kos," developed the basics of modern medicine by favoring observation over myth and superstition. He defined the Code of Ethics for the medical profession, still used and known as the Hippocratic oath. He also established a comprehensive diagnostic questionnaire and wrote many treatises including *Corpus Hippocratum*, especially devoted to the treatment of illness through the use of plants.
- **Cato the Elder**, or Marcus Porcius Cato (234–149 B.C.), was a politician and a writer who tried to stop the decline of Roman civilization. He was called "the Censor" because of his legendary severity. He advocated, among other things, a return to the land to counter slackening morals. He grew medicinal plants, which he mentions in his treatise on agriculture entitled *De re rustica*.
- **Pliny the Elder**, or Gaius Plinius Secundus (23–79), was a Roman writer. In the 37 volumes of his *Natural History*, he compiled more than 2000 works. He often describes with passion the medicinal virtues of plants.
- **Pedanius Dioscorides** (40–90) was originally a Greek physician in Nero's army. He wrote an important treatise on phytotherapy entitled *De Materia Medica* in which he describes 600 plants and their therapeutic uses.
- **Galen** (131–201), a Greek physician, became famous in Rome by treating the emperor Marcus Aurelius and his sons. He wrote approximately 500 medical treatises. He was the first to describe the human anatomy, and to reveal the usefulness of metals and the importance of the bad humors regarding illness. His theories influenced medical thinking for 10 centuries. He gave his name to galenical (the area of pharmacy that deals with the creation of pharmaceutical products by extracting one or more active

constituents of a plant). He fearlessly combined up to 100 substances in his absolute or cure-all remedies.

The Middle Ages

- **Avicenna**, or ibn Sina (980–1037), a physician originally from Persia, author of the *Canon of Medicine* and the *Book of Healing*, finally brought an original vision to medicine, an approach imbued with North African philosophy to which he added a pharmacopoeia (a list of drugs and their uses).
- **Hildegard of Bingen** (1098–1179) was a highly educated, German, Benedictine abbess and visionary who treated others using plants and prayers. She wrote 3 major treatises on healing and left a mark on the history of phytotherapy through her global approach regarding health. She was called the "healing saint."
- **Trotula Plantearius**, a woman physician, worked during the 12th century at the medical school in Salerno, Italy. This was an exceptional nonreligious medical school where the study of plants was encouraged. Very able, Plantearius became famous thanks to her treatise on gynecology entitled *Les Maladies des femmes avant, pendant et après l'accouchement* (Female Ailments Before, During and After Childbirth).

The Renaissance

- **Theophrastus Philippus Aureolus Bombastus von Hohenheim**, or Paracelsus (1493–1541), referred to himself as Paracelsus ("better than Celsus"), for he asserted that his theories were better than those of Greek and Roman medicine, which had become outdated. This Swiss physician was also an alchemist and a philosopher. He formulated the theory of signatures, in which he ascribes certain virtues to plants based on their similarity to organs. Nevertheless, he manufactured dangerous metal-based medications. He was also called the "Luther of Medicine."
- **Rembert Dodoens** (1517–1586), a Dutch physician, worked for the emperor Maximilian, and then for his son, Rudolf. His best friends included Clusius (1526–1609) and Lobelius (1538–1616), two countrymen and famous botanists of that era. Dodoens wrote *Cruydeboek* (*Herball*) and *The Medicinal Practice of Simples*, outrageously plagiarized later on by Englishman John Gerard (see below).

- **Pietro-Andrea Mattioli** (1500–1577), an Italian physician and a famous botanist responsible for the botanical garden in Florence, is the author of several treatises on botany and medicine including *Di Pedacio Dioscoride*, published in 1507, which explains the works of Dioscorides.
- **Olivier de Serres** (1539–1619). Committed to a form of mixed farming ahead of its time, this French agronomist was a very competent herbalist. He wrote a marvelous treatise entitled *Théâtre d'agriculture et ménage des champs* (Cultivation and the care of our fields).
- **John Gerard** (1545–1612) was an enthusiastic gardener who traveled extensively. Gaining a wealth of medicinal experience during his travels, he brought exotic plants back to England and began working for an aristocrat. Gerard was mostly known as a barber-surgeon. His treatise, *Gerard's Herball*, was more or less a translation of Rembert Dodoens's *Herball*, and his illustrations strangely resembled those of Tabernaemontanus, a German herbalist of that era.
- **Nicholas Culpeper** (1616–1654), an herbalist and English physician, was a living paradox: aristocrat yet antimonarchist, Protestant yet passionate about astrology. His ambition was to make medicine accessible to all. He succeeded, since his treatise, *The Complete Herball*, was reprinted more than 100 times since its publication in 1652.
- **Nicolas Lemery** (1645–1715), a French chemist and physician, is the author of two longtime authoritative works in France: *Le Traité des drogues simples* and *La pharmacopée universelle* (Treatise on simple drugs; The Universal Pharmacopeia).

The Enlightenment
- **Samuel Thompson** (1760–1843), an English settler, studied medicine with Indian shamans (high priests) and midwives. He cured his daughter of a bad fever. Imprisoned for illegally practicing medicine, he remained, however, very popular. He began a line of thinking which closely follows traditional native medicine that has had millions of supporters. He founded the Reformed Medical Society, a school that trained the first American naturopaths.
- **Carolus Linnaeus** (1707–1778), a Swedish naturalist, is known worldwide

because of his system for classifying plants, which has since been significantly modified. Initially extremely critical of his country, he died in Sweden after becoming Botanist emeritus and official physician to the king.

The 19th Century

- **Sebastian Kneipp** (1821–1897), a German priest and healer, cured himself of tuberculosis by taking cold baths. He developed an effective treatment method based on hydrotherapy, dietetics and phytotherapy. He cared for thousands of the sick, most notably Pope Pius IX.
- **Jean Kunzle** (1870–1955), a Swiss abbot from the Valais, published several books on plants including *Le Grand Ouvrage: Plantes médicinales* (The Great Work: Medicinal Herbs), an illustrated atlas: *Bonnes et Mauvaises Herbes* (Good and Bad Herbs), a calendar, a monthly magazine and a series of plant-based remedies sold throughout the West.
- **Maud Grieve**. Born towards the end of the 19th century, this enthusiastic English gardener, who died in the 1950s, grew several hundreds of plants described in her remarkable treatise on phytotherapy *A Modern Herbal*. Published for the first time in 1931, it has been often reprinted.
- **Dr. Edward Bach** (1886–1936). Initially a conventional physician, then a homeopath, this English visionary discovered, through experience and his extreme sensitivity, the effects of flowers on the soul. Today, his 38 elixirs and homeopathic vaccines are still used throughout the world.
- **Jethro Kloss** (1863–1946). This American was truly the pioneer of vegetarianism in the United States. He began manufacturing natural products, published a magazine and established a sanatorium. His work, *Back to Eden*, covers all areas of health. He has been republished about 10 times since 1939 and has many supporters.

European Contemporaries

- **Maria Treben**. An Austrian, born at the beginning of the 20th century and who died a few years ago, Treben was a highly talented, self-taught herbalist. Her work, *Health from God's Garden*, sold more than 8 million copies worldwide.
- **Dr. Alfred Vogel**. This formidable Swiss naturopath was named doctor

honoris causa by an American university. Two treatises on naturopathy assured his fame: *Le Petit Docteur* (The Little Doctor) and *Nature Doctor: A Manual of Traditional and Complementary Medicine*. A huge traveler, he revealed many exotic plants to the world, most notably Echinacea.

- **Dr. Jean Valnet**. A physician in the French army during the war in Indochina, he became a firm believer in naturopathy, an ardent defender of medicinal plants and a producer of famous essential oils. His three major works (included in the bibliography) are recognized as significant reference sources in phytotherapy circles.
- **Maurice Mességué**. A pioneer in the renewal of popular phytotherapy, ecologist and philosopher, this likable herbalist is also a highly regarded, prolific author and formidable businessman.
- **Dr. Henri Leclerc**. Recently deceased, this generalist became a convincing proponent of naturism. His books, such as *Guérir par les plantes* (Curing with Plants) and *Précis de phytothérapie* (A Short History of Phytotherapy), are remarkable.
- **Raymond Dextreit**. First and foremost a naturopath and hygienist, this very prolific author has written dozens of brochures on different illnesses and their treatment. He gives full credit to plants.

American Contemporaries

- **John Lust**. A nephew of Benedict Lust, a great German naturopath who emigrated to the United States, he opened the first chain of natural food stores and sanatoriums in North America. In 1974, he published a remarkable treatise entitled *The Herb Book*.
- **John Christopher**. An ardent defender of phytotherapy, he was imprisoned several times before being recognized as an expert. He founded the famous herbalism correspondence school and wrote the comprehensive guide *School of Natural Healing*, which has often been plagiarized.
- **Dr. Varro Tyler**. A researcher and teacher specializing in pharmacognosy (the science of drugs relating to medicinal products in their natural or unprepared state), this scientist has a very rational view of plants and their active principles. His work is interesting, especially *The Honest Herbal* (1982) and *Herbs of Choice* (1994).

- **Michael Tierra**. He represents the new generation of American herbalists open to all the positive effects of plants on health. A specialist in the Chinese approach to herbs, he demonstrated a true passion for his subject in his book *The Way of Herbs*.
- **David Hoffman**, a medicinal herbalist living in California, is a true fan of plants and a great phytotherapist recognized by his peers. He wrote *The Holistic Herbal* (1983).

The Best North American Herbalists

- **Alma Hutchens**. A student of the Tretchikoffs, a Russian herbalist couple renowned in their own country, she traveled extensively. To perfect her knowledge of plants indigenous to North America, she consulted with North American Indian herbalists. She was also interested in the Russian empirical and scientific approach (see bibliography).
- **Jeanne Rose**. The approach used by this American herbalist is varied, erudite and sensitive. Her two illustrated treatises—two tiny jewels that are easy to use—deal with beauty and well-being: *Herbs and Things* (1972) and *Jeanne Rose's Herbal Body Book* (1976).
- **Susun Weed**, herbal healer, has a New Age side to her, tinged with the esoteric and the feminist. Two of her books are, moreover, devoted solely to women. She is very knowledgeable, witty and humorous, and her books are very nicely illustrated (see bibliography).

- **Rosemary Gladstar**, an American originally from Armenia, has been renowned for over 20 years primarily as a popular teacher. Gardener, herbalist and therapist, she also wrote a comprehensive gynecological treatise entitled *Herbal Healing for Women*, New York, Five Side Books, 1993.
- **Danièle Laberge**. Initially a psycho-educator in Quebec and Mexico, she became a biodynamic farmer in Michigan. She received an eclectic education from a Ukrainian healer, from Dr. Christopher and from a Hopi shaman. Since returning to Quebec 15 years ago, she has been growing the most beautiful flower and medicinal plant garden in the province. She founded her own manufacturing and distribution company, and has written several exceptional works on physical, mental and spiritual health. She offers the only comprehensive correspondence course in herbalism in French North America.

CHAPTER 2

Harvesting and Processing Wild Plants

We do not inherit the land of our ancestors,
We lend it to our children.
—NORTH AMERICAN
INDIAN SAYING

*M*ore than ever, we need to be conscious of the limited number and variety of plant species we can pick, and of their natural habitat that is shrinking everywhere on earth. We must restrict harvesting to meet our basic needs.

ECOLOGY AND ETHICS

In this vast land of Canada, I have seen about 20 precious medicinal plants located within a radius of 12 mi (20 km) around my home decrease in number or disappear altogether, in particular, because of intensive farming, urban sprawl and the development of regional tourism. This phenomenon exists worldwide. With the anticipated growth in population and technology, the only way to stop the destruction of plant life is through a clear understanding of the problem and the taking of appropriate action. Fortunately, citizens everywhere are increasingly conscious of the beauty and the vast wealth of nature, and are firmly working towards the preservation of the most beautiful wild areas.

In Europe the "green" parties are growing in force and number. In Quebec, the government has been consulting with experts and will soon legislate the preservation of endangered plant species. In no way do I wish to contribute, either through my teaching or my writing, to the plundering of the treasures that can be found in our forests and fields. On the contrary, I want to sensitize you to the characteristics and unique and irreplaceable nature of wild plants. If you want to pick the plants mentioned in this book, try to limit yourself to a reasonable quantity. Who knows, maybe you too will help preserve a species and its natural habitat, or even help it spread.

INTELLIGENT HARVESTING

Here are some of the basic principles for picking plants while respecting nature.

Preferred locations: wild prairie, large forests, hills and mountains. All of these must be located as far as possible from any city, village, heavily traveled road, domestic-animal herds and polluted lakes and streams.

Live and let live: With wild public places increasingly rare, especially in Europe, it is acceptable to request the permission of the property owner to explore his or her land, and, for believers, to thank the Creator, the local spirits and also the soul of the plants for sending their energy to you so that you might increase yours tenfold.

Quantity: Limit yourself to 1 plant for every 10, or 1 for every 20 in the case of roots and rare species. Encourage the manufacture of mother tinctures instead of herbal teas: they require a much smaller quantity to be equally, if not more, effective. In the fall, reseed by digging the seeds in around the plant that has been removed. If it is a perennial, leave the roots; if not, leave the sprouts as well as part of the roots in the soil.

The right time: Each species develops at its own rate and reaches a state of maturity appropriate for picking. For more information, consult the calendar and monographs. There are, however, common rules that must be respected: choose a sunny day, pick after the dew has evaporated, and do not mix different species in the same bag or basket—this has to breathe, therefore, it should be made of thick paper or wood—and then cover the plants if picking for an extended period of time.

In general, each part should be picked separately:
- Roots, in the fall or early spring;
- Leaves, just before flowering, in the second year for biennials;
- Flowers, when they begin to blossom, never withered;
- Seeds, in the fall when they are ready to leave the mother plant;
- Fruit, when it is ripe and colorful;
- Bark, on adult trees, at the end of winter: limit to 1 small rectangle per person—cauterize the tree with clay or mud—or choose a small branch.

The Best Tools

Below are indispensable tools for a successful harvest:
- Clean hands to handle all the delicate parts such as the flowers and seeds;
- Gloves for thorny species;
- Sharp pruning shears to handle tough stems;
- A small, easily managed shovel for roots;
- A canvas bag, a willow basket and thick paper bags for transporting.

If the outing is going to be long, think about wearing the proper footwear, protecting your legs and head, and bringing water, food, a lighter, even a map of the area or a compass if you do not know the countryside. It goes without saying that the best way to find the plant that you are looking for is to know the area you are traveling to and the type of habitat the plant prefers. If this is not the case, take along a guide of the area.

Basic Rules For Processing Plants

The word "drug" gave rise to the words "drugs" and "drugstore." This term comes from the German word *trocknen* or "to dry."

Some tips

- Never wash a whole plant before drying.
- Rinse only the roots, then brush and spread them out in the sun for a few hours to disinfect them before chopping and storing. They should dry for 2 weeks before bagging them in paper. For larger quantities, the paper bag is slipped inside a plastic bag or into a glass jar stored away from light.
- The leaves are trimmed to start the drying process. Sometimes they are left on the plants hung in bouquets in a ventilated attic by covering them with cotton or paper. Generally, 1 week of drying in a dry, dark and ventilated place is adequate.
- The flowers are spread out, often individually, on tissue paper. They are covered with the same paper and then turned daily so that they preserve their color, scent and properties.
- The fruit is quickly dried to retain its color, flavor and vitamins. A well-ventilated rack in a warm attic will do, but if there is persistent humidity, an oven set at a low temperature or an electric dehydrator may be required.

It is easy to make a homemade dryer from wood and plastic racks. The important thing is to maintain good air circulation. Remember that the preservation, effectiveness and wholesomeness of plants depend on good drying. This operation requires air, warmth, darkness, time, care and experience!

My Preferred Method

A mother tincture remains the best way to treat ailments using plants, as it needs only very small quantities of ingredients. There is no loss of active principles, and it takes up less space and time. This preparation is easy to carry in a small vial and can be consumed as is. Still, you can plan ahead and prepare a few "classics" based on dried plants for warm, honeyed infusions that are so comforting in winter.

QUALITY CRITERIA

In order for medicinal plants to be effective, they must be of optimal quality. Their marketing is regulated by standards specific to each country. On the other hand, the stamp "Demeter" and the mark of the Organic Crop Improvement Association (OCIA) are internationally recognized standards. Of course, the reputation of a producer or distributor is especially important. When shopping, trust your senses and check the freshness and the drying method used. If the texture, color, smell and taste can guide you fairly accurately, experience and prudence will do the rest.

29

Preservation

- Flowers and leaves remain effective, sometimes for up to 2 years.
- Better-quality bark, seeds and roots remain active for a period of 3 years, and up to 5 years if they are properly preserved.

- Alcohol-based mother tinctures remain effective for a period of 5 years, those in wine or vinegar, for up to 3 years maximum.
- Pills, capsules, extracts and nebulisates are all subject to manufacturing standards specific to each product.
- Cerates, salves and ointments stay active from 6 months to 1 year, longer if they have been stored in a cool place and they contain preservatives.

CONSUMERS, IMPORTING AND GLOBALIZATION

The market for medicinal plants is growing rapidly and represents billions of dollars worldwide. Although this business affects the health of individuals, production and sales standards are far from being safe and reliable. Below are some examples.

- Some major producers such as Morocco, Mexico and Poland have an extremely high rate of pollution. They often use insecticides and pesticides purchased at low cost from northern countries that view these products as dangerous and outdated.
- Many plant stocks imported into developed countries undergo a battery of fumigations, microbicidal sprays and irradiation when they reach Customs. Popular plants such as chamomile, mint, linden and vervain are consumed the most and are, therefore, polluted by these treatments.
- Phytosanitary checks and analyses are relatively safe, sometimes even overly so, but chromatographic (HPCL) or chemical analyses to detect heavy metals or pesticide levels are not carried out, as they are too costly, complex and tedious for both government and business.

To determine the quality of the plants you are using, choose one of the following solutions:
- Buy a product that has been identified on the label as meeting organic farming standards, or is from a reputable local or regional producer.

- Grow and process your own plants: it's fun, good for you and increasingly encouraged for ecological, psychological and health reasons.
- Pick plants yourself, using common sense and the advice of this guide!

The following is by no means an exhaustive list of plants headed for extinction. By referring to this list, however, you will know which ones to treat with care by protecting their habitat, by limiting the amount you pick and by helping them reproduce and thrive in their natural surroundings.

Table 1.1 *Endangered Wild Plants*	
Agrimony	*Agrimonia eupatoria*
Angelica	*Angelica archangelica*
Avens	*Geum rivale*
Barberry	*Berberis vulgaris*
Bearberry	*Arctostaphyllos uva ursi*
Catnip	*Nepeta cataria*
Coltsfoot	*Tussilago farfara*
Common elder	*Sambucus nigra*
Common juniper	*Juniperus communis*
Elecampane	*Inula helenium*
European linden tree	*Tilia cordata*
Figwort	*Scrofularia nodosa*
Hawthorn	*Craetaegus oxyacantha*
Indian tobacco	*Lobelia inflata*
Maidenhair fern	*Adiantum capillus veneris*
Mallow	*Malva moschata*
Meadowsweet	*Filipendula ulmaria*
Mullein	*Verbascum thapsi*
Pennyroyal	*Mentha pulgum*
Rosehip	*Rosa eglanteria*
Slippery elm	*Ulmus rubra*
Tansy	*Tanacetum vulgare*
Valerian	*Valeriana officinalis*
Violet	*Viola odorata*
Wild ginger or European wild ginger	*Asarum canadense* or *europeanum*
Wild thyme	*Thymus serpyllum*

Table 1.2 Wild Medicinal Plant Harvest Calendar

Month / Parts to Harvest	April	May	June	July	August	September	October
Balsams Resins	Balsam, fir, Oak						
Sprouts	Birch, Oak, Willow	Balsam fir, Hawthorn					
Leaves & Stems	Chickweed, Dandelion, Ground ivy, Wild strawberry	Angelica, Burdock, Comfrey, Curled dock, Horsetail, Motherwort, Raspberry, Willow, Wood sorrel	Ash, Bedstraw, Bramble, Celandine, Cinquefoil, Fern, Kelp, Maidenhair fern, Mint, Mugwort, Nettle, Plantain, Tansy, Watercress	Avens, Birch, Bearberry, Catnip, Chicory, Figwort, Hawthorn, Mullein, Oak, Quitch grass, Shepherd's purse, Slippery elm, Wild thyme	Alfalfa, Bearbind, Coltsfoot, Indian tobacco, Lettuce, Prostrate knotweed		

Flowers	Coltsfoot, Violet	Dandelion, Hawthorn, Mustard, Speedwell, Wild pansy	Angelica, Common elder, Mallow, Rosehip, St. John's Wort, Woundwort	Angelica, Chamomile, Evening primrose, Joe-pye weed, Meadowsweet, Yarrow	Agrimony, Burdock, Common thistle, Eyebright, Fireweed, hawkweed, Loosestrife, Mouse-eared	Goldenrod	
Roots	Wild ginger					Avens, Cinquefoil, Elecampane, Horseradish	Agrimony, Burdock, Dandelion, Fern, Valerian, Wild carrot
Fruit				Blueberry, Chokecherry, Raspberry, Strawberry	Common elder, Hop		Juniper
Seeds					Angelica, Indian tobacco, St. John's Wort	Burdock, Evening primrose, Plantain, Wild carrot	All plants reseed

Note: Harvests in Europe sometimes precede those in North America by 1 month. This table shows the average between the two continents.

33

CHAPTER 3

How to Use Wild Medicinal Plants

*T*raditional herbalists use plants in a thousand different ways, the simplest and most effective having survived the passage of time. However, few natural alchemists still collect the dew of the common lady's mantle to prepare holy elixirs, or recover the latex from the dandelion to make a viricide ointment. We have moved away from magic to industry. Often we unwittingly ingest medicinal plants on a daily basis. Below are some of the areas in which they can be readily found.

- In cooking in the form of seasoning (aromatics), in salad (watercress) and in fruit (strawberries).
- In beauty and personal-hygiene products: bubble bath, toothpaste, soap, powder, mascara and lipstick. The best perfumes are made from essential oils derived from distilled flowers (lavender, jasmine, neroli, rose).
- In farming, as a fertilizer (seaweed), a compost activator (chamomile, horsetail, valerian) and a pesticide (garlic, pyrethrum).
- In medicine: about 40% of synthetic medications are derived from plants. Cardiotonic is made from foxglove, a remedy for cancer (tamoxifen) is derived from yew, and that for leukemia is taken from periwinkle. This does not include the many menthol-based external analgesics and thyme-based local antiseptics.

EATING FRESHLY PICKED PLANTS

To eat plants that are alive and uncooked as animals do is the simplest way to benefit from nature's goodness. However, it is important to rinse them well, since the excretions from wild animals contain many parasites. For example, you could make a digestive and remineralizing spring salad by taking the young leaves of daisy, mint, chickweed, sheep sorrel, dandelion, plantain and violet plants, and seasoning them with a good vinaigrette. In this way, you retain almost all the active principles, antioxidants, enzymes and vitamins contained in the plant. Do not overeat, for your energizing cure might just become a drastic purge. One portion of salad per day is adequate.

The juice extracted from plants is also effective. For example, the juice made from the leaves of quitch grass purifies the skin and blood.

DECOCTION

Since we do not have either the enzymes or the 3 rumens (stomachs) that herbivores have to digest fiber and some organic acids, we cook our vegetables to make them easier to assimilate. Decoction is a good way to crack the outer protective coating of the plants and to dissolve the active principles in water. Place the freshly picked plants in a saucepan: 1 tablespoon for every cup (250 ml) of water is adequate. Bring to a boil and cover. Do not cook for more than 3 minutes for the tender parts of the fresh plants. You can, however, macerate them for a certain amount of time before straining. Eat small mouthfuls or use in a compress.

MOTHER TINCTURE

Mother tincture remains the best way to preserve the active principles of the plant longer. It is mostly used by specialists and experienced herbalists, particularly in Europe, where nebulisates and herbal teas are still preferred. This

is, however, the simplest and most effective way to benefit from all the therapeutic qualities of the plant.

This method is easy to understand and to use: pick a mature plant; finely shred (without creating a mash) in an electric blender with twice the amount of spirits (between 60% and 80% alcohol). Pour everything into a glass jar and macerate for 1 month (or 1 moon, as the ancients used to say!), away from light. Vigorously shake every 2 to 3 days. Carefully strain the mixture through a fine sieve, a coffee filter or a cheesecloth, squeezing it so as to keep as much of the concentrate as possible. Instead of alcohol, some herbalists use plant glycerine (glycerol), apple cider vinegar energized with honey (oxymel), dry honey wine with 12% alcohol (mead), or even dry white wines or astringent red wines. All of these are traditional methods, and the results vary according to the talents of the producer and the quality of the raw materials.

INFUSIONS (OR HERBAL TEAS)

For a long time, this way of consuming plants was associated with grand-mothers sitting in a corner by the fire on long winter nights. Today, all cafés and restaurants offer herbal teas to meet growing consumer demand. Unfortunately, in the eyes of an herbalist, it is difficult to find good-quality dried plants, whether in natural food stores, European shops that carry herbal products or pharmacies that carry a few "harmless" varieties! I am some-what of an expert in this area and, in France as in Quebec, I have rarely found organic plants that were well dried and properly packaged (protected from both air and light), let alone plants harvested in the same year. Only certain natural food stores whose owners are well informed offer them. By now you will have understood that in order to be truly good and effective, a dried plant needs to be handled carefully.

Once you have chosen a plant, prepare an infusion using 1 teaspoon in 1 cup (250 ml) simmering water. Infuse for 3 to 5 minutes in an earthenware or terra-cotta teapot if possible. To preserve the taste and the properties, avoid prolonged contact between the plants and metal. If the strainer is not integrated with the teapot, use a China cap strainer made of willow or plas-tic. Hot or warm infusions—just like decoctions—are more effective if taken on an empty stomach. They are absorbed into the blood more quickly through the intestines. White sugar, especially in large quantities, interferes with the virtues of the plant. Honey, even if it serves no purpose, is added in its churned, unpasteurized form when the herbal tea has cooled to preserve the enzymes as much as possible.

In my opinion—and many patients can vouch for this—2 to 3 cups (500 to 750 ml) infusion daily, taken over an adequate amount of time, can control even the most chronic diseases. Remember your grandmothers: in all their wisdom, they knew how to properly use the remedies of a "good woman," in Latin *bona fama*, which means of good repute!

INDUSTRIAL METHODS

Practiced on a large scale in the laboratory, industrial methods produce adulterated products. The extracts, nebulisates and essential oils are increasingly available in pharmacies.

Standardized Extract
The plant is dried quickly and mechanically ground. It is diluted in an alcoholic solvent that is allowed to evaporate. The plant is now in the form of a concentrated powder that can be used to make capsules or pills. There is one advantage to this: the plant is absorbed in a practical way. But processing requires a lot of liquid and heat, thereby eliminating enzymes, vitamins and other active principles of the plant in favor of one constituent deemed to be essential.

Nebulisate
This product is obtained by quickly drying an unstrained tincture in an electric turbine. The pulverized particles are then turned into capsules or diluted in alcohol or glycerine. Whether used to make a spray, a lyophilizate (a freeze-dried substance), an extract or a nebulisate, I am convinced that the plants lose their best qualities in this high-tech processing. Long live the apothecary's good old marble mortar!

Essential Oil
Distilling plants to obtain the essential oils is a technique that dates as far back as the earliest civilizations. Their therapeutic power resulting from the tremendous concentration of active principles is undeniable.

As an herbalist, I regret the huge loss of nutritive elements due to distillation and a certain unawareness of the ecological and energy problems caused by this method. On average, between 200 lbs (100 kg) of thyme or 1000 lbs (500 kg) of juniper are required to produce 4 cups (1 liter) of essential oil. I question the irresponsible harvesting of tons of plants at a time when preserved wild areas are disappearing everywhere in the West in favor of rampant urbanization that is gobbling up wild spaces and natural habitats.

Nonetheless, aromatherapy, when practiced with discretion and professionalism, represents an extremely effective and powerful healing art.

Here's the simpler way to do it: the plant is heated to 212°F (100°C) in a still similar to the type used to make brandy; the water vapor, rising through a tower, condenses, thus allowing the essential oils to concentrate on its surface.

EXTERNAL TREATMENTS

Poultice
This procedure requires whole herbs, crushed or diluted in water, or prepared in some other form (powder, tincture). The mixture is applied directly to the skin to promote scarring or to solve a skin problem. It can be used hot or cold.

- To treat a bee sting: after removing the stinger, apply crushed or chewed plantain leaves to the wound and wrap with a clean cotton bandage or, if you are in the forest, with a burdock leaf.
- To heal a boil: make a paste by combining 3 T (20 g) freshly crushed figwort with 1 ¼ T (20 g) slippery elm; dilute the mixture with 1 ¼ T (20 ml) boiling water. Apply to a piece of gauze and maintain the poultice for 1 whole night.

Compress
Prepare an infusion or strained decoction. Soak a piece of cotton to be applied to the skin.

A chamomile tea compress is excellent for treating conjunctivitis.

Medicinal Oil
It is generally used in a poultice in the event of arthritic or muscular pain and water retention. It can also be used as a primary ingredient in a cerate. Medicinal oil is produced using high-quality oil, ideally, one that is certified organic and first cold-pressed, and preferably relatively inoxidizable at room temperature. For example, olive, castor or sesame oil, or even a mix of all 3,

would do. It is important to always pick healthy plants on a dry day, and to dry them well to avoid any excessive fermentation. Otherwise, heat the oil and herbal mixture at very low heat in a double boiler for several hours.

Medicinal oil should be prepared using 1 plant at a time, macerated for at least 1 month, strained and subsequently combined with other plants. It should always be stored away from light and used within 9 months. It is used for rubs and massages, or for poultices.

Examples of treatment oils:

- Garlic: pain, fungi, rheumatism, warts;
- Marigold: chilblain, sores, erythema, redness;
- Comfrey: burns, fractures, varicose ulcers;
- Joe-pye weed: wounds, cuts, swelling;
- Indian tobacco: eczema, hives, psoriasis;
- Mint: otitis, muscular pain, migraine headaches;
- St John's Wort: burns, neuralgia, spasms;
- Black walnut: dermatosis, infection, mycosis;
- Plantain: conjunctivitis, eczema, insect bites;
- Rose: rosaceae, dry skin, wrinkles.

Cerate and Ointment (or salve)

These are practical semisolid preparations used for all sorts of skin ailments and are easy to keep. The cerate is a thick salve made from medicinal oil cooked with beeswax in a double boiler: 1 ¼ T (20 g) wax for approx. 5 T (80 ml) oil.

Ointment is a mixture of fats and plant concentrates (in powder form, macerated or simmered). Currently, the following animal fats are used: lard or pork fat, lanolin or sheep fat, beef tallow, goose or bear fat. Often, fresh or dried plants are placed in the fat and allowed to simmer for a long time at low heat. To save time, essential oils, tinctures or plant powders can be added.

My Recipe for Protective Balm for the Skin

8 T (80 ml)	Olive oil with St. John's Wort
8 T (80 ml)	Olive oil with rosehip (flower)
8 T (80 ml)	Castor oil with comfrey flowers
5 T (50 g)	Pure beeswax
50 drops	Balsam fir essential oil
10	Amber glass jars, 2 T (30 ml) each

Combine the 3 oils. In a saucepan, melt the beeswax and stir in the floral oil mixture, then the drops of essential oil. Combine again, pour into the small jars and let cool before sealing.

This balm promotes scarring, hydrates, regenerates and protects. A tiny, well-dispersed amount is enough to fight dry, sensitive skin on the face, hands or feet.

HERBAL BATHS

This is a pleasant treatment, easy to do and effective. I have personally cared for my children, even as newborns, with much success, by submerging them in therapeutic baths. Hydrotherapy is highly recommended, especially in France, to treat a large number of illnesses.

All plants are water soluble. The easiest way to use this method is to pour an infusion or decoction directly into the bath. The skin absorbs the active principles and circulates them throughout the bloodstream and lymphatic system. Mother tinctures are also highly soluble in fresh water. Fresh or dried herbs wrapped in a thin piece of cloth (to avoid plugging the pipes) and simply infused for the duration of the bath will release their active principles into the water. Soaking the hands or feet, a practice updated by Maurice Mességué, one of the French fathers of the new plant medicine, are very effective and recommended for people who suffer from gastric problems and for those who do not respond to herbal teas. In fact, all plants in a concentrated decoction (50% plant to 100% water*) can be used in baths. Following are the most popular:

- Balsam fir: pulmonary infection, constipation, nervousness.
- Chamomile: hypertension, indigestion, insomnia;
- Motherwort: anxiety, palpitations, neuromuscular spasms;
- Summer flowers: rheumatism and unpleasant sweating;
- Thyme: bloating, fatigue, infection;

ANAL INJECTION, ENEMA, BOLUS OR PESSARY

Problems concerning the colon and elimination are increasingly common. Two of the best ways to treat them are anal injections and enemas, wrongly abandoned today after centuries of abuse.

For a simple anal injection, use a small rubber or plastic bulb with a stylet tip that has been disinfected well, and then choose the recommended plant liquid.

Examples
- Chronic constipation: olive oil emulsion and mallow decoction (half of the mixture);
- Intestinal parasites: garlic and black walnut decoction. Boil 5 garlic cloves and 3 T (5 g) black walnut leaves in 2 cups (500 ml) water. Strain and cool. Inject after having a bowel movement;
- Colitis, diarrhea: 1 cup (250 ml) oak bark decoction with 1 T (10 ml) linseed oil and 4 T (60 g) slippery elm powder.

Enemas require greater quantities of liquid, sometimes several liters, and a relatively simple yet precise drainage system with a tap. For more information, consult the work of Dr. Jensen (see bibliography). These purges are repeated over several consecutive days. It is preferable to fast during this

43

*Throughout this book, this formula, in particular for mother tinctures, means measuring ½ cup (125 ml) leaves and 1 cup (250 ml) alcohol, wine or water.

time. Garlic, coffee, ginger and marsh mallow are the most popular plants for use as additives to these healthy purges.

The bolus, or pessary, is a paste made from herbal powder that is inserted into the rectum or the vagina for a prolonged regenerating effect.

Bolus Against Vaginitis and Monoliasis

(enough paste for 30 boluses)
¼ cup (60 ml)	Boiling water
¼ cup (60 g)	White clay
¾ cup (150 g)	Slippery elm powder
10 drops (1 t)	Figwort tincture
50 drops (1 t)	Wild thyme tincture

Combine all the ingredients and roll the paste to form a small cylinder weighing approximately 1 T (15 g) and incorporate a fine cord (similar to a tampon string). Insert the bolus into the vagina and leave overnight. Remove upon waking and perform a vaginal douche with a raspberry decoction. The boluses can be kept in the refrigerator to harden and keep them longer.

Simpler method: dip a tampon or vaginal sponge in the mixture.

EXCEPTIONAL USES FOR MEDICINAL PLANTS

Inhalations
- Inhale the steam of a decoction. For example, use a mint or balsam fir decoction against nasal congestion.
- Inhale the smoke from a plant burned on a coal fire and placed in a metal container. To combat asthma, use chamomile, mint, mullein, coltsfoot. Try one type at a time and beware of allergies.

Protective Pouches

Sew small fabric pouches and fill with plants. Wear them to protect against illness and evil spirits. The following are the most widely used plants: yarrow, hawthorn, mugwort, oak, fern, St. John's Wort, nettle. You can also slide these pouches into your pillow to sleep better.

FLORAL ELIXIR OR PSYCHOTHERAPY USING FLOWERS

Dr. Bach, an English physician practicing at the beginning of the 20th century, relaunched the production and use of floral elixirs. He created several and recommended the use of 38. A floral elixir is made from a flower picked at its peak. Ideally, two quartz crystals should be used to cut each corolla individually.

For example, to prepare an elixir made from yarrow, pick each small flower separately. Put the flowers in pure water in a crystal bowl left exposed to the sun for 2 to 3 hours when the sun is at its highest point. This process may seem complicated, but it is key to ensuring a quality product. Carefully strain and preserve the mixture with a little cognac, or a benzoin or myrrh tincture. It can be diluted up to 100 times its volume. It is then energized[*] by shaking it, much like homeopathic products.

Each flower has its own personality and can have an influence on us by transfusing, drop by drop, its virtues thanks to four elements: the earth contained in the silica in a crystal bowl; the fire of the sun that acts a catalyst; the air that serves as an exchanger and oxidizer; and the pure water that serves as a vehicle. I do not personally prepare floral elixirs, but I recommend them on a regular basis and use them on occasion. I am always amazed at their strength and the preciseness of their effect.

In the next chapter, I will occasionally highlight the psychotherapeutic benefits of the plants. I am convinced that they sometimes transmit their qualities to us when all we do is simply admire them.

45

[*]Energization: increasing the effectiveness of a remedy by following specific homeopathic preparation methods: dilution, trituration.

SOLAR HERBAL TEA OR ENERGIZED MACERATION

Some plants release their active principles through simple maceration in cold water. This is the case with delicate flowers such as mallow and violet, and with seeds and sticky roots such as plantain and comfrey. To obtain energized water, simply put the plants in a transparent glass jar filled with water and leave them in the sun for 1 to 2 hours.

SYRUP

Generally used to treat pulmonary problems, syrup is enjoyed by both children and men who are less appreciative of the strong or mild tastes of other
preparations. The main problem with syrup is the huge amount of sugar
required to preserve and stabilize it. Use honey or choose organic sugar: it is
costlier, but it tastes better and is healthier. In this case, store the syrup in the
refrigerator.

Pectoral Syrup

2 cups (500 g)	Honey or raw sugar
1 T (5 g)	Mallow (flower)
2 T (10 g)	Balsam fir shoots
1 T (15 g)	Elecampane root
2 cups (500 ml)	Water

Boil the plants for 15 minutes, evaporating half the water. Macerate for 15
minutes. Strain, add the honey or sugar and simmer for 10 minutes, stirring
constantly. Refrigerate, strain and bottle. Keeps fresh for up to 6 months.

Depending on the age of the person, take 1 t or 1 T of syrup, pure or
diluted, before each meal.

ELECTUARY OR MEDICINAL HONEY

Typically, this therapeutic product is a combination of honey and essential
oil. The ancient herbalists often used medicinal honeys made from whole
plants and applied them internally or externally, especially to treat children.

Digestive Electuary

1 cup (250 g)	Creamy honey
½ cup (25 g)	Peppermint, pulverized
2 T (10 g)	Slippery elm powder
½ cup (25 g)	Comfrey leaves powder

Heat the honey in a double boiler. Add the plant powders, stirring constantly. Pour the mixture into small jars. Swallow 1 teaspoon or tablespoon as needed of the pure or diluted medicinal honey, being sure to add a lot of saliva to absorb the active principles better.

I have tried to provide an overview of the most widely known ways to use medicinal plants and to benefit from their many virtues. I hope that I have done them honor and I wish you much success as you try these methods.

CHAPTER 4

Wild Medicinal Plants

1. Agrimony   *Agrimonia eupatoria*
2. Alfalfa   *Medicago sativa*
3. Angelica   *Angelica-archangelica*
4. Avens   *Geum rivale*
5. Balsam   *Abies balsamea*
6. Barberry   *Berberis vulgaris*
7. Bearberry   *Arctostaphylos*
8. Bearbind   *Convolvulus sepium*
9. Bedstraw   *Galium aparine*
10. Blueberry   *Vaccinium myrtillus*
11. Catnip   *Nepeta cataria*
12. Celandine   *Chelidonium majus*
13. Chamomile   *Anthemis nobilis*
14. Chickweed   *Stellaria media*
15. Chicory   *Cichorium intybus*
16. Chokecherry   *Prunus cerasus*
17. Cinquefoil   *Potentilla anserine*
18. Coltsfoot   *Tussilago farfara*
19. Comfrey   *Symphytum officinale*
20. Common ash   *Fraxinus excelsior*
21. Common burdock   *Arctium lappa*
22. Common elder   *Sambucus nigra*
23. Common juniper   *Juniperus communis*
24. Common speedwell   *Veronica officinalis*
25. Common thistle   *Cirsium vulgare*
26. Curled dock   *Rumex crispus*
27. Dandelion   *Taraxacum officinale*
28. Elecampane   *Inula helenium*

49

29. Evening primrose	*Oenothera biennis*
30. Eyebright	*Euphrasia officinalis*
31. Fern	*Dryopteris filix mas*
32. Figwort	*Scrofularia nodosa*
33. Fireweed	*Epilobium arviflorum*
34. Goldenrod	*Solidago virgaurea*
35. Grape vine	*Vitis vinifera*
36. Ground ivy	*Glecoma hederacea*
37. Hawthorn	*Craetaegus xyacantha*
38. Hop	*Humulus lupulus*
39. Horseradish	*Cochlearia armoracia*
40. Horsetail	*Equisitum arvense*
41. Indian tobacco	*Lobelia inflata*
42. Joe-pye weed	*Eupatorium aculatum*
43. Kelp	*Fucus vesiculosis*
44. Linden	*Tilia Americana*
45. Loosestrife	*Lythrum salicaria*
46. Maidenhair fern	*Adiantum pedatum*
47. Mallow	*Malva moschata*
48. Meadowsweet	*Spriraea ulmaria*
49. Motherwort	*Leonorus cardiaca*
50. Mouse-eared hawkweed	*Hieracium pilosella*
51. Mugwort	*Artemisia vulgaris*
52. Mullein	*Verbascum thapsus*
53. Nettle	*Urtica dioica*
54. Oak	*Quercus alba*
55. Pennyroyal	*Mentha pulegium*
56. Peppermint	*Menta piperita*
57. Plantain	*Plantago major*
58. Prostrate knotweed	*Polygonum aviculare*
59. Quitch grass	*Agropyron repens*
60. Raspberry	*Rubus idaeus*
61. Red clover	*Trifolium pratense*
62. Rosehip	*Rosa eglanteria*
63. Shepherd's purse	*Capsella bursa*
64. Slippery elm	*Ulmus rubra*
65. St. John's Wort	*Hypericum erforatum*

66.	Tansy	*Tanacetum vulgare*
67.	Valerian	*Valeriana officinalis*
68.	Violet	*Viola odorata*
69.	Walnut	*Juglans regia*
70.	Watercress	*Nasturtium officinale*
71.	White birch	*Betula alba*
72.	Wild carrot	*Daucus carota*
73.	Wild ginger	*Asarum canadense*
74.	Wild pansy	*Viola tricolor*
75.	Wild strawberry	*Fragaria vesca*
76.	Wild thyme	*Thymus serpyllum*
77.	Willow	*Salix alba*
78.	Wood sorrel	*Oxalis acetosella*
79.	Woundwort	*Prunella vulgaris*
80.	Yarrow	*Achillea millefolium*

AGRIMONY

Latin name: *Agrimonia eupatoria*

Common names: Church steeples, philanthropos

History: Traces of the cultivation of agrimony have been found in the gardens of the first cities built near lakes some 10,000 years ago. Its name stems from the Greek word *agrimonos* meaning "blinker"—the Egyptians used it for treating eye infections—and "Eupator," the name of a Persian physician-king who used it as a depurative (a plant that purifies the blood). Soldiers also used agrimony for many years to promote the scarring of war wounds. In 1476, the physician Philippe de Comines recommended it as the main ingredient in *eau d'Arquebuse*, a tincture made from agrimony, mugwort and a vinegar base. Saint Hildegard praised it for its ability to treat intermittent fevers and even amnesia. Several centuries later, John Gerard and Dr. Hill both became convinced that agrimony was remarkably useful in draining the liver.

Whether used to treat worms in children or diabetes in the elderly, agrimony is a reliable ally in controlling serious digestive problems.

Maurice Mességué tells of a decisive experience. He treated a famous singer who regained his voice after gargling with a mouthwash made from agrimony, 8 to 10 times a day. Mességué also recommends agrimony for general ulcerations of the mouth and throat.

Habitat: In poorly drained, clay soils, in sparse grazing lands, in grassy clearings, and along wet, shady forest trails.

Description: A perennial that grows 12 in to 28 in (30 cm to 70 cm) in height. It has a hairy, cylindrical stem that ends in a cluster of beautiful golden flowers. The root is thick, small but deep, brown on the outside and yellowish inside. The seeds bristle with small hooks that latch onto animal fur and clothes, thus allowing the plant to spread.

Parts Used: All the aerial parts towards the end of June and the roots in fall.

Chemical Composition: Essential oils, tannins, carbohydrates, vitamins A, C, P and K, minerals (calcium, silicon), phytosterine, bitter principles, xanthophyllite (yellow pepper), protein.

Medicinal Properties: Antidiarrheic, hypoglycemic, astringent, vulnerary, cholagogue, choleretic, diuretic, decostruent, emmenagogue, hemostatic, nutritive, tonic, parasiticide, vermifuge.

Applications: Agrimony can be used

diarrhea. Agrimony is excellent as part of a long-term cure against diabetes, for it lowers sugar levels and quenches thirst. It also treats hepatitis by intensively detoxifying the liver. It slows peristalsis and repairs the mucous membranes of those suffering from colic. For external use: prepare a concentrated decoction by boiling or infusing 1 whole plant and root for several minutes in 1 cup (250 ml) water. It is excellent for treating conjunctivitis, hemorrhaging and pathological suppurations from fungi to weeping eczema.

Anecdote: Agrimony is part of the famous remedies for the soul recorded by Dr. Bach. It is best suited to people in pain and to drug addicts who want to kick their habit.

whole, freshly boiled or infused in an herbal tea at 1 T per 1 cup (250 ml) dried leaves (the whole plant is hung up to dry for 1 week): works against ulcers, diarrhea and diabetes. The mother tincture (made from the whole plant or just the root) is interesting because of the extended treatments possible in winter, with the leaves and roots acting against

 ANTACID WINE

3 cups (750 ml)	Red wine
1 cup (40 g)	Fresh agrimony leaves
½ cup (20 g)	Alfalfa leaves
¼ cup (10 g)	Oak bark

*M*acerate the crushed plants in the wine for 1 month. Strain. Drink 2 T (25 ml) 3 times daily to eliminate stomach hyper-acidity.

ALFALFA

Latin name: *Medicago sativa*

Common names: buffalo grass, Chilean clover, purple medicle

History: Its French name is derived from *lucerne*, a mixture of Celt and French meaning "the plant that glimmers." The original variety from the Middle East was yellow and grew taller than its neighbors. The Arabs called it *al-fac-facah*, which means "father of all food," for alfalfa was also the favorite food of their Thoroughbreds.

Two thousand years ago, the Chinese were intrigued by the cows that grazed on alfalfa with delight. They quickly recognized the nutritive value of this plant: not only did it form part of their food, but it was also used to treat emaciation and ulcers. In Europe, it was grown primarily as fodder. Throughout North America, alfalfa sprouts are sold for salads. In natural food stores, liquid chlorophyll derived from alfalfa extract is sold as a blood depurative. Thanks to alfalfa, the antihemorrhagic vitamin K was discovered.

*This charming legume is a
low-cost source of energy and can really
help you live longer!*

Habitat: Fairly acidic and clay farmland, rich in nitrates and phosphate. It can also be found on nearby fallow land.

Description: An herbaceous perennial with round, erect stems. The leaves are a dark green and the flowers range from pale mauve to deep purple. The oblong fruit contains dozens of small, striated and shiny, brown seeds.

Parts Used: The young shoots that grow after germination, the aerial parts when the plants start to flower.

Chemical Composition: Proteins, sugars, chlorophyll, plant estrogens, minerals (calcium, iron, magnesium, phosphorus, potassium, silicon), beta-carotene, vitamins B, C, E and K, enzymes.

Medicinal Properties: Appetizer, fortifying, cicatrizant, hemostatic, digestive, nutritive, galactogogue, fertilizing, cholesterol-lowering, cardiotonic, remineralizing, restorative.

Applications: The best way to eat alfalfa is to eat it raw, in a salad or sandwich. Adult alfalfa leaves picked in fields are, however, richer in chlorophyll and minerals. They help in treating ulcers, sore throat, stomach ulcers, lack of appetite and anemia. They also lower the level of bad cholesterol. Herbal tea made from alfalfa can be drunk over the long term, but in small doses because it can cause bloating if more than 3 cups

form is a good way to meet the daily requirement of minerals and proteins.

Caution: Do not eat alfalfa seeds: they contain a dangerous enzyme called canavanine that can stop blood regeneration. Also, avoid this plant if you suffer from lupus, breast or uterine cancer, if you just became pregnant or if you are taking anticoagulants.

Anecdote: Carrying dried alfalfa around with you drives away your financial worries.

This charmine legume is a low-cost source of energy and can really help you live longer!

(750 ml) or 5 g of leaves are consumed per day. Ingesting it in capsule or pill

NUTRITIVE SALAD

2 T (10 g)	Alfalfa seeds
4 cups (1 liter)	Water
1	Plastic net
1	Elastic
1	Glass jar

Soak the seeds in the water for 24 hours, then drain. Using the elastic, attach the plastic net to the top of the glass jar. Rinse the seeds in the jar under the tap and drain. Store the jar away from light. Repeat this procedure every morning and night for 3 to 4 days. Shoots will appear on the sixth day. Soak the sprouts in a salad bowl, rubbing gently to remove the seed coats and to remove those that are still hard. Drain and store in the refrigerator. Consume within 1 week.

Try this alfalfa salad with homemade vinaigrette.

Note: Two tablespoons of seeds produce 3 cups of alfalfa sprouts.

Latin name: *Angelica archangelica*

Common names: archangel, herb of the angels, dead nettle, masterwort

History: For centuries, angelica has been used in India as a general tonic and in China as a uterine tonic. The Chinese use a particular variety, namely *Sinensis*, which they call dong quai, to fortify the womb before and after childbirth. Men also use it against rheumatism and flu, and to fortify their ch'i or vital life force contained in the breath.

Relatively unknown in Europe before the invasions by the Scandinavian barbarians, angelica was initially grown in Bohemia and used by the monks after the archangel Michael revealed to one of them its effectiveness against the plague. It is also said that its name is derived from the date on which the flowers bloom around the time of the feast day of Saint Michael on May 8, the date on which renewal was celebrated. Angelica was held in such high esteem that it was called the "root of

Angelica is among the elixirs for a long life. Beautiful, tall and fertile, it generously transfers its qualities to those lacking in energy.

the Holy Spirit." North American Indians recommended it against respiratory, infectious and obstructive ailments, from asthma to tuberculosis.

As angelica was considered a Christian herb, the women who grew it in their gardens could not be viewed as witches. Peasants made angelica necklaces for their children to keep them safe from misfortune. Angelica was part of the most famous digestive, pectoral and tonic curealls. However, in the 19th century, angelica fell into disuse. Roques, quoted by Jean Palaiseul in *Our Grandmothers Knew*, stated: "It causes us great pain to see a plant so rich in properties used so little today whereas exotic remedies that everyone talks about and whose worth lies in their rarity and expens, are easily adopted."

Habitat: In Europe, in moist, mountainous and relatively temperate areas. In Canada and the United States, near shaded streams and in moist ditches.

Do not confuse angelica with sweet flag (*Acore calamus*), which is very different and belongs to another family, or with water hemlock (*cicuta maculata*). (See the chapter on poisonous plants.)

Description: This plant grows between 3.3 ft and 8.25 ft (1 m and 2.5 m) high, is normally a biennial (it may bloom twice in the same year, or 4 years in a row if the conditions are right). Its

tall stem is a purplish-green, hollow and divided. Its leaves are somewhat triangular and attached to the stem by way of a long petiole. The flowers are clustered in a whitish terminal umbel. They give off a sweet, musky scent. The pale yellow fruit contains oval-shaped seeds. The fleshy taproot is brown on the outside, whitish on the inside, and has small branches.

Parts Used: The whole plant: leaves, stems, then flowers, seeds and, finally, in fall, the first year's roots.

Chemical Composition: Essential oil, valeric acid, iridoid psoralens. Seeds: fucocoumarin. Roots: estrogens, tonics, organic acids, salt minerals (potassium, zinc), coumarinic derivatives.

Medicinal Properties: Antispasmodic, bitter tonic, appetizer, carminative, cholagogue, stomachic, emmenagogue, depurative, expectorant, mucolytic, diuretic, lipotropic, galactagogue, oxytocic.

Applications: The first year, only pick some of the leaves so as not to kill the plant. The stems are picked at the same time, with the largest ones being the most interesting because of their taste and texture, especially for making preserves (see the recipe). Dried in a decoction or in an herbal tea: approx. 2 oz (50 g) in 2 cups (500 ml) water will treat indigestion, fatigue or water retention.

The flowers are picked mid-May and can be quickly dried in the shade and used in an herbal tea, or fresh in a decoction or mother tincture.

ANGELICA PRESERVE

8 oz (250 g)	Angelica stems
13 oz (400 g)	Raw sugar (organic)
approx. ⅓ cup (100 ml)	Water
1	Terracotta terrine

Cut the angelica stems all the same length and steam in a little water to tenderize. Remove and peel them before steaming until they are dark green. Drain and let dry.

Place the cooked stems in the terrine. Cover with 8 oz (250 g) sugar. Let stand for 3 days. Then, cook the mixture for several minutes at high heat. Strain the plants and the syrup, taking care to save the liquid.

Simmer the syrup again with the rest of the sugar. Place the stems in the syrup and boil for a few minutes. Drain and dry in a cool spot away from flies. Preserve in a glass jar, away from light and use as a cake decoration, as flavoring in a compote or flan, or as a digestive treat between meals.

The seeds are collected in the middle of summer when the fruit is brownish. They are dried in the shade or prepared in a wine-, vinegar- or alcohol-based mother tincture: ¾ oz (20 g) seeds in 2 cups (500 ml) water. Their taste is full-bodied. If preparing an herbal tea, limit the amount of seeds to 5 seeds in 1 cup (250 ml) water, for, in larger quantities, the seeds numb the taste buds. They help with digestion, especially the stomach.

The roots also contain a maximum number of active principles. It is recommended that they be dried first to neutralize the psoralens that can provoke dermatitis (wear gloves when picking). The roots are the most active. Take 1 t (5 g) in 1 cup (250 ml) boiling water, 3 times daily as a digestive, tonic and diuretic.

Warning: Angelica is not recommended during the early stages of pregnancy, nor for people who have clear, sensitive skin, and for those who suffer from cancer and diabetes, because it is a tonic for the adrenal glands and promotes hyperglycemia.

Anecdote: North American Indians used angelica in three different situations:

- The singers gargled with decoctions made from the stems before long, sacred powwow ceremonies.
- Old Indians took large quantities of angelica root to end their lives.
- Hunters and players put the dried root in their pockets for good luck.

59

ROSACEAE FAMILY

Latin name: *Geum rivale*

Common names: chocolate root, herb bennet, way bennet, goldy star

History: The Latin name *Geum rivale* comes from the Greek word *geno*, which means "I smell good." Indeed, the freshly dug root smells like cloves. Roman apothecaries also called it *Radix caryophylata* (clove root).

Monk-healers of the Middle Ages maintained that it had to be picked on March 25 while praying to St. Benedict.

There where the root resides, Satan cannot take hold and must flee. This is why it is blessed among all the herbs and he who wears it, remains harmless from any venom.
Ortus Sanitatis
Latin medical treatise
for monk-healers

John Gerard recommended taking a mother tincture made from the avens root prepared in wine to treat snakebite

The root truly has the power to purify all our emunctories. According to Culpeper and Father Kunzle, avens fortifies the heart and even makes us happy.

and stomach discomforts, and chewing the root to combat bad breath. Culpeper prescribed its use to fight chest and pulmonary ailments, sharp side pains, spitting up blood, and even the plague!

In the 18th century, the avens root in powder form was used instead of quinine and Peru balsam to combat epidemic fevers, and also as a light sedative when combined with valerian. As Father Kunzle said: "God gave to avens the virtue of chasing out from the eyes, nose, teeth, brain and even the heart, all that should not be there: it cures eye, head, and tooth ailments, as well as head colds and even diarrhea."

Habitat: Moist and shaded areas, such as the edge of the forest, the banks of lakes and streams.

Description: A perennial plant with a single round stem divided into 3 branches that become petioles for yellow and pale pink flowers. The leaves are smaller towards the top. The thick, brown root smells of cloves.

Parts Used: The aerial parts at the beginning of summer, uncovered roots in fall or early spring, on March 25, the feast day of St. Benedict in Europe.

Chemical Composition: Glucosides, lactones, tannins, essential oil, gum, minerals (calcium, sodium, iron), trace elements.

good for making the tannins and minerals more soluble; a tincture prepared in alcohol enhances the essential oil.

The root is chosen mostly for its concentrated medicinal virtues. Scald and macerate it for a few hours before using: 1 t (5 g) in 2 cups (500 ml) water. It acts against food and other types of poisoning, for example, from alkaloids and heavy metals, and diarrhea.

Anecdote: Avens's reputation as a powerful poison antidote began during the Middle Ages: according to legend, St. Benedict, through his passionate prayer, may have neutralized a poison that should have killed him.

Medicinal Properties: Antibiotic, antiputrid, anti-infective, antiseptic, astringent, antidiarrheic, depurative, antitoxic, febrifuge, refreshing, remineralizing, tonic, sedative, antispasmodic, stomachic, antacid, vulnerary, regenerating.

Applications: The flowers and leaves are used in a mother tincture or dried in an herbal tea to treat minor infections of the mucous membranes.

Tincture: ⅔ oz (20 g) in 1 cup (250 ml) alcohol, and strained: 20 drops, 3 times a day.

Herbal tea or decoction: 1 plant in 1 cup (250 ml) water.

In a skin compress: boil 2 plants in 1 cup (250 ml) water. Strain and apply. Excellent against weeping eczema and topical allergies.

The mother tincture in vinegar is

TONIC TINCTURE BLEND	
1 ½ oz (50 g)	Avens root
1 oz (30 g)	Angelica root
1 oz (30 g)	Cinquefoil root
1 ½ oz (50 g)	Dried raisins
4 cups (1 liter)	Brandy

Combine all the ingredients in a large jar. Store away from light for 1 month. Shake every 2 or 3 days. Strain.

Take 1 oz (25 ml) before each meal in case of a lack of appetite or a weak stomach, and 1 hour after each meal in the event of sluggish digestion or flatulence. It is used as a pick-me-up when convalescing or overcoming fatigue, and also as an antidiarrheic.

61

BALSAM FIR

Latin name: *Abies balsamea*

Common names: fir

History: North American Indians worshiped the balsam, for, according to them, it is the home of a powerful spirit. In German mythology, Vogesus, the god of the forest, hides in a majestic fir tree to spread his virtues among the branches.

All men of the forest know the disinfecting qualities of the resin and the antitoxic virtues of the inner bark. The Indians made "pine beer" from black spruce and added maple syrup for the fermentation process. In Quebec, everyone knows the famous "nuns' syrup," a pectoral syrup made with 20% balsam resin gum.

Father Kneipp created a concentrated balsam extract in the form of a relaxing bubble bath. He recommended eating pure resin pellets to cure pneumonia and pleurisy.

For many northern peoples, the balsam fir is a symbol of eternity, notably

for all Christians who associate the celebration of Christmas with it.

Habitat: Shady areas, acidic soils, cool climates and the pure fresh air of the north.

Description: A majestic tree with a conical shape that can attain a height of 66 feet (20 meters). The trunk is covered with a smooth, grayish bark and dotted with resin-filled vesicles. The grayish-green branches are adorned with flat, dark evergreen needles on the top, that are whitish underneath.

The balsam, with its conical shape pointing up to infinity, represents eternity beyond the ephemeral.

Parts Used: The young shoots in the middle of spring, whole branches, the outer and inner bark, and the gum that is harvested in the fall.

Chemical Composition: Resin: terpene acid and bitter principles, essential oil. Young shoots: some of the resin components, mucilages, vitamins A and C, minerals (calcium, iron, fluorine). Bark: minerals, tannins, resin.

Medicinal Properties: Antiseptic, bactericide, analgesic, antispasmodic, bechic, pectoral, cholagogue, laxative, astringent, regenerating, diuretic, dissolvent, emollient, counterirritant, immunostimulant, viricide, adrenal tonic.

Applications: In an herbal tea or a decoction (3 shoots in 1 cup [250 ml] water), the balsam shoots are recommended for pulmonary infections, coughing and constipation.

In a decoction for the bath: 3 oz (100 g) per 4 cups (1 liter) boiling water for 4 minutes. The adult branches cure muscular spasms and joint pain. Clean both the bath and the saucepan well following the treatment, for the essential oils contained in balsam will stain.

The inner bark treats difficult urinary infections and gastrointestinal inflammation. Boil 1 t (5 g) bark in 1 cup (250 ml) water for 5 minutes. Strain. Drink 3 cups (750 ml) daily, before each meal.

Balsam gum or "Indian glue" can be applied unadulterated to an abscess, an open wound or even a wart. Cover with a bandage to prevent it from sticking to clothes. Change the dressing at least twice in 24 hours. Continue the treatment for up to 1 week, for example, in the case of a plantar wart.

It can be used to treat toothache in the case of an abscessed root. As a

BALSAM FIR SYRUP

2 cups (500 ml)	Water
8 oz (250 g)	Balsam shoots
1 cup (250 ml)	Creamy honey
1	Tinted glass bottle

In an enamel and stainless-steel covered saucepan, simmer the balsam shoots for 15 minutes. Let stand for 1 hour. Strain. Add the honey and cook at low heat for 15 minutes. Let cool and bottle. Store in the refrigerator. Consume pure or diluted in water, within 3 months, at a rate of 1 T (15 ml) daily, before each meal. Excellent for coughs, and for clearing the lungs and intestines.

Note: When made with sugar, the syrup will keep for 9 months.

medicinal oil (20% liquid resin and 80% olive oil), it calms joint and muscular pain, is used to treat bacterial infections of the skin and hemorrhoids.

Instructions for using the essential oil: For use in the bath, the essential oil must be diluted in alcohol, milk or oil (15 drops in ¼ cup or 60 ml). For massages, dilute to 10% in vegetable oil. To inhale or use indirectly with an essential oil diffuser, put no more than 20 drops at a time in 4 cups (1 liter) hot water. Ideal for treating nasal and pulmonary congestion.

Balsam gum can be purchased commercially in capsule form. It is recommended to stop smoking, clean the lungs, relieve constipation and facilitate sleeping.

The dark honey of the spruce tree or honeydew, unique in France in the Vosges region, is a delicious pectoral nectar.

Warning: In large doses, balsam gum is indigestible: do not take more than 1 t (5 g) daily.

Anecdote: Breathing in the scent of balsam restores vigor to the lungs and blood. In the past, many tuberculosis sanatoriums were located in the middle of a pine forest. Do not throw away your Christmas tree. Boil a branch and inhale.

BARBERRY

BERBERIDACEAE FAMILY

Latin name: *Berberis vulgaris*

Common names: jaundice berry, pepperidge bush

History: The Egyptians used diluted barberry juice to treat the symptoms of the plague, and Hindu ayurvedic physicians used it to cure hepatic diarrhea. In America, the Indians used barberry against infection, fever and bad wounds. Herbalists of the Renaissance relied on the signatures theory of Paracelsus: based on the yellow color of the bark and the shape of the vesicle of the fruit, they deduced that this plant was effective in treating the liver and gallbladder. According to the Eclectics, the fruit is a cholagogue and a laxative, while the bark is an astringent. Paradoxically, as is the case with several other plants, barberry also stops bleeding. In many countries, barberry bushes were pulled out because it was believed they harbored black rust, which attacks grains. Fritz

Barberry is a shrub that has been falsely persecuted because it is said to have formed part of Christ's crown. It serves as a protective hedge, not only for esthetic but also therapeutic reasons.

Weiss, the great German-American herbalist, confirms its antibiotic and regenerating benefits against eye infections. In homeopathy, Nepal barberry is used to treat liver infections, whence its name jaundice berry.

Habitat: Old mixed forests and along the edge of pasturelands. It is sometimes used as an ornamental hedge.

Description: Perennial shrublike hedge 6.6 to 9.9 feet (2 to 3 m) in height. Has gray stems and, at the axil of the deciduous leaves, tiny, sharp, orange-colored thorns. The flowers are a pale yellow, hanging in clusters. The egg-shaped red and tart fruit contains 2 or 3 tapered brown seeds.

Parts Used: Ripe berries in the fall, the bark of the stem and the roots in fall or early spring.

Chemical Composition: Bark: berberine, berbamine, oxyacanthine, resin, tannins. Fruit: acid, sugars, pectin, vitamin C.

Medicinal Properties: Antibiotic, bactericide, astringent, hemostatic, cholagogue, choleretic, hypoglycemic, depurative, immunostimulant, prophylactic, nutritive, remineralizing.

Applications: In a decoction: 1 t of bark or fresh or dried root in 1 cup (250 ml) water: to gargle, against ulcers and sore throat; drink 1 cup (250 ml) before

each meal in the case of stomach ulcers and allergic diarrhea; use in a compress to treat bacterial eye infections.

Using the ripe fruit, prepare jams, tarts, compotes or jelly for sensitive intestines. Choose the mother tincture prepared in alcohol to treat biliary insufficiency, infections of the lower abdomen or metrorrhagia: take 1 t, 3 times daily for 10 days or more.

Anecdote: According to many French scientists, the berberine from the barberry has a chemical makeup that is close to that of morphine. It could be used successfully detoxify opium addicts.

DEPURATIVE WINE AND TONIC

4 cups (1 liter)	Red wine
1 cup (150 g)	Freshly crushed barberry berries
1 cup (250 ml)	Raw brown sugar

Combine the wine and the berries. Macerate for 1 month away from light. Stir regularly. Strain and add the sugar. Shake well. Can be stored for 6 months. Drink 1 oz (25 ml), pure or diluted in water, before each meal to enrich the blood, drain the gallbladder, increase the number of platelets or combat a microbial infection.

Note: The sugar is optional as it only serves to improve the taste. It can adversely affect the purity of the mixture.

BEARBERRY

Latin name: *Arctostaphylos uva ursi* or *Arbutus uva ursi*

Common names: bear's grape, upland cranberry

History: Bearberry is nicknamed the "bear's grape," for this animal adores its berries and semi-evergreen leaves. According to legend, it was Marco Polo who brought bearberry seeds back from China in the 13th century. Among Chinese herbalists, it had the reputation of being a genital and urinary antiseptic. In the 16th century, physicians at the medical faculty in Montpellier, France, praised its effect on venereal disease. Rabelais, a French physician and writer in the 16th century, lauded it thusly: "He took a hot piss that strongly tormented him but his physicians saved him with a strong diuretic drug that made him piss his pain away." North American Indians used it in a decoction to treat urinary infections. They dried the berries for their vitamins and smoked its leaves in a calumet, in a mix-

---

Bearberry is one of the best urinary and genital antiseptics, all the more precious because it is increasingly rare.

---

ture called kinnikinnik in the United States, and *sapack homi* in Canada. In the 18th century, it was officially entered into the *British* and the *American Pharmacopeia*.

Habitat: The sunny trails of peat bogs and mountains, and on the edge of forests containing a thick, humusy, acidic soil.

Description: Small crawling shrub with long hairless stems adorned with shiny leaves. The flowers are clustered in loose, terminal bunches of 3 or 4 blooms. The fruit is red, shiny and fleshy.

Parts Used: The leaves in the spring or fall, after the fruit has fallen; since bearberry is endangered, take no more that 2 stems per plant.

Chemical Composition: Hydroquinones (including arbutin), tannins, minerals (calcium, potassium), citric acid, flavonoids, essential oil.

Medicinal Properties: Antiblennorrhagic, fungicide, antilithic agent and diuretic, astringent, antiseptic, cholagogue, choleretic, febrifuge, sudorific.

Applications: In an herbal tea or in a decoction: 1 t (2 g) in 1 cup (250 ml) water 3 times daily; in a mother tincture: ⅔ oz (20 g) in 1 cup (250 ml) alcohol: take 20 drops in ½ cup (100 ml) water, 3 times a day.

The leaves should be soaked for

69

several hours before boiling. Avoid storing them in a metal container. Excellent against urinary and venereal infections.

Warning: Limit yourself to 1 antibiotic cure every 15 days maximum. Avoid bearberry in the case of a stomach ulcer, chronic constipation, and if pregnant.

Anecdote: The North American Indians that smoke bearberry during their rituals maintain that it is a visionary's herb that heightens the psychic faculties.

70

 ANTISEPTIC CURE FOR THE LOWER ABDOMEN

3 oz (10 g)	Bearberry leaves
4 cups (1 liter)	Water
1 t (5 g)	Sodium bicarbonate

Lightly chop the bearberry leaves and soak for 12 hours in a large bowl of cold water. Then boil the leaves in a saucepan for 3 minutes. Pour this mixture into the bowl and infuse until the liquid is drinkable. Add the sodium bicarbonate and shake. Drink 1 cup (250 ml) at a time, warm or cold, several times during the day. Repeat over 10 consecutive days. This bitter herbal tea has a powerful effect on small kidney stones, purulent cystitis, gout, hypotrophy of the prostate and bacterial venereal infections such as blennorrhagia.

Note: Bearberry is the color of greenish urine because of the concentrated tannins.

BEARBIND

CONVOLVULACEAE FAMILY

Latin name: *Convolvulus sepium*

Common names: hedge bind weed, old man's nightcap

History: Originally from North Africa, bearbind was already prized as a purgative by Dioscorides. Long popular, it was dethroned by its cousin, jalap, originally from South America, and by *scamoine* from Syria. The herbalist Meyrinck (quoted by Mrs. Grieve in *A Modern Herbal*) maintains that hedge bearbind is an excellent cholagogue, very useful in treating jaundice, ascites and all the internal organs lacking bile. English peasants long used its boiled root in beer as a purgative. The concentrated mixture provoked brief nausea. This treatment was reserved for ardent partygoers and for those with the strongest constitutions.

Habitat: Everywhere it can grow, but it needs the support of taller herbs, hedges or trellises, and good acidic and moist soil.

Description: Perennial herbaceous plant with a climbing, coiling stem bearing alternating leaves. Trumpet-shaped flowers are white or pale pink with white stripes. The seed is a capsule, and the root a fleshy tubercle that forms at the end of the stem, drops off in fall to spend the winter underground.

Parts Used: The parts exposed to the air in summer and the root in fall.

Chemical Composition: Glucoside, chlorophyll, minerals (iron, magnesium)

Medicinal Properties: Antiseptic, cicatrizant, cholagogue, choleretic, emmenagogue, antispasmodic, uterine, febrifuge, refreshing, hypotensive, relaxant, laxative, purgative.

Applications: In a decoction: choose 1 of the following combined with 1 cup (250 ml) water: 3 leaves, 2 flowers or 2 g of the stem and 1 g of the root (honey can be added to take away the bitterness). The stems and the flowers act as laxatives. The leaves are also emollient and regenerating agents of the digestive system. If, in addition to being constipated, you have delicate intestines, simply bathing the hands and feet would suffice: 1 oz (30 g) for 16 cups (4 liters) water. This remedy relieves liver ailments such as ascites due to cirrhosis. The fresh sap of the plant when crushed is an effective treatment for fevers relating to infections such as tonsillitis, sinusitis, otitis, etc.

This beautiful little pale pink bell catches our eye and helps us to untangle our intestines.

Take 1 T (15 ml) juice, 3 times daily for 3 to 7 days.

A mother tincture made from the root is used primarily to treat hepatic constipation.

Anecdote: Bearbind follows the path of the sun in reverse: it opens in the morning, facing west. When bearbind is cut, it re-forms its stem starting from the top towards the bottom. What a contradictory and fascinating plant!

THREE-FLOWER LAXATIVE

2 T (5 g)	Bearbind flowers
2 T (5 g)	Mallow flowers
2 T (5 g)	Common elder flowers
3 cups (750 ml)	Pure water

Simmer the flowers in water for 3 minutes, cover and infuse for 15 minutes. Strain and drink between meals to fight constipation.

BEDSTRAW

RUBIACEAE FAMILY

Latin name: *Galium aparine*

Common names: cleavers, catch-straw

History: The French name *"gaillet"* is taken from the Greek word *gala*, which refers to its coagulating properties. Pliny said that a bowl of soup made from bedstraw with a little oatmeal and mutton eliminated fat and promoted thinness. John Gerard recommended a bedstraw gruel as a remedy against bites from venomous animals, such as wasps and snakes. Later, his countryman Culpeper recommended using it to cleanse the liver, reinforce the kidneys and to prepare the body for difficult seasonal changes. Over the centuries, in the French countryside, a bedstraw plaster was used on burns, sores and wounds. It was drunk as an herbal tea to treat pain, insomnia and nervousness. Recent American experiments confirm the surprising virtues of the raw poultice, stabilized in freshly ground oatmeal, to treat tumors and the hardening of the skin caused by ganglia.

Bedstraw acts as a small, tenacious broom that clears away all concretions and cleanses the whole body.

Habitat: Bedstraw grows in colonies in acidic, moist soil, along streams and shaded ditches.

Description: Bedstraw is a perennial that grows 8 in to 12 in (20 cm to 30 cm) in height, with climbing stems adorned with whorled leaves. All the stems bear small thorns that grab onto animal fur and onto clothes. The flowers are white and very small.

Parts Used: The stems and leaves, preferably before flowering.

Chemical Composition: Vitamins A, C and K, minerals (iron, silica, sodium and potassium), acids, asperulin, coumarin, flavonoids.

Medicinal Properties: Antispasmodic, antiseptic, antithyroid, astringent, blood depurative, dissolvent, diuretic, immunostimulant, sudorific, parasiticide, viricide.

Applications: The whole plant is used, preferably fresh and crushed, in a poultice (1 handful or 10 g) on a wound, age spots, and even on a skin tumor.

In a decoction: drink 2 to 3 cups (500 ml to 700 ml), or 1 plant in 1 cup (250 ml) water, of fresh bedstraw daily. This is a powerful depurative of the blood, the lymph, the kidneys and the prostate. Prepare a mother tincture (1 part plant to 2 parts alcohol, vinegar or wine) against skin or kidney ailments: 5 to 10 drops, depending on the concentration,

before each meal. When diluted in water to 20%, it can also be applied to many skin disorders and even on freckles.

Warning: Avoid bedstraw in the case of diabetes, hypothyroidism and large kidney stones.

Anecdote: The elixir made from bedstraw flower helps in opening new internal passages of understanding and in focusing on the essential. A simple flower, it clarifies difficult moments and removes obstacles.

STONE-CRUSHING TINCTURE

1 cup (250 ml)	White wine (12%) alcohol content or something similar
¼ cup (15 g)	Fresh bedstraw

Finely chop the bedstraw by hand or in a vegetable mill and macerate in the wine for 1 month away from light. Strain. Consume as needed. To prevent kidney stones, take 1 t (5 ml) before each meal for 1 month. It can also be used in a compress applied to wounds and persistent cysts.

BLUEBERRY

ERICACEAE FAMILY

Latin name: *Vaccinium myrtillus*

Common names: bilberry, huckleberry, whortleberry

History: Blueberries have existed since the earliest days of humanity, as fossilized seeds at prehistoric sites have shown. American Indians used them dry, in a paste, and mixed with meat, most notably in pemmican, a dish based on wild game. They applied the boiled leaves to wounds and used the dried flowers in their ritual fumigations to chase away evil spirits that cause madness. Dioscorides said that the blueberry firms up the tissues, and calms the flow of the stomach; he used it to treat diarrhea, dysentery and inflammation of the bile.

During the Second World War, the regenerative power of blueberries on the cornea was noticed, for bomber pilots could see their targets much better during the night, after having eaten the berries.

This dear little woodland grape is now sold in pill form at the cost of its weight in gold, but nothing can replace the good old blueberry pie of our grandmothers!

Habitat: Acidic, moist, deciduous forestlands, swamps and forests after a fire.

Description: A subshrub that grows 12 in to 16 in (30 cm to 40 cm) high with several straight stems. The leaves, slightly dentate around the edge, are light green and shiny. The light pink flowers bloom in the spring. The fruit is a fleshy, blue berry whose color tends towards purple.

Parts Used: The leaves in the spring, the fruit in early or midsummer depending on the region, and the roots in the fall.

Chemical Composition: Fruit: sugars, anthocyanidins, fatty acids, pectin, beta-carotene, vitamin C, myrtillin, minerals (iron, copper, manganese), tonics. Leaves and roots: tannins, chlorophyll, mucilages, arbutin, acid, quinine.

Medicinal Properties: Antidiabetic, antibiotic, astringent, antiseptic, antiuric, diuretic, antioxidant, regenerating, ophthalmic, vulnerary, remineralizing, general and venous tonic.

Applications: The fresh leaves are used in a light decoction (1 t in 1 cup or 250 ml water) or dried in an herbal tea. It is an antidiarrheic, antacid or diuretic (internal use) and, in skin compresses, it is antiseptic and aids scarring. It also treats urinary infections, hyperacidity

against night vision, weak capillaries and diabetes. Otherwise, freeze the fruit, gently dry it in the oven or prepare a blended or pure mother tincture. Tinctures can be made using the fruit, leaves or roots (50% plant, 100% alcohol).

Anecdote: Blueberry elixir helps to fight memory loss by purifying the blood and irrigating the brain.

FATHER KNEIPP'S ELIXIR

2 cups (500 ml)	Brandy
7 oz (200 g)	Crushed, raw blueberries
2	Cinnamon sticks
5	Cloves

Combine all the ingredients and macerate for 1 month away from light. Stir from time to time. Strain.

Drink 1 oz (25 ml), pure or diluted, in the case of diabetes, gastritis, enteritis, colic and intestinal gas, or poor night vision, or simply as a full-bodied and delicious digestive!

---

of the mucous membranes or the blood.

The root acts even more as an astringent and intestinal antiputrid (same dosage): it treats diarrhea, ulcers and suppuration.

It is good to do an intensive cure with raw fruit when it is at its prime: useful

CATNIP

LAMIACEAE FAMILY

Latin name: *Nepeta cataria*

Common names: catmint, catswort, field balm

History: Since the Old Kingdom in Egypt (2700–2300 B.C.), catnip has been a symbol of fertility; it was dedicated to the goddesses Bast and Sekhmet, the cat and the lioness. Catnip was believed to help women transform themselves into cats at night. In reality, catnip attracts primarily tomcats, for it contains nepetalactones, chemical substances that are similar to the hormones released by felines in heat. English peasants planted some catnip around their storeroom to attract cats and keep away rats, which detest this smell.

Culpeper advised using it in a compress mixed with animal fat to treat abscesses, swelling, and war wounds. He maintained that rinsing the head with a decoction eliminates crusts, scabies and dandruff. According to Dr. Aldéi Lanthier and Dr. Henri Leclerc, catnip herbal tea is one of the best remedies against hiccuping.

The Chinese consider it bitter, cold and spicy. They use it to harmonize the liver, nerves and lungs, and in the case of nervous tension due to too much emotional upheaval. For overexcited children, they recommend a mixture, in equal parts, of catnip, chamomile and balm herbal tea.

Currently, North American herbalists often suggest catnip as a tranquilizer and mild sedative, especially effective in children.

Habitat: Gravelly or rocky soil, acidic, fallow lands and limestone hills, preferably in full sun.

Description: Herbaceous perennial that grows up to 3.3 feet (1 m) in height with a square, slightly hairy stem. Its oval, serrated leaves are also covered with a thin down. The flowers are a pinkish white. The catnip has a lemony mint scent, a strong, bitter taste, and it feels soft to the touch.

Parts Used: The aerial parts, especially the leaves and the flowery tops.

Chemical Composition: Methyl acetate, nepetalic acid, nepetalactones, essential oil, iridoid, tannins, minerals (calcium, potassium, silicon).

Medicinal Properties: Anodine (which soothes pain), antiseptic, antispasmodic, sedative, aromatic, carminative, diaphoretic, febrifuge, digestive,

This aromatic and velvety plant truly deserves to regain its noble status.

astringent, emmenagogue, uterine tonic, pectoral, antihistaminic.

Applications: To obtain the best results, consume catnip raw in a spring salad or fresh in a decoction. Do not boil it, but macerate it longer in hot water: 3 leaves in 1 cup (250 ml) water. It can be drunk cold in the case of fever and digestive migraine, or hot in the case of colic or diarrhea. As an enema, it can be used against intestinal pain, even in a young child: place 1 flowery top or 2 leaves in 1 cup (250 ml) water, then infuse and strain.

Catnip is excellent for treating excessive nervousness: bronchospasms, hyperactivity and insomnia. After a meal, as an herbal tea or mother tincture: place 3 leaves in 1 cup (250 ml) water; take 10 drops at a time. It is digestive and antiflatulent.

Warning: Catnip is a powerful tranquilizer and muscle relaxant. Avoid taking it during the day, especially before performing a job that requires a lot of concentration and dexterity. Limit to small doses of hot herbal tea, otherwise, it becomes emetic.

Anecdote: The *Master Book of Herbalism*, a treatise on popular magic, recommends burning dried catnip and bloodroot to eliminate a serious defect or stop an alienating addiction. Write on a piece of paper the condition you want to get rid of and throw the paper into the fire. At the same time, invoke the name of a protective spirit.

ANTISPASMODIC ENEMA

1 whole plant or 20 g	Fresh catnip
2 cups (500 ml)	Very hot water
1	Pyrex bowl
1	Disinfected enema bulb

Place the shredded plant in Pyrex bowl. Pour in the hot water. Infuse and let cool for 10 minutes, then strain. Use all the infusion by filling the bulb several times, according to the usual method. For a baby less than 2 years old, divide the quantities by 4. This recipe overcomes colic, fever, migraines and spasms of the plexus.

CELANDINE

Latin name: *Chelidonium majus*

Common names: garden celandine

History: The origin of its name remains unclear. According to the Ancient Greeks, the name comes from *chelidon* or "swallow," for this bird rubs the eyes of its young with this plant so that they will see faster and fly sooner. The alchemists of the 16th century may have referred to it as *coelidonum* or "gift from heaven": they consumed it in the form of a mother tincture in white wine to ward off jaundice. Paracelsus praised its orange sap for treating blood impurities and its flower for curing biliary congestion.

According to John Gerard, celandine simmered in good honey, strained and then applied to the eyes, cures blindness and clears the cornea blocked by a cataract. Clusius (1526–1609), a Dutch physician and herbalist, maintained that the celandine sap could treat excessive bile and yellowish-green suppurations of the skin and the mucous membranes. Dr. Mességué advised bathing the hands and feet, harmless but effective, against allergies, arthritis, sores, eczema, hypertension, sciatica and conditions of the prostate.

The Russian researcher Denissenko, quoted by Maurice Mességué (*Herbier de santé*, 1975), reveals that it may have cured various cancers. Celandine is extremely popular in homeopathy as a major drainer of the liver and gallbladder.

Habitat: Near human habitation: stables, gardens, shady walls. Empty lots and city lanes sometimes become home to very developed colonies.

Description: Herbaceous perennial between 12 in and 20 in (30 and 50 cm) high. Its leaves are a beautiful light green. Its golden flowers with 4 petals grow in flared umbels. The fruit is a brown clove that contains several dozen small, dark brown seeds.

Parts Used: The whole plant before the seeds are produced in May and June, the root in fall.

Chemical Composition: Leaves and sap: viricidal alkaloids, pigment, bitter principles, carotenes, chelidonic acid, essential oil, proteolytic enzymes.

Medicinal Properties: Antiseptic,

80

Celandine is a powerful plant to be used with care. Its floral elixir strengthens the throat and the voice, and makes oral communication and even the sharing of thoughts between partners much easier.

anesthetic, antiscorbutic, antihistaminic, choleretic, cholagogue, emmenagogue, oxytocic, fungicide, viricide, hypotensive, sedative, laxative, purgative.

Applications: Fresh sap: in the case of conjunctivitis or genital warts, use celandine diluted in boiling water ($\frac{1}{20}$). To treat a wart, apply the fresh sap, which forms beads at the stem axil, 2 times daily for several consecutive days. The entire plant can also be used in a poultice on a wound. In a mother tincture, take 5 drops, 3 times a day in water or apply directly onto a wart or corn; for external use, diluted in 1 cup (250 ml) boiling water to clean an open wound or in the case of infected mucous membranes.

A decoction made from the fresh plant—1 leaflet for 1 cup (250 ml) water—3 times a day to cleanse the liver and gallbladder. Add chamomile, mint or dandelion to improve the bitter, acrid taste of celandine. Doing this type of cure for 3 weeks is an excellent way to treat eczema, psoriasis and even arteriosclerosis (hardening of the arteries).

Warning: Celandine taken in strong doses over a prolonged period of time can have a dangerous narcotic effect accompanied by respiratory spasms or an irritating cough. It can also lead to severe liver poisoning.

Anecdote: According to superstition during the Middle Ages, if celandine is placed on the head of a seriously ill person, the one who will die will begin crying, while the one who will live will laugh!

ANTI-WART TINCTURE

$\frac{1}{3}$ oz (10 g)	Freshly crushed celandine
1 cup (250 ml)	Apple cider vinegar

Combine and let stand for 1 month in a glass jar away from light. Shake every 2 to 3 days. Strain.

Apply undiluted onto the warts 2 times a day or, use a pad soaked in tincture and held in place with a bandage. Change regularly over the course of 1 week.

Can be taken internally at a rate of 5 drops in $\frac{1}{2}$ cup (150 ml) of water before the 3 meals to cleanse the liver.

CHAMOMILE

ASTERACEAE FAMILY

Latin name: *Anthemis nobilis* or *chamomilla matricaria*

Common names: German chamomile, garden chamomile, ground apple, pinheads

History: Its main name comes from the Greek "Kamaï" and "melon" meaning "potato," and which becomes manzanilla in Spanish meaning "little apple," evoking its scent of ripe apple.

The Egyptians, who worshiped it for its virtues and dedicated it to Ra, the Sun God, used it against malaria. The Romans, who introduced it into the northern countries, called it the "plant of doctors." It owes its name *matricaria* to its regenerating qualities for the uterus; for centuries, it has soothed premenstrual pains, and acute and postnatal uterine infections. Culpeper recommended its use for inducing menstruation and for treating an impressive variety of "hot" ailments (fever, jaundice, diarrhea, migraine); for treating all types of headaches, he advocated rinsing the head with a chamomile decoction. In 1656, John Parkinson wrote in *Paradise on Earth*: "Chamomile is good for everything, for the sick and the healthy, especially in regular baths as much to cure oneself as to stay healthy!" The Germans, who are the biggest consumers of chamomile in the world, call it *alles zutraut* or "the one that is capable of everything." The great American herbalist John Christopher and many other specialists maintain that chamomile is one of the most precious medicinal herbs for good health.

Habitat: Wild grasslands, untreated grass fields, dirt roads and rubble, earth embankments and slopes, always in full sun.

Description: Perennial between 20 in and 30 in (50 cm and 75 cm) in height, remarkable for its terminal flower head with its bomb-shaped, yellow center and its white petals that rise or droop according to the amount of sun.

Parts Used: The flower heads, harvested at maturity on a sunny day when the petals are in a horizontal position and the ligules (the "tongues" of the corolla) are a deep yellow.

Chemical Composition: Chamazulene, essential oil, glycosides, glucosides, coumarin, phytosterine, mucilages, minerals (calcium, sulphur, iodine), vitamins A, C and F.

Recent research has shown its ability to effectively combat *Candida albicans* (yeast infections) and staphylococcus. In addition, it stimulates our antibodies, especially the lymphocytes and macrophages.

Medicinal Properties: Anodyne, antispasmodic, antiseptic, emmenagogue, oxytocic, tranquilizing, sedative, carminative, choleretic, febrifuge, sudorific, laxative, emollient agent, relaxant, regenerating, remineralizing, vulnerary.

Applications: The simplest and most effective way to use chamomile against a multitude of ailments is in an infusion: no more than 3 heads in 1 cup (250 ml) water, for at a higher dosage it becomes emetic. Strained chamomile infusion can be used as an external lotion against eye infections, a variety of wounds, dry skin, premature wrinkling and as the final rinse to soften and lighten blond hair. As a mother tincture: ⅔ oz (20 g) in 1 cup (250 ml) water: take 20 drops, 3 times daily. It treats all sorts of pain including hepatic, intestinal and nervous. It can also be administered as a concentrate to young children who are colicky or teething.

A bath prepared from a chamomile decoction is beneficial (even for children) against fever, itching, neuralgia and excessive nervousness.

The active principles in chamomile dissolve well in oil. It is an ingredient in many creams and salves for treating wrinkles and minor skin irritations.

Warning: Those allergic to pollen, especially ragweed, may react to chamomile, in particular, garden-chamomile.

Anecdote: The more you step on chamomile, the stronger it gets and the more it spreads. As an elixir, this small flower restores confidence, strength and hope.

SUNSHINE OIL

1 cup (250 ml)	Organic virgin olive oil
1 oz (30 g)	Dried chamomile flowers
30 drops	Lavender essential oil

Place the flowers and the oil in an airtight jar. Macerate for 1 month, shaking regularly. Carefully strain, add the lavender. This calming oil will keep for 6 months. Use in the event of minor skin irritations, neuralgic and muscular pain, dry skin, and even to reduce wrinkles!

85

CHICKWEED

CARYOPHYLLACEAE FAMILY

Latin name: *Stellaria media*

Common names: satin flower, star-weed, stitchwort

History: According to John Gerard, chickweed macerated with flaxseeds and marsh mallow works wondrously against all kinds of swelling, while the sap of its leaves cures scurvy and its decoction cleanses infected eyes, clears congested lungs and blocked intestines. His countryman Culpeper maintained later "chickweed is a sweet, gentle and subtle plant, influenced by the moon, for it is white, calming and refreshing, even for an overheated liver, when contained in a wet poultice made from the crushed plant, and even more effective with a prayer and divine blessing."

Father Kneipp used it to fight pulmonary infections and, in 1954, the American researcher F. K. Fitzpatrick confirmed its effectiveness against the tuberculosis microbe. Popular wisdom says that it is useful against obesity in

elderly women and, today, it is used in plant-based slimming formulas. In China, chickweed has been used internally for a long time to combat flu and aching joints, and externally to treat skin disorders. Susun Weed adores chickweed and devotes more than 10 pages praising it in her famous treatise *Healing Wise*.

Habitat: Loose, fertile soil, and the rich soil of vegetable gardens.

Warning: The common pimpernel, a plant commonly found throughout Europe, is potentially toxic.

Description: An annual that grows 4 in to 3.3 ft (10 cm to 1 m) in height and consists of several stems, each bearing small flowers at the axil of each division. The white, star-shaped flowers are terminal. Chickweed is sensitive to both pressure and time, for it only opens when the weather is good, between the hours of 9:00 a.m. and noon!

This tiny "weed" is greatly underestimated. Once we get to know it better, we will begin to grow it in our vegetable gardens.

Parts Used: All the aerial parts.

Chemical Composition: Carbohydrates, proteins, oil, saponins, minerals (calcium, magnesium, iron, silica, sodium), vitamins B_1, B_2, B_3 and C (375 mg per 100 g), chlorophyll.

Medicinal Properties: Antiseptic, resolvent, antiscorbutic, dissolvent, diuretic, lithotriptic, normotensive, depurative, nutritive, remineralizing, refreshing, counterirritant, pectoral, antitubercular, cardiac and nervous tonic.

Applications: The young plants can be eaten and even blanched and frozen for the winter, or preserved in marinades. In a poultice (.35 oz [10 g] or a handful), freshly chopped or scalded, chickweed treats abscesses, itching, skin eruptions, boils and other skin lesions. Taken as an herbal tea (0.105 oz or 3 g in 1 cup or 250 ml water), fresh chickweed is a good remedy for slimming, because it also drains excess fats, minerals and proteins. Simmer in water for 1 minute and do not infuse too long, for its properties disappear when exposed to heat.

In a lotion, it regenerates the skin, even facial skin. Chickweed is excellent for bathing the eyes against conjunctivitis, and in enemas for treating colitis and hemorrhoids. Chickweed is useful for any excess heat due to menopause, a brief fever, a hot abscess or jaundice. It absorbs and calms all inflammations.

Anecdote: Chickweed elixir brings peace of mind and raises consciousness, thereby allowing sound choices to be made. It stimulates the libido and increases fertility.

AROMATIC AND DIURETIC MARINADE

½ cup (125 ml)	Water
1 cup (40 g)	Raw chickweed
1	Fresh celery stick
½ cup (125 ml)	Apple cider vinegar
½ t (2 g)	Dill seeds
1 pinch	Salt

Pour the boiling water onto the chopped chickweed. Thinly slice the celery and blanch separately. Add the blanched celery, the vinegar and the dill seeds. Sterilize or refrigerate. Consume within 1 month as a garnish on chickpeas or pâté, or in a salad.

CHICORY

Latin name: *Cichorium intybus*

Common names: wild succory

History: Chicory is first mentioned in the Ebers papyrus (1500 B.C.). The Egyptians used it in soups and as a vegetable, and even used the dried root in powder form to make bread. Pliny recommended chicory for refreshing the blood, and Dioscorides suggested its use for fortifying the stomach and helping with urination. Later, Galen called it "the friend of the liver." It is to Olivier de Serres, the agriculture minister under French king Henry IV, that we owe the "chicory syrup blend," a mixture of chicory, rhubarb, cinnamon, cape gooseberry, hart's tongue and sandalwood. He said "this chicory syrup blend is good against vermin, therefore, worms." Chicory has been grown for almost a millennium, from Arabia to England, including Belgium, which is one of the biggest producers of chicory "coffee." Charles Dickens, in *Household Words*, describes at length the cultivation and use of this marvelous dietary

and therapeutic plant. Dr. Leclerc, in particular, recommends it to his patients experiencing urination problems due to a hepato-renal syndrome.

Habitat: Uncultivated land throughout the northern hemisphere, limestone and silicious soils, along roadsides and paths, where stones have been dumped, and along embankments.

Description: Perennial plant 5 ft (1.5 m) high. The flowers at the base resemble those of the dandelion. The flowers are a sky blue. The root is a deep, brown, thick taproot.

Parts Used: In the spring, the leaves, then the entire plant.

Chemical Composition: Bitter principles, chlorophyll, sugars, minerals (calcium, copper, iron, magnesium,

The chicory root drains digestive and blood toxins.

88

manganese, potassium, phosphorus), vitamins A, C, P and K.

Medicinal Properties: Appetizer, digestive, cholagogue, choleretic, depurative, diuretic, basifying, hypoglycemic, hypotensive, stomachic, vermifuge, remineralizing, tonic.

Applications: The young leaves are tasty in a salad. In a decoction, they treat sensitive intestines and help to cleanse the blood and gallbladder, even in the case of jaundice. Most of the active principles are concentrated in the root: the fresh root is used in a decoction, dried or roasted, to treat diabetes and water

89

DEPURATIVE SALAD

15	Springtime chicory leaves
5	Endives
10	Black olives
	Garlic, olive oil and lemon juice vinaigrette (to taste)

Wash the salad, finely chop and sprinkle with vinaigrette. Toss and garnish with the pitted olives. Consume at the beginning of each meal for several consecutive days to cleanse the gallbladder, soften the intestines and deacidify the blood.

retention: 1 t in 1 cup (250 ml) water. The roots of the hybrid variety (*Cichorium endivia*) are forced to produce endives. These are eaten cooked or in a salad. They have a bitter taste, a watery consistency and are very effective as a diuretic.

Anecdote: The chicory flower opens at sunrise and shuts at noon. Its elixir, made popular by Dr. Bach, helps fight selfishness combined with jealousy and possessiveness, and replaces them with altruism.

CHOKECHERRY

ROSACEAE FAMILY

Latin name: *Cerasus vulgaris* in Europe, *Cerasus virginiana* or *pennsylvanica* in North America

Common names: Black cherry

History: The Roman Lucullus brought chokecherries back from the city of Cerasus in Persia after his victory over Mithradites in 66 B.C. Pliny tells of the Greeks who used large quantities of cherries to treat gout due to excessive drinking and eating of meat. Throughout time, North American Indians and Russians have used the bark as an analgesic, a diuretic and a febrifuge. The gum oozing from the trunk was renowned for curing sores and eliminating the dry crust resulting from eczema.

In the early 20th century, in Quebec, the nuns of Kamouraska advised drinking an herbal tea made from chokecherry bark, stripped from the bottom to the top of the tree, to stimulate lactation.

In 1920, in the United States, black cherries were recommended for treating cysts, and red cherries for clearing the lungs.

Habitat: In Europe, in orchards, in North America, in sunny, old fallow lands, along the edge of young forests and forest soil after a fire.

Description: The chokecherry can reach up to 33 ft (10 m) in height (except some American varieties which resemble shrublike hedges). The bark, a beautiful dark brown, is smooth and easily stripped from the trunk, especially in winter. The pinkish-white flowers grow in terminal clusters. Wild American varieties bear smaller, darker and more numerous cherries; however, they are not as fleshy, sweet or juicy as those in Europe.

Parts Used: The cherry stem, the fruit and the inner bark.

Chemical Composition: Bark and young leaves: cyanogenic glycoside. Fruit, stem and leaves: coumarin. Fruit and stems: tannins, potassium. Fruit: vitamin C, iron, acids, fructose (sugar which can be assimilated even by diabetics), lignin, pectin.

Medicinal Properties: Antiarthritic, anti-gout, diuretic, lithotriptic, refreshing, pectoral, remineralizing, laxative, regenerates the mucous membranes and the skin, blood and lymphatic depurative.

Applications: The cherry stem is the most widely used part due to its diuretic effect. It should be dried well to eliminate the hydrocyanic acid. A light herbal tea—1 t (5 g) stems for 4 cups (1 liter) water—is recommended for arthritis, uric acid, cystitis, edema and urinary retention. Take 1 cup (250 ml), 3 times daily, before each meal.

The raw fruit can be eaten in moderate quantities, but avoid drinking any water and, in particular, any soft drink, to prevent diarrhea. A cherry cure for two days may be recommended to treat gout, diabetes and obesity, or simply to cleanse the lymph and blood.

The inner bark is collected from young branches in early winter. Dry well for 1 month in a dry and ventilated spot. In a decoction 1 cup (250 ml) taken 3 times a day, it can be used to treat fever, migraine and a variety of neuralgias. Limit the cure to 10 days.

Anecdote: In China, the cherry blossom is the symbol of love, purity and renewal.

REJUVENATING CHERRY MASK

| 1 lb (450 g) | Cherries |
| 2 lb (1 kg) | Clay |

*P*it the cherries, coarsely crush and combine with the clay to produce a thick facial mask. Recline and relax for 10 minutes. Rinse with warm water.

Note: In the case of headache, spread a thicker layer on the forehead.

CINQUEFOIL

Latin name: *Potentilla anserina*

Common names: biscuits, flesh and blood, shepherd's knot, silverweed

History: Hippocrates and Dioscorides both advised using cinquefoil for jaundice, ulcers, rheumatism and tooth abscesses. Its name comes from the Latin *potens* meaning "powerful." Roman soldiers used it to make a poultice to stop bleeding and to promote scarring. Culpeper recommended its use to treat epilepsy by eating it in a soup at a rate of 3 oz (100 g) daily for one month. During the 16th century, it was called the "herb of alchemists" due to its gold and silver colors, and it holds the noblest virtues that allow humans to purify themselves. It was even grown in the 18th century in northern Europe. About the same time, John Salmon, an English physician, nicknamed it "every woman's friend"; he advised using it against white discharges and abnormal hemorrhaging. He maintained that it overcame oral ulcers and dental pyorrhea, benefits confirmed by

Olivier de Serres. According to him, a decoction combining cinquefoil and horseradish even prevents premature tooth loss.

Habitat: Fallow land, rocky shorelines and alongside roads.

Description: Small perennial 0.4 in to 12 in (1 cm to 30 cm) in height. Its leaves are divided into numerous leaflets. The flowers are a beautiful bright yellow.

Parts Used: The whole plant flowering starts, about mid-June. However, the leaves are also active in summer and the active principles are more concentrated in the fall.

Chemical Composition: Tannins, resins, starches, glycine, tormentol, choline, amino acids, minerals (calcium, iron sulfate, magnesium, potassium, silica, sodium), red pigment, vitamin C, bioflavonoids.

Medicinal Properties: Analgesic, antiscorbutic, antidiarrheic, astringent, antispasmodic, cicatrizant, hemostatic, nutritive, remineralizing, stomachic, antacid, tonic, restorative, vulnerary, detoxifying.

Applications: The young plants can be eaten raw, finely chopped, mixed in a salad or cooked (hotpot, soup). Dry the whole plant in the shade or use it fresh in a decoction (1 plant rinsed in 1 cup [250 ml] water) for external compresses:

94

A great disintoxifying plant,
it quickly cleanses the blood of any
traces of nicotine and
other drugs.

> ### PAIN-RELIEVING DECOCTION
>
> | 4 t (10 g) | Fresh cinquefoil leaves |
> |---|---|
> | 1 t (5 g) | Fresh valerian roots (if dried, use 3 t) |
> | 4 cups (1 liter) | Water |
>
> Boil the fresh plants for 5 minutes (or infuse for 15 minutes if they are dried). Drink 1 cup (250 ml), 4 times daily, before meals.
>
> Effective against all kinds of pain stemming from headaches, diarrhea, neuralgia, premenstrual cramps and even contractions during childbirth.

in the case of hemorrhaging, suppurations or bruising. For internal use (1 root in 1 cup [250 ml] water): against diarrhea, gastritis or uterine hemorrhaging. It is also very useful in treating fractures or osteoporosis. It can be used without fear for extended treatments lasting 1 or 2 consecutive months by combining it with other plants richer in chlorophyll, such as plantain, and richer in vitamin C, such as watercress and common sorrel. This allows an increase in the amount of minerals and tannins that are absorbed. An excellent detoxifying plant, it helps addicts wean themselves from alkaloids such as nicotine and cocaine.

Anecdote: Simply, cinquefoil is a powerful plant. Its root liberates us from our torments and helps us to live life to the fullest.

95

COLTSFOOT

ASTERACEAE FAMILY

Latin name: *Tussilago farfara*

Common names: coughwort, ass'-foot, bullsfoot

History: All the great physician-herbalists of antiquity recommended inhaling the smoke of coltsfoot to treat pulmonary infections, a practice followed for a long time by the English and the Swedes. Coltsfoot can be found in 2 famous mixtures in *British Pharmacopeia*, the one using the pectoral flowers, and the other the vulnerary flowers. From the 12th to the 17th century, the coltsfoot flower appeared as the emblem on the signs of Parisian apothecaries.

The flower was also among those simples that were used against tuberculosis, but it is especially one of the best pectorals. Dr. Leclerc advises its use as a gentle mucolytic in the case of obstructive bronchitis to release purulent mucus.

Habitat: Rubble, poorly drained, fallow land, along the edge of ditches and streams, and always in sunny areas.

Coltsfoot personifies well
the idea of renewal: it brings hope,
and dissipates, at the end of
winter, psychic and
physical congestions.

Description: A cousin of the dandelion with its reddish stem composed of overlapping scales. The bright yellow flowers bear several ligules that change into flying aigrets when the first leaves appear. These are especially thick, soft, waxy and green on the top and covered with a whitish down underneath.

Parts Used: Flowers that were not pollinated when the stamens are still a golden yellow, just before they completely open, and the leaves towards the month of June when they reach the size of a large hand.

Chemical Composition: Yellow colorant (xanthophyll), essential oil, biofilm, minerals (calcium, potassium, sulphur, silicon, zinc), inulin, alkaloids, tannins, rutin, vitamin C.

Medicinal Properties: Antibiotic, antiseptic, antihistaminic, bechic, astringent, emollient, depurative, tonic, expectorant.

Applications: Fresh flowers that have been boiled a few minutes are excellent for combating congestion, pulmonary inflammation, benign coughing, emphysema, and asthma attacks caused by allergies: 3 flowers in 1 cup (250 ml) water, 3 times daily for 3 to 10 days.

The smoked flowers (ideally com-bined with lavender or rosemary) can be used to treat pulmonary blockages: ⅓ of each type, 3 cigarettes a day. The smoke inhaled from coltsfoot burnt on cedar or

97

on cypress wood has the same properties. In a poultice (1 leaf softened in water or steamed and replaced 3 times a day) held in place with a bandage : apply on abscesses, cysts or other purulent wounds; in a decoction : 1 leaf in 1 cup (250 ml) water, 3 times a day, will treat colitis and diarrhea. If the leaves are combined with oak bark and mallow flowers (⅓ of each), the results will be achieved even faster.

In a mother tincture made from spring flowers or the leaves picked in summer (50% plant, 100% alcohol) : take 15 drops, 3 times daily, to treat asthma, bronchitis, diarrhea or suppurations.

Anecdote : In Quebec, the growth of coltsfoot spread around hospitals from simple plantings brought by French settlers. Children with rickets were fed and treated using the grilled and buttered leaves of coltsfoot.

DECONGESTIVE SYRUP

1 oz (30 g)	Coltsfoot leaves
⅓ oz (10 g)	Marsh mallow root
¾ oz (25 g)	Balsam shoots
¾ oz (25 g)	Ground ivy
⅓ oz (10 g)	Licorice
4 cups (1 liter)	Water
2 lb (1 kg)	Natural honey

Boil this mixture in 4 cups (1 liter) water for 15 minutes. Strain and add 2 lb (1 kg) natural honey. Gently melt, simmering at low heat for 20 minutes. Cool before bottling. Store in refrigerator. Consume within 3 months.

Treatment : 1 T (15 ml), 2 to 3 times a day. Even children will enjoy it!

This syrup is most effective when the 3 native plants have been freshly picked, and the cultured plants (marshmallow and licorice) have been dried.

COMFREY

BORRAGINACEAE FAMILY

Latin name: *Symphytum officinale*

Common names: gumplant, knit bone, slippery root

History: The Romans nicknamed it *conferva* ("that which knits together"). Pliny tells of its root that, when boiled with pieces of meat, comfrey binds them together into one solid block. Since antiquity, animals and humans have eaten the leaves of this plant rich in proteins. The elderly in England have been known to eat it in a soup or with their mutton stew to promote digestion.

In *De Materia Medica*, Dioscorides advises using soaking comfrey root against hemorrhoids and the spitting of blood from the stomach and the lungs. Wet nurses during the Middle Ages applied it regularly to their cracked breasts. Jean Fernel (1497–1558), physician to French king Henry II, systematically recommended its use to surgeons to treat trauma and fractures, and to accelerate scarring after an operation.

Dr. Leclerc used it against stomach ulcers and Dr. Vogel produced a commercial powder made from the root. Both advised its use to treat bronchitis and anal infections.

Habitat: Heavy, moist clay soils, dry grassland, and along streams and rivers, always in full sunshine.

Description: Comfrey is a perennial plant with stems 3.3 ft (1 m) in height. The leaves are hairy and rough in texture, and can reach 12 in (30 cm) in length. The white, pink or purple flowers are bell-shaped and cylindrical. The fleshy, brown root spreads out over an area that is several square yards.

Parts Used: The leaves, the flowers and the roots in the fall.

Chemical Composition: Leaves: proteins, choline, complex B vitamins, tannins. Rhizome: mucilage, asparagines, starch, sugars, proteins, vitamin B_{12}, minerals (calcium, silica, iron), essential oil, tannins, saponins, pyrrholizidine.

Medicinal Properties: Astringent, antibiotic, cicatrizant, emollient, nutritive, regenerating, pectoral, vulnerary.

Applications: The young leaf can be consumed in soup, in a gratin, a quiche or an omelette. Lightly cooked, comfrey represents a good source of chlorophyll, mucilage and starch. It acts as an emollient and a laxative, and has regen-

Comfrey allows one to remain firmly grounded. Its energy is reassuring. It also promotes neuro-locomotive coordination and eliminates muscular tension.

boil 1 part plant in 3 times its volume of water for 3 minutes. Macerate and strain.

The flowers can be eaten in a salad or used to make a floral elixir.

The root releases its mucilage in cold water. After brushing and rinsing the root, slice it into sections and let stand for 30 minutes or more. Drink the slightly warm water used to soak the root. The roots can also be stored: after brushing, shaking and drying the roots in the sun for several hours, spread them out in the shade in a well-ventilated spot. After 2 or 3 weeks, store them in an airtight jar. They are useful in treating chronic bronchitis, fractures and stomach ulcers.

The leaves generally dry in about a week during dry weather. These are effective in poultices for wounds. The herbal tea has a remineralizing effect in the winter, a season when finding any greens is rare.

erating qualities, in particular for the mucous membranes of the digestive tract. In the form of an enema or vaginal douche, it can treat minor infections:

RECONSTITUTING OINTMENT

To prepare this ointment, first macerate 3 oz (100 g) comfrey root, cut and dried, in 3 T (50 ml) good-quality olive oil for 2 weeks.

1 cup (250 ml)	Castor oil
20 drops	Lavender essential oil
1 ¼ oz (40 g)	Beeswax

Strain the olive oil and comfrey. Melt the wax in a saucepan. Stir in the 2 kinds of vegetable oils, then the drops of essential oil. Pour into small, dark green jars. Let cool.

This is a multipurpose ointment: it is effective against cuts, wounds, contusions, tendonitis, fractures and even wrinkles!

The leaves and roots become concentrated in a mother tincture: 1 part roots to 3 parts alcohol or 1 part leaves to 2 parts alcohol (the roots contain the active principles).

Warning: The young leaves and roots contain pyrrholizidine, an alkaloid that promotes the growth of abnormal cells and blocks the veins of the liver. Comfrey is not recommended for long-term treatment (more than 20 days), nor in large quantities (1 t [5 g] per day). For pregnant women, newborns and people suffering from cancer, limit to external use only.

Anecdote: Many nomadic peoples of the northern countries put their comfrey leaves in their shoes to avoid blisters, but also to protect against illness and misfortune while traveling.

COMMON ASH

Latin name: *Fraxinus americana* (Quebec), *Fraxinus excelsior* (Europe)

Common names: European ash, weeping ash

History: This very old tree already existed during the Tertiary Period. Moved there by the glaciers, it became acclimatized to the southern hemisphere. There are more than 50 different species, half of which grow in Asia. The hardwood of the ash is prized in carpentry and its flexibility allowed it be used to make bows and arrows. According to Homer, Achilles' bow was made of ash. Dioscorides recommended applying a medicinal wine made from white wine in which ash leaves had been macerated, to treat snakebite. He told of how snakes detest this tree so much that they even avoid slithering by in its shadow! A Viking legend maintained that the world was sheltered by a large ash called Yggdrasil and that the gods held council at its feet.

Since the 18th century, it has been referred to as the "cinchona of Europe"

We inherit the attributes of
the fertile and hardy ash by consuming
its many parts.

because of its fever-reducing attributes. Professor Binet, as have many other therapists before him, praised its antirheumatic properties and its effectiveness against gout.

Habitat: Alkaline and moist soils, along the edges of woods and well-aerated grasslands where the plant can take up a lot of space to grow.

Description: Ash is a slender tree that grows between 33 ft and 99 ft (10 and 30 meters) high. Its branches are hairless and a grayish-green. The bisexual flowers have no petals, but reddish stamens appear before the leaves open. The fruit (key fruit) contains a single seed.

Parts Used: The leaves in May and June, the mature seeds and inner bark at the beginning or the end of winter.

Chemical Composition: Leaves: vitamin C, sugar, coumarin, minerals (iron, copper, potassium), bioflavonoids. Bark: bitter principles, tannins, rutin, resin.

Medicinal Properties: Aphrodisiac,

promotes fertility, diuretic, antiuric, febrifuge, sudorific, laxative, purgative, nutritive, tonic.

Applications: The dried leaves are used to produce herbal teas that are diuretic and fever-reducing. In the fall, use the fruit to prepare a mother tincture: 1 part fruit crushed in 4 parts alcohol. Macerate for 1 month, then strain. Men can take up to 10 drops, 30 minutes before sexual intercourse, but only once a day! Ash aids reproduction, but must be used in moderation, for its virilizing effect is very strong.

The inner bark—1 T in 1 cup (250 ml) boiling water—represents a power-ful diuretic and febrifuge. Consume at most 3 cups (750 ml) per day for no more than 10 consecutive days.

Warning: Avoid ash if being treated with anticoagulants, during the early stages of pregnancy and in the event of acute renal infection. Ash, especially its seeds, is not recommended for anorexics and people suffering from any sexual obsession.

Anecdote: To treat a wart, prick it with a needle, then prick the trunk of an ash and recite: "Ash, ash, keep it." The ash will take it away!

SPARKLING WINE

16 cups (4 liters)	Water
2 oz (60 g)	Ash leaves
1 ¾ oz (50 g)	Chicory root
4 lb (2 kg)	Raw sugar
1 lb (500 g)	Tartaric acid or cream of tartar
1 ¼ oz (40 g)	Champagne yeast

*B*oil the ash and the chicory in water for 10 minutes at low heat. Infuse for 2 hours. Add sugar, tartaric acid and yeast. Dissolve and allow to ferment about 10 days at 68°F (20°C) in a covered pot, but not completely closed (if not, the cover could fly off). Bottle. Wait 3 months. For a slimming or diuretic cure, drink small amounts (1 oz or 25 ml) before each meal for a period of 10 days. This homemade champagne treats fevers, gout and water retention.

COMMON BURDOCK

Latin name: *Arctium lappa*

Common names: great burdock, burr, batweed, love leaves, philanthropos

History: Dioscorides and Pliny both gave it the qualifier of *philanthropos* ("friend of man") because of its many depurative attributes including purifying the blood, kidneys and even the respiratory passages. The Romans called it *personnata* ("person"): using its leaves, they produced masks for actors. After their feasts, they would take the roots of the burdock as a gentle purgative. Its nickname, "the herb of ringworm sufferers," dates back to France in the Middle Ages. It was famous for treating highly visible skin disorders such as ringworm and scrofula. St. Hildegard recommended it against problems involving phlegm that blocks the lungs, such as chronic bronchitis and even tuberculosis. Culpeper advised using the juice from freshly crushed leaves against sinus congestion and snakebite, and the grated and salted root against the bite of a rabid dog. During the Middle Ages, in England, this plant was also referred to as *bardona* and used in a decoction made from seeds to eliminate kidney stones. The preserved root was very popular as a sweet. Henry III of France may have been cured of syphilis thanks to the burdock root. In France, in the 18th century, the healer Lazare Rivière became famous for his magic "Rivière's potion" to treat venereal disease. Relatively recent American scientific research has confirmed its depurative and hypoglycemic virtues (eliminates heavy metals in the blood) and its antistaphylococcal and antistreptococcal benefits.

The Chinese have been using it for thousands of years against very "yang" illnesses (accumulation, overflowing) such as diabetes, hypertension and boils. They say that it is capable of sapping negative nervous energy and of stimulating the libido. The Japanese have been growing it extensively under the name *gombo*. They eat it steamed.

Habitat: In clearings, among rubbish, in heavy and poorly drained soils, and along paths.

Description: Biennial plant capable of reaching 6.6 ft (2 m) in height, with a lush floral stem. The large leaves are a beautiful dark green on top and covered with fine whitish hairs underneath. The purple flowers become thorny balls that

Burdock, from which Velcro was formed, is symbolic of tenacity and vitality.

grip onto animal hairs and clothes. By spreading in this way, the seeds promote the continued existence of the species. The root is dark on the outside and thick, whitish and woody on the inside.

Parts Used: During the first year, the leaves in summer and the roots in fall. In the second year, the flowers in summer and the seeds in autumn.

Chemical Composition: Leaves: iron, bitter principles, resin, tannins, riboflavin. Roots: inulin, starch, mucilages, potassium nitrate. Seeds: glucosides, essential oil.

Medicinal Properties: Antiseptic, bactericide, aphrodisiac, hormonal stimulant, diuretic, lithotriptic, depurative, lipotropic, emollient, regenerating, hypoglycemic, tonic, nutritive, restorative.

Applications: The leaves are particularly recommended as a skin remedy: fresh, reduced to a purée or steamed, they are directly applied to the skin (on average, 1 fresh leaf per wound). Their bacteria-killing and bitter properties rapidly treat acne, burns, eczema, boils, impetigo, ulcers and oozing psoriasis. The steam from the burdock decoction removes blackheads and even milium. Burdock also purifies oily skin and

urinary incontinence. Follow the treatment during the day to avoid disturbing restorative sleep, since mother tincture is a diuretic: ½ t of seeds or 1 flowery top in 1 cup (250 ml) water.

The root is famous for its depurative effect, hypoglycemic virtues and nutritive qualities. This legume that tastes like the heart of an artichoke is consumed in large quantities in Japan and as survival food in the event of war (cooking time: 20 minutes). In a mother tincture (⅓ roots to 3 times the amount of alcohol or white wine), burdock works against diabetes, gout, chronic blood and skin diseases.

Anecdote: The burdock root is rich in growth hormones. It stimulates hair growth if applied as a lotion every day for 40 days or more.

cleanses normal the skin. Repeated applications of a simple fresh herbal tea will have the same effect. It is excellent for skin disorders in a decoction: 1 leaf for 1 cup (250 ml) water (boil for 10 minutes).

The burdock flowers and seeds, boiled or in a mother tincture, are recommended against kidney and bladder infections due to the poor assimilation of proteins, gout, cystitis, nephritis and

SKIN-SAVING POULTICE

| 1 | Egg white, beaten until stiff |
| 1 | Burdock leaf |

*U*sing a piece of cloth, prepare a poultice by combining the egg white and the crushed burdock leaf. Replace 2 to 3 times a day.

In the case of a recent burn or painful wound, apply this poultice quickly.

COMMON ELDER

CAPRIFOLIACEAE FAMILY

Latin name: *Sambucus nigra*

Common names: black elder, bore tree, hylantree, pipe tree

History: The botanical name of common elder is derived from the Greek *sambuca*, a wind instrument that requires pipes made from the branches of the elder tree. Pliny was the first to call it this.

During the Middle Ages, people were convinced that Judas had hung himself from a common elder; for this reason, it was called the "Judas tree." Rumor also had it that the crucifix on which Christ died was made from elder wood. Even the Gypsies respected and feared this plant: they forbade camping near an elder or the burning of its leaves in the campfire.

In 1644, an English military surgeon, Martin Blackmich, published a treatise entitled *Anatomy of the Common Elder* in which he mentions, among other things, that eating a mushroom parasite called

Elder is a magical shrub with many curative virtues. In many ways, it deserves to become popular once again.

"Judas's ears" was a remedy against hysteria, sore throat and tonsillitis.

Aubrey (1626–1697), a French pharmacist, summed up its principal properties: "Our fathers used it against erysipelas and rheumatism; it is truly an appetizer and a digestive, and its berries provoke urinating, and cure gout and syphilis when taken in 1 or 2 drams. It also acts as a laxative when taken in two doses or more; the common elder truly stimulates all the secretions of fluids and natural wastes."

Today, elder is still very much appreciated and grown in England and Switzerland; elder is the principal ingredient in a slimming and cleansing cure called "Sambu."

Habitat: In acidic, moist soils, near old barns and stables.

Description: Slender shrub capable of reaching 10 ft (3 m) in height; its leaves have long petioles. The creamy white flowers are grouped in corymbs and flower at the end of May and early June. Upon maturity, the fruit resemble red or black berries and contain a single seed.

Parts Used: The flowers, just before completely flowering, the ripe fruit, the bark and branches, in early spring.

Chemical Composition: Leaves: alkaloid, glucosides, acids, coniine, potassium nitrate. Bark: tannins, acid,

resin. Flowers: essential oil, mucilage, potassium, choline, tannins. Fruit: organic acids (eldrin, sambucine), glucosides, aminoacids, vitamin C.

Medicinal Properties: Alterative, appetizer, bronchodilator, mucolytic, depurative, immunostimulating, diuretic, lithotriptic, febrifuge, sudorific, nutritive, tonic, purgative, vulnerary.

Applications: In a decoction: ¾ oz (20 g) inner bark per 4 cups (1 liter) water: to be taken several times a day as an antiasthmatic or purgative.

Only the dried leaves are used externally in an antiscrofular ointment, or in a pulverized decoction against parasites and insects. Common elder even keeps moles and mice away from the garden.

Placed under a hat, the fresh leaves keep mosquitoes away.

The flowery tops are picked and then dried spread out on fine paper, in the shade in a well-ventilated area, and then cooked. In an herbal tea: 1 top in 1 cup (250 ml) water acts as a diuretic and works against colds. Fresh, in a quick decoction: against all acute infections of the mucous membranes, lungs and kidneys. The whole flower is used to make doughnuts or crushed in a cake batter to lighten it.

Eat the raw fruit in small amounts (3 oz or 100 g), for it acts as a laxative. It can be used in fruit salad, jam, a compote, syrup or liqueur. In a mother tincture, the fruit is diuretic, fortifying and tonic. Dried in a dehydrator and used in an herbal tea, the berries are effective against diarrhea and cellulite: 1 t in 1 cup (250 ml) water, 3 times daily. In this instance, do a longer cure by using the elderberry in an herbal tea, a mother tincture or simply by chewing it as is.

Mother tincture: 50% plant, 100% alcohol. Take 20 drops, 3 times a day.

10-day cure: diarrhea.

30-day cure: obesity, edema.

Anecdote: The antirheumatic virtues of elder were accidentally rediscovered in 1899. An American sailor who got drunk on port spiked with elderberry juice was completely cured of his rheumatism!

OLD-FASHIONED ELDERBERRY WINE

16 cups (4 liters)	Water
2 lb (1 kg)	Elderberries
1 oz (30 g)	Toasted bread
1 T (15 g)	Wine yeast
2 lb (1 kg)	Brown sugar
1 t (5 g)	Allspice
5	Cloves
1 T (15 g)	Pieces of ginger
1	Earthenware or glass jar

Crush the berries, place them in the water, add the spices and gently boil for 30 minutes at low heat. Pour everything into the jar and add the toasted bread and the package of wine yeast. Store the container at 68°F (20°C) until fermentation is complete (10 to 20 days). Then strain, bottle and store in the cellar or in a cool place for at least 2 months.

Drink 1 oz (25 ml) before meals. In the case of anemia, this is an excellent stimulant and tonic for the immune system.

111

COMMON JUNIPER

CUPRESSACEAE FAMILY

Latin name: *juniperus communis*

Common names: dwarf juniper, field juniper, Geneva, juniper berries

History: In Switzerland, archeological digs have revealed the presence of juniper berries in prehistoric caves. Cavemen probably ate them for nourishment and for treatment. In Athens, during the great plague, Hippocrates contributed to containing the disease by advocating purifying fumigations for which juniper berries, lavender, hyssop and sage were used. The Romans used it in their cooking and as a digestive herb. Pliny and Galen both recommended a hot juniper wine to purge the liver.

The monks of the Salerno school praised it: "Good for the lungs, this aromatic berry still eliminates the possibility of getting a sharp, chronic cough. It expulses from the body a dangerous venom and its burnt seed calms a terrible malady." Here is what the great Dr. Lemery said in the 14th century: "Juniper berries are the correct cephalic

This precious conifer, found everywhere on the planet, is one of the most widely consumed and recognized remedies the world over.

drugs to fortify the heart, the nerves, the stomach, and to stimulate a woman's month, resist any venom and to soothe renal pain." Gin, made famous by the Dutchman De Kuyper, is an English invention resulting from the distillation of a tincture made from juniper berries in brandy. There have always been medicinal wines made from juniper in Scandinavia and *Wacholder* ("the watchman") beer in Germany.

Habitat: Limestone and siliceous soils, rocky hills in temperate areas.

Description: Small shrub 20 in to 30

in (50 cm to 75 cm) high and covered with short, evergreen, stiff grayish-green needles. The tiny flowers that appear in April and May are a greenish-yellow. The fruit consists of blue berries that take 3 years to reach maturity on female plants: they have an aromatic and sweet taste. Juniper gives off an aromatic spicy balsam scent typical of resin plants.

Parts Used: The wood and denuded stems later in the fall or in early spring, the thorns (when picked with the small branches, they are easier to dry) and the ripe berries, in late autumn and in winter, every third year.

Chemical Composition: Leaves: vitamin C, essential oil. Fruit: sugars, vitamins A, B, C and F, minerals (calcium, cobalt, iron, magnesium, manganese, potassium, selenium, silica, zinc), essential oil, acid, proteins.

Medicinal Properties: Antiscorbutic, antiseptic, appetizer, stomachic, antilithic agent, diuretic, antirheumatic, anti-inflammatory, cholagogue, emmenagogue, uterine tonic, insect repellent, pectoral, immuno-neural stimulant.

Applications: Once the branches, leaves and berries are dried, they are burned over a wood fire or scented vegetable charcoal. It is used for disinfecting a room or for neutralizing contagious diseases.

Slightly boil and macerate the

113

branches for one whole night (1 t of needles in 1 cup [250 ml] water): this is an antiseptic drink for the kidneys and the bladder, and a diuretic; it helps to stop arthritis and gout attacks. The simplest way to consume the berries is to chew them. Start with a small amount: 4 per day, up to 40 berries taken over several helpings. They treat kidney infections, rheumatism and stomach ailments. To fortify the stomach, cleanse the kidneys or purify the breath, simply chew a few berries. The mother tincture in gin or in apple cider vinegar is excellent against flu, water retention and rheumatism.

Juniper berries with their smooth, resin-like taste are used in many traditional cooking recipes such as Brunswick stew or sauerkraut with meat. They help digest protein.

Warning: Avoid juniper if suffering from an acute urinary infection and in the early stages of pregnancy. Do not use in a cure for longer than 1 month and do not exceed the prescribed doses.

Anecdote: According to Father Kneipp, "Our body, our most loyal and precious home, needs juniper fumigations and vapors at certain times during the year: this purifies the organism and soothes the respiratory system."

STONE-CRUSHING DECOCTION

1 T (15 g)	Juniper berries
2 t (10 g)	Marsh mallow root
2 t (10 g)	Parsley root
2 T (5 g)	Horsetail leaves
1 t (5 g)	Angelica seeds
4 cups (1 liter)	Water

Boil all the plants in the water for 7 minutes. Infuse 30 minutes and strain. Drink all the liquid in 3 servings, before meals, and extend the cure from 7 to 21 days to pass kidney stones, and to relieve all types of water retention and rheumatism.

COMMON SPEEDWELL

SCROPHULARIACEAE FAMILY

Latin name: *Veronica officinalis*

Common names: black root, culver's root, physic root

History: The origin of its Latin name has been the subject of much debate. According to the ancient polytheist Greeks, the word *veronica* comes from *phero*, "I bring," and *niki*, "victory," for *veronica officinalis*, triumphed over all ailments; the orthodox religions translated it into Latin as "true icon"; finally, Catholics dedicated it to St. Veronica, humble and modest but devoted and efficient. North American Indians used it in a decoction in case of poisoning to provoke vomiting; during sacred rituals, they made those who could not tolerate hallucinogenic herbs drink it.

In Culpeper's time, French peasants used it against bronchitis, hemorrhaging, water retention and skin disorders. In 1690, Johannes Francus, a German herbalist, devoted an entire 300-page treatise to the plant: *Polchresta Herba Veronica*. Subsequently, this plant was

forgotten until Maria Treben trumpeted its excellent ability to cleanse the blood, and drain the bile and bad cholesterol, which Danièle Laberge in Quebec has also confirmed.

Habitat: Acid and moist grasslands, fallow land and the edge of moist, deciduous forests.

Description: Small perennial herb 6 in to 12 in (15 cm to 30 cm) high with a semi-climbing stem, adorned with dentate, oval flowers and a short petiole. The small flowers are a light blue with darker blue stripes, and grow in lateral clusters.

Parts Used: The whole plant before flowering is complete, but in case of emergency, the leaves.

Chemical Composition: Organic acids, sugars, red pigment, flavonoids, bitter principle, resin, tannins.

Medicinal Properties: Astringent,

Discretely self-propagating yet everywhere in our organic gardens, speedwell is endowed with a great purifying power.

diaphoretic or sudorific, dissolvent, diuretic, emmenagogue, nutritive, pectoral, tonic, vulnerary.

Applications: Many people eat it raw in a salad in early spring, or added to soup. In a decoction: 1 flowering stem or ¹⁄₁₀ oz (3 g) in 1 cup (250 ml) water helps to treat edema, digestive discomfort and, over the long term, chronic skin disorders. These can also be treated with external lotions: ⅔ oz (20 g) of the whole plant in 1 cup (250 ml) boiling water and strained in a compress applied to the area to be treated.

Anecdote: Father Kunzle advises overtaxed intellectuals who suffer from headaches to drink speedwell and to rest for 1 week near a stream in a mountain forest.

MULTIPURPOSE SPRINGTIME TINCTURE

1 cup (250 ml)	Slightly acidic white wine
1 ¾ oz (50 g)	Whole, fresh speedwell (at the beginning of summer)

*C*hop the plant in a food processor. Combine with the wine. Let stand for 1 month, shaking the container every 2 or 3 days. Strain. Consume over the course of a year. In the event of sluggish digestion, intestinal insufficiency or eczema, take 1 t (5 ml) before each meal.

COMMON THISTLE

Latin name: *Cirsium vulgare*

Common names: cotton thistle, woolly thistle

History: The French name *chardon* comes from *carder* meaning "to comb" or detangle fibers. In Ancient Greece this plant was used to comb out sheep's wool before spinning. There are 2 sides to the common thistle: on the one hand, it represents misery and neglected land (some countries even imposed fines on property owners who let it grow); on the other hand, it became the royal emblem of Scotland in 1458, and is still used as its symbol today. Pliny and Dioscorides maintained that the thistle leaves helped in straightening bent backs and twisted necks as well as reinforcing the bones of weak children. In many European countries (England, Scotland, Denmark), since the Roman Conquest, the practice was to eat the young peeled stems as well as the disk floret of the flower head steamed just like artichokes, their cousins.

Under the forbidding
thorns of the common thistle, hidden
deep in its cottony head, are many
benefits for good health.

Habitat: Dry, limestone soil, pastureland and its nitrogenous soil.

Description: Biennial plant that grows 3.3 ft to 4.95 ft (1 m to 1.5 m) high. The central stem is solid and prickly. The leaves end in long, pointy beige-colored thorns. The abundant seeds are equipped with aigrets and attached to the base by a ring until they reach maturity. The roots are slender and deep.

Parts Used: The leaves, flowery tops, seeds and the cooked roots in September, after flowering.

Chemical Composition: Leaves: sugars, chlorophyll, bioflavonoids, minerals (iron, silica, potassium), bitter principles, mucilages, tannins. Seeds: acids, polyunsaturated oil. Root: inulin, bitter principles.

Medicinal Properties: Antimitotic, antibiotic, cholagogue, choleretic, hypoglycemic, fortifying, hypotensive, blood depurative, immunostimulant, viricide, refreshing, cooling, tonic, remineralizing.

Applications: Thistle often served as survival food, for its leaves can be eaten once the thorns have been removed. It is used to prepare a nutritous bittersweet soup. Finely shredded and used in a poultice, thistle cures suppurating wounds. When boiled whole (1 leaf in 1 cup [250 ml] water), the leaves act as a

diuretic and gently drain the liver and soothe fevers caused by an overtaxed liver. The roots lower blood sugar levels, reduce blood pressure and cholesterol levels. Taken in an herbal tea—1 t in 1 cup (250 ml) water—3 times a day for 10 days before meals constitutes a seasonal cleansing.

Popular medieval beliefs praised the thistle decoction as a miracle lotion against baldness. The woolly aigrets of the thistle have long served as a dressing for wounds as well as stuffing for pillows. The cold-pressed oil of the seeds was used for cooking and as lamp oil for many years.

Anecdote: To treat a beloved pet, an ancient ritual called for a thistle to be placed at each of the compass points around the animal and to invoke the god, totem or patron saint of the animal.

ANTIVIRAL DECOCTION

1	Thistle flower head picked at the start of flowering
3 cups (750 ml)	Pure water

Boil the flower head for 3 minutes. Infuse for 15 minutes.

Drink during the day before meals. Effect a cure for 10 to 30 consecutive days in the case of a viral infection to nourish and stimulate the immune system.

CURLED DOCK

POLYGONACEAE FAMILY

Latin name: *Rumex crispus*

Common names: parell, patience herb, sour dock, yellow dock

History: North American Indians have used curled dock for a long time as survival food and as a purifying cure at the end of winter.

Culpeper, Paracelsus and, before them, the monks at the Salerno school, all used curled dock against bilious humors, venous blood and all kinds of pustules and scrofulas. Culpeper noted that the "Curled dock, falls under the patronage of Jupiter, as do all plants of a similar type, and all these are drying, yet refreshing and useful against all the abnormal leakages of vital fluids, from excessive bile to loss of blood, and the boiled seeds are the best part for this use. As for the roots, they treat all itching and ruptures of the skin and their distilled water will wash away freckles."

In numerous *Codices*, notably the American and the French ones, curled dock is described as cathartic, laxative,

depurative and reliably tonic. The great American herbalists Jethro Kloss, Alma Hutchens and Penny C. Royal commonly use it as an antiseptic used externally and as a cholagogue and tonic when taken internally.

The Academy of Minsk recommends it be used in a poultice against burns, ulcers and infected wounds that are slow to heal. Marie Provost claims it is ideal for cleansing the uterus in case of infection or hemorrhaging, and regenerating as a vaginal douche used after childbirth.

Curled dock is symbolic
of generosity, tenacity and fertility:
1 plant produces 30,000 seeds that can
wait 50 years to germinate!

Habitat: Everywhere in the northern hemisphere except in very cold climates; prefers very wet, shady areas, uncultivated and rocky soil, fallow land, rubbish and ditches. It often grows in colonies, which can be seen from afar because of the plant's reddish, abundant mane.

Description: A very hardy, perennial plant that grows 3.3 ft (1 m) in height. It has a central, channeled stem and large, alternating lanceolate leaves. The flowering, rust-colored tops grow in clusters. The three-sided fruit in the shape of a pyramid holds 3 seeds. The taproot is brown on the outside and golden on the inside.

Parts Used: The leaves, from spring until summer, and especially the root, harvested in the fall or the spring; the seeds are rarely collected.

Chemical Composition: Leaves: chlorophyll, vitamins A and C, oxalic acid. Roots: tannins, chrysophanic acid, rumicin, minerals (calcium, iron, magnesium, phosphorus), tonic, bitter principle.

Medicinal Properties: Appetizer, digestive, astringent, cicatrizant, choleretic, cholagogue, depurative, diuretic, emmenagogue, laxative, purgative, nutritive, tonic, pectoral, mucolytic, remineralizing, immunostimulant, uterine tonic.

Applications: The soft, steamed leaf makes a good poultice in the event of infectious skin problems such as acne, sores and eczema. The young leaf can also be eaten raw in a salad (a maximum of 3 leaves per serving), or boiled and drunk in a decoction over several days to purify the liver and the blood.

The root, in particular, has an effect on the lower digestive system and the intestines which it helps to regulate: for a laxative effect, 1 T (15 g) root in 1 cup (250 ml) water; as an astringent, 1 t (5 g) in 1 cup (250 ml) water.

The root and seeds boiled or prepared in a mother tincture, taken regularly (at a rate of 1 t in 1 cup [250 ml] water), combat anemia, reinforce the nervous system and increase fertility, especially in women.

Warning: Given its high level of oxalic acid and iron, curled dock is not recommended for those suffering from rheumatism, hypersideremia (too much iron in the blood), osteoporosis and kid-

---

NAVAJO SYRUP

4 cups (1 liter)	Water
2 lb (300 g)	Fresh curled dock roots
2 cups (500 g)	Wildflower honey

Slowly boil the roots until half the water has evaporated. Strain and melt the honey in the liquid, heating slowly. Keep this syrup cool: it's ideal in the fall for treating respiratory ailments. Take 1 t (5 ml), 3 times daily, as a pectoral, cholagogue and laxative syrup.

ney stones, nor for pregnant women nearing the end of their pregnancy.

Anecdote: Curled dock personifies a mother's goodness and renders the heart more tender.

DANDELION

ASTERACEAE FAMILY

Latin name: *Taraxacum officinale*

Common names: lion's tooth, cankerwort, piss-a-bed, priest crown, puffball, swine snout, wild endive

History: Chinese and ayurvedic physicians have used dandelion for thousands of years against all kinds of infections (colds, pneumonia, etc.) and to treat hepatic ailments, and those caused by poor control of fats (atherosclerosis, breast cancer, etc.). In the West, starting in the Middle Ages, it began to be referred to as "urinary." According to the signatures theory, the yellow flower of the dandelion is a remedy of choice for the liver and the production of bile. Culpeper recommended it as the ultimate herb for treating all "harmful disorders of the body."

This plant may have been brought to the United States when European settlers from Germany (the evangelists)

A few incredible figures: the dandelion is foraged by 93 different types of insects; during the winter of 1907, 30 metric tons of roots were sold at the New York market, and there are about 60 varieties around the world!

and England (the fundamentalists) arrived in the 16th century. They used it as food and as a remedy for liver and kidney ailments. In Brazil as in Quebec, in Alsace as in Italy, all nature lovers eat it in salad to cleanse and invigorate. English, Chinese and Swiss studies confirm its exceptional antidiabetic, cholagogue and diuretic virtues.

Habitat: Lightly treated lawns, moist fallow and pastureland, vacant lots in cities and sparse, mountain grasslands.

Description: Perennial plant that grows 6 in to 20 in (15 cm to 50 cm) in height. Plant bears irregular, dentate leaves that radiate out from the stem. The flower, which blooms from May to July, is a golden yellow: in fact, it consists of 200 minuscule flowers clustered around a single flower head. The double root is actually 2 roots, one a dark brown, fleshy rhizome, and the other a taproot filled with latex. The fruit is an achene that grows in the shape of an umbrella.

Parts Used: The whole plant, but especially the leaves in spring when their base is still white and the central stem has not yet grown. The root in spring and fall.

Chemical Composition: Chlorophyll, pectin, gluten, latex, lactone, vitamins A, C and F, bioflavonoids, minerals (iron, calcium, potassium, sodium, silica), proteins, acids, sugars, choline, lecithin, tannins, bitter principle, resin.

Medicinal Properties: Antiscorbutic, antifungal, cholagogue, choleretic, depurative, remineralizing, diuretic, lithotropic, nutritive, bitter tonic, ophthalmic and vulnerary.

Applications: The root, pulled in the spring and fall, is the best part, especially for draining biliary and hepatic toxins

DANDELION WINE

16 cups (4 liters)	Boiled water
4 cups (250 g)	Dandelion flowers picked around noon on a sunny day
2	Untreated oranges (without the juice)
2	Untreated lemons (without the juice)
3 lb (1.5 kg)	Honey (dandelion honey, if possible)
1 T (15 g)	White wine yeast, dry

Pour the boiling water on the flowers. Dilute the honey in the mixture. Cut the citrus fruit into cubes and add to the mixture. Allow to ferment in an earthenware jar or in a large glass pitcher in a dark location at 68°F (20°C) for 3 weeks and stir with a large wooden spatula every 2 to 3 days. When fermentation is complete, strain using a clean cheesecloth. Bottle the wine and seal with a cork.

Age in a cool area for 9 months.

This wine is excellent for the gallbladder, for treating gout and uric acid, and is highly recommended for a prediabetic condition.

Drink half a glass before meals: it is delicious, has an original taste and adds zing!

Note: For those who are lazy, here is the modified recipe: Macerate 1 cup (60 g) flowers in 4 cups (1 liter) white wine for 1 month. Strain and sweeten to taste. It's ready!

and for cleansing the kidneys. It can be eaten raw and grated in a salad, boiled or steamed, or even roasted in a frying pan just like coffee made from grains. In a mother tincture (between 15 and 20 drops in water, 3 times daily), it is diuretic and choleretic. To dry the plant, wash it first, then spread it out on a wire tray, in the shade, in a well-ventilated area for about 2 weeks.

Eating the fresh leaves in a salad is the best way to preserve their properties. They can be added to soup, to an omelette or a hotpot. In a mother tincture or dried, they act as a depurative and treat skin disorders, anemia and demineralization.

The pure latex is used on warts or even on infected wounds and, when diluted by half, can be used to treat eye infections. Repeat the applications. Use a fresh stem for each application.

Eaten raw or prepared in a decoction, a mother tincture or a medicinal wine, the flower is recommended against bile retention and constipation.

The dandelion leaf cleanses the lymphatic system, clears up edema, fights cellulite and stimulates the immune system.

Anecdote: According to an ancient magical belief, if you cover the body in dandelion juice, you attract the sympathy of all those who are like you. If you blow a tufted seed in the direction of your lover, all your thoughts will be sent to him or her!

ELECAMPANE

ASTERACEAE FAMILY

Latin name: *Inula helenium*

Common names: elf dock, horse-heal, velvet dock

History: Elecampane is said to have been born from the tears of Helen who was kidnapped by Paris, whence its Latin name. Dioscorides and Galen both recognized its digestive, emmenagogue and pectoral attributes. The Romans carried it to northern Europe during their campaigns. Pliny maintained that regularly chewing elecampane purifies the breath and fortifies the gums and teeth.

St. Hildegard praised it for its benefits: "Elecampane is beneficial and healthy for the intestines." At the market and the apothecary, candies made from elecampane could be found to treat asthma and contagious diseases.

The name "horseheal" comes from the plant's powerful therapeutic effects on equine skin infections. But it also cures chronic skin suppurations in humans and, according to John Gerard,

The great purifying power of this endangered sunny plant is reason enough to encourage its growth.

poisonous snakebite. Culpeper said that elecampane cured pulmonary ailments, epidemic fever, gout and sciatica.

In the United States, the Eclectics advised using it to induce menses, to treat lithiasis and chronic pulmonary ailments.

In 1885, in Germany, pharmaceutical research proved that elecampane neutralized Koch's bacillus (tuberculosis). European scientists recently confirmed the antiparasitic qualities of elecampane, in particular, against yeast parasites, giardiasis and pinworm.

Habitat: Moist, clay soils, fallow land on the edge of forests, acidic yet stony grasslands, nitrogenous (from animal excretions) pastureland and also near rivers.

Description: Hardy perennial plant that grows up to 3.3 ft (1 m) in height. The plant has a central, cylindrical stem adorned with terminal, golden flowers in the shape of the sun. The oval leaves are rough on the top, cottony and whitish underneath. The fleshy root can weigh several pounds.

Parts Used: Essentially, only the root is taken from a 2- to 3-year old plant, dug up in the spring or fall; the leaves can be used at the beginning of summer, before flowering.

Chemical Composition: Inulin, essential oil, hydrocarbons, saponins,

albumin, resins, pectin, inositol, vitamin C, mineral salts (calcium, magnesium, potassium, sodium phosphate), mucilages, bitter principles.

Medicinal Properties: Antiseptic, antibiotic, aromatic, deodorizing, antifungal, pesticide, choleretic, febrifuge, dechlorinating, uricosuric, emmenagogue, dissolvent, hypoglycemic, digestive, pectoral, viricidal, tonic, depurative, vermifuge, vulnerary.

Applications: The fresh root is used in a pectoral decoction, an antiparasitic enema or a digestive drink at the rate of 2 g in 1 cup (250 ml) water. Traditionally, it is used in a mother tincture in alcohol, white wine or vinegar: 1 oz (25 g) in 1 cup (250 ml), strained, taken at a rate of 20 drops, 3 times daily, it treats

VERMIFUGE WINE

1 cup (250 ml)	Gin or vodka
7 oz (200 g)	Elecampane root, fresh or dried, chopped
4 cups (1 liter)	Red wine
¼ cup (75 g)	Cane sugar

*M*acerate the elecampane in alcohol for 1 week in an amber-colored jar, away from light. Add the wine and sugar. Shake regularly and strain at the end of 1 month. Drink in a liqueur glass—1 oz (25 ml)—before meals, for 3 consecutive days. Wait 10 days. Repeat the treatment 3 times. This aromatic wine also has aperient, digestive and tonic attributes. Avoid drinking in the case of an ulcer, diarrhea and in the early stages of pregnancy.

coughing, fungi, infections and fatigue. For infusions, preserve by cutting into strips to activate drying (at least 2 weeks). It must be used quickly, for after 1 year the essential oil and inulin will have evaporated.

The dried leaves can also be smoked. Besides chasing away insects, the smoke kills aerobic or airborne parasites. It also acts as an external antiseptic.

The flowers, grown in the West for use as decoration, are used in China in a hepatic herbal tea and, in North America, as a floral elixir because of their purifying attributes.

Anecdote: Elecampane is connected to the planet, to the metal and to the god Mercury. It stimulates the imagination and allows those who have gone mad to return to their senses!

EVENING PRIMROSE

Latin name: *Oenothera biennis*

Common names: evening star, fever plant

History: Theophrastus, an ancient Greek physician, it seems, named evening primrose. Its name of *oenothera* appears to have come from *oïnos*, which means "wine," and from *thera*, meaning "to chase." It evokes the ability of the plant to counter the effects of intoxication. Strangely, evening primrose is a native plant of North America. It is believed to have reached the ports of Holland in 1614, when the colonization of America began. North American Indians had been using it for some time in a poultice and in lotion form to stop bleeding, treat wounds and regenerate damaged skin (scars and malignant eruptions). In Europe, in the 17th century, it was called the "the king's panacea" and was used against all kinds of pain (menstrual, rheumatic, etc.).

In 1917, a German researcher, Dr. Unger, revealed that the seeds of the evening primrose consisted of 15% oil.

This evening star that only blooms at dusk is capable of regenerating the entire body.

From 1919 on, the discoveries followed one upon the other, notably that of gamma-linoleic acid. Dr. John Williams marketed concentrated evening primrose oil under the name Naudicelle. Serious experiments have proven the effectiveness of evening primrose oil in treating major ailments such as schizophrenia, multiple sclerosis and chronic asthma. It is now commercially grown and consumed around the world.

Habitat: Uncultivated land, poor pastureland, sandy shores and along paths, in full sunshine.

Description: Biennial plant that grows 3.3 ft (1 m) in height with a hardy, round and slightly hairy stem with red

131

spots, and divided near the top. It bears solid spikes of bright yellow flowers. The fruit is joined to the stem at the leaf axil. The taproot is fleshy and reddish. Dried, the plant emits a red-wine scent.

Parts Used: All the parts of the plant including the root.

Chemical Composition: Essential fatty acids, plant sterols, ceryl alcohol, mucilages, tannins, minerals (calcium, magnesium, manganese).

Medicinal Properties: Astringent, cicatrizant, anti-inflammatory, antispasmodic, depurative, laxative, immunostimulant, antioxidant, lubricating, nutritive.

Applications: The first year, the young leaves and root can be eaten raw or steamed, or applied to the skin to treat a minor wound. The second year, the stems and leaves can be used in a decoction to treat diarrhea, nervous, pulmonary or asthmatic spasms, or panic attacks. The flowers can be used to prepare a floral elixir or to garnish salads. The young fruit can be steamed and eaten in large quantities. As for the seeds, they can be ground and used to prepare a mother tincture (50% plant, 100% alcohol): take 20 drops, 3 times daily. They can also be eaten dried and swallowed with water after being thoroughly chewed.

The evening primrose oil (concentrated in capsules) is excellent for treating arthritis, multiple sclerosis, dry skin, hot flashes due to menopause, premenstrual syndrome, and immunodeficiency disorders. It is more effective if taken with vitamin E. As with all polyunsaturated fats, it must be stored in the refrigerator.

Warning: Avoid giving evening primrose oil to epileptics and in the case of persistent nausea. Ideally, the liver should be cleansed before consuming evening primrose to assimilate it better.

Anecdote: Evening primrose elixir repairs the chakra of the heart and treats a stomach that has been irritated for a long time.

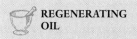

REGENERATING OIL

¾ cup (20 g)	Evening primrose flowers
1 cup (250 ml)	Organic olive oil
40 drops	Lavender essential oil

*D*ry the flower petals for 1 week and gently shred. Add the olive oil and the essential oil. Macerate for 1 month, away from light; shake occasionally. Strain.

This oil promotes scarring and hydrates. It should be used in small quantities on the face (and occasionally on the body) to treat sores, wrinkles and dry skin.

EYEBRIGHT

SCROFULARIACEAE FAMILY

Latin name: *Euphrasia officinalis*

Common names: Eyebright

History: The Latin word *euphrasia* comes from the name of one of the three Greek Graces, Euphrosyne, meaning "delight." St. Hildegard of Bingen said that eyebright fortifies the brain, memory and eyes. In 1313, Arnaud de Villeneuve, a great Italian physician, wrote a treatise glorifying eyebright. John Gerard recommended combining it with fennel to reinforce eyesight, and in a white-wine tincture against cataracts. Olivier de Serres grew it and called it "little light" because of its ability to improve eyesight. The signatures theory perceived an open eye in the shape of the heart of the flower, and homeopathy still uses *Euphrasia* to treat sensitivity to sunlight and lacrimation brought on by inflammation of the eye due to an infection or allergies. Dr. Vogel produced and recommended a simple eyebright tincture to treat the

eyes: it is still available under this name in a 50 ml format.

Habitat: On the edge of poor pastureland, along roadsides and paths, in full sun.

Description: A small annual 2 in to 10 in (5 cm to 25 cm) high, with oval leaves that literally wrap around the flower spike. The main corolla is white and mauve with purple stripes.

Parts Used: The whole plant at the

You need good eyesight
to find eyebright, but it is worth
the effort if you want to
continue to see it!

start of flowering, at the end of August, or early September.

Chemical Composition: Tannins, phenolic acid, glucosides, essential oil, choline.

Medicinal Properties: Antiseptic, cicatrizant, astringent, antidiarrheic, anti-inflammatory, basifying, expectorant, pectoral, ophthalmic, immune system tonic.

Applications: Eyebright is truly the most famous plant for soothing and treating eye disorders: conjunctivitis, glaucoma, keratitis and iritis. Perform an eye wash using a cold decoction: 1 t (5 g) of the fresh or dried plant, boiled in 1 cup (250 ml) water for 5 minutes. Compresses can be reapplied after repeatedly dipping them in the decoction. Or, rinse the eyes with 1 T (15 ml) of the cool liquid. The eyebright decoction can also be drunk: 3 whole fresh plants in 1 cup (250 ml) water or 1 t of dried plants in 1 cup (250 ml) water. It fights diarrhea, sinusitis and seasonal allergies that provoke painful nasal and ocular discharges.

Anecdote: In *A Modern Herbal*, Mrs. Grieve quotes the great English poet John Milton, who tells of the archangel Michael who commanded Adam to wash his eyes with eyebright and rue (*Ruta graveolens*) to regain his sanity after committing the original sin!

134

OPHTHALMIC SOLUTION

1 ½ oz (2 g)	Fresh or dried eyebright
1 cup (250 ml)	Spirits (gin, brandy)

In a mixing bowl, shred the plant in the alcohol. Put the mixture in a jar, shake every 2 or 3 days. Strain after 1 month.

Use as an eyewash at a rate of 30 drops in 1 cup (250 ml) boiled water. Used internally, this solution soothes seasonal allergies, catarrhs and the common cold.

FERN

Latin name: *Dryopteris filix mas* or *Aspidium filix mas*

Common names: aspidium, British fern, male fern, sweet brake

History: It was ferns, fossilized more than 350 million years ago, that generated the largest mass of coal. According to Dioscorides and Galen, the male fern root was one of the best vermifuges known. North American Indians used it to reduce pain during childbirth and to increase lactation in wet nurses. John Gerard provided a recipe for expelling long, flat worms: "Eat little at night, drink a decoction made up of ½ oz of fern root in 2 cups of honeyed water, also eat fresh garlic and, in the morning, take a purgative to be sure of getting rid of these dirty creatures immediately." A famous healer, Mme Nauffer, may have sold Louis XVI a secret vermifuge remedy worth its weight in gold, and whose principle ingredient was fern. The peasants of Berri, the Sami of Norway and the trappers of Quebec all ate the young

Ferns, the generous pioneer plants rich in carbon and oxygen, purify the air that nourishes all living organisms.

fiddleheads in spring and slept on beds of fern to keep away insects, relieve rheumatism or prevent children from bedwetting.

Habitat: Old and marshy, moist deciduous forests of the northern hemisphere.

Description: A plant with deeply cut leaves and equipped with orange-colored spores (reproductive corpuscles) stuck on the nervures.

Parts Used: The young, hairless stems of the leaves at the beginning of spring, the leaves in summer, and the rhizome in fall.

135

Chemical Composition: Aspidinol, flavaspidic acid, essential oil, oleoresin, sugars, chlorophyll.

Medicinal Properties: Analgesic, antirheumatic, cholagogic, fungicide, deodorizing, diuretic, emmenagogue, oxytocic, galactagogue, remineralizing, vermifuge, parasiticide.

Warning: Avoid absorbing the fern root during the early stages of pregnancy and while breastfeeding, in the case of severe cardiopathy or serious hepatic disorders. Do not combine with alcohol or oil. A too-strong dosage can cause blindness. For internal use, take only under supervision. In the case of a deworming cure, always mix with a water-soluble vermifuge.

Anecdote: According to an ancient belief, carrying fern seeds around with you makes you invisible or helps you to pass unnoticed. They keep away evil witches who will try to harm you.

FATHER KUNZLE'S OIL

5	Fern fronds, well dried
⅘ cup (200 ml)	Olive oil

*D*etach the dried leaflets from the stems and macerate in the oil for 1 month. Carefully strain. This oil can be kept for 6 months away from light. This is an ideal massage oil for muscular pain.

FIGWORT

SCROFULARIACEAE FAMILY

Latin name: *Scrofularia nodosa*

Common names: throatwort, kernelwort

History: In 1623, the German botanist Otto Brunfels gave this plant the name "figwort," undoubtedly because of its round and greenish appearance and its therapeutic properties against suppurating indurations. One of its names in French, "siege herb," goes back to the 100 Years War. The armies of Louis XIII ate the roots and leaves for 13 months during the siege of La Rochelle.

Here is the treatment recommended by John Gerard against water retention: "Every morning, on an empty stomach, eat a piece of bread with butter and covered with powdered figwort root and drink two cups of water; dress in wool garments and walk briskly until you sweat profusely; follow this treatment for 7 consecutive days and you will be cured."

Pietro-Andrea Mattioli, an Italian

botanist and healer, also called it "anti-scrofuloso." He advocated its use, in particular, to treat abscesses due to diabetes and tuberculosis.

Recently, Dr. Leclerc confirmed the depurative and hypoglycemic qualities of this plant and, because of this, its usefulness in treating the symptoms of diabetes.

Habitat: Acidic and shaded soils, moist areas, the edges of forests and along the edges of ditches where figwort grows in dense colonies.

Description: Large perennial plant

Although ugly and smelly, figwort detoxifies the blood and skin thanks to its depurative properties, and bees love it!

3.3 ft (1 m) in height with a square stem bearing large dentate and lanceolate oval leaves. The abundant flowers are a strange greenish-yellow mixed with purple.

Parts Used: All the parts exposed to the air at the beginning of flowering, sometimes the root in fall.

Chemical Composition: Acids, flavonoids, glucosides, iridoids, pectin, rhein, saponins, sulphur, alkaloid, vitamin C.

Medicinal Properties: Antiscrofulous, analgesic, depurative, diuretic, lithotriptic, hypoglycemic, nutritive, hypertensive, tonic, purgative, antiseptic, vermifuge, fungicide, vulnerary, rubefacient.

Applications: Figwort must always be taken in moderation. The leaves and stems are used in a weak decoction: 1 oz (30 g) per 4 cups (1 liter) water. Do not exceed 3 cups (750 ml) daily. Eventually it can be combined with a complemen-

tary or more aromatic plant (raspberry, common elder, meadowsweet): it treats arthritis, skin disorders and constipation.

In a mother tincture and diluted in fruit juice (10 drops, 3 times daily): carry out a cure in the case of skin disorders or diabetes.

In a compress or a poultice, the raw plant is applied to cysts, nodules, ulcers or wounds.

In the case of vaginitis, insert a whole leaf, rolled up, into the vagina at bedtime. Allow the petiole to remain visible. Remove upon waking in the morning. Follow this treatment for 10 consecutive days.

Figwort is also a good insecticide: macerate the plants in rainwater (5% plant). Spray on infected plants.

Warning: Avoid figwort in the case of colitis and diarrhea, hypoglycemia, hypertension, tachycardia as well as severe cardiac lesions.

Anecdote: For more than a thou-

ANTISCROFULOUS OINTMENT

⅓ oz (10 g)	Fresh figwort leaves
⅓ oz (10 g)	Beef tallow or fat
⅔ oz (20 g)	Lard or pork fat
1	Glass jar, about 2 oz (50 ml)

Dry the shredded leaves in a frying pan until they become powdery. Add the two types of fat. Gently stir until this mixture is completely blended. Pour into jar. Let cool. Can be refrigerated for 3 months.

Despite its greenish color and unpleasant smell, this ointment is very effective against adenitis, cysts, abnormal indurations, fungal ailments and weeping eczema.

sand years, in Alsace and in England, figwort has been viewed as a protective herb against misfortune. It is hung on doors and around the necks of children to attract the graces of the good fairies and to keep evil spirits away.

FIREWEED

ONAGRACEAE FAMILY

Latin name: *Epilobium augustifolium* or *parviflorum*

Common names: blooming sally, blood vine, flowering willow, purple rocket

History: North American Indians used fireweed to make compresses to apply to burns, wounds and swelling. In 1820, the Eclectics demonstrated that several Nordic peoples used it in a fresh decoction against intestinal problems in the summer, such as diarrhea due to food poisoning. In northern Russia, a fireweed herbal tea is drunk instead of regular tea and, in times of famine, the young steamed shoots are eaten. In Kamchatka, a hallucinogenic beer using fireweed and yellow-orange fly agaric is produced. The Austrian herbalist Maria Treben provoked renewed interest in the little fireweed (*Epilobium parviflorum*) by asserting that she had cured several prostate cancers thanks to this plant, a fact confirmed by Danièle Laberge in Quebec.

The recent discovery of concentrated

Fireweed represents
renewal after a difficult time:
it cools all fires!

beta-sitosterol in this plant reinforces these facts.

Habitat: Moist areas, ditches, recently burned areas in wet forests and along rivers.

Description: Perennial plant 28 in to 5 ft (70 cm to 1.5 m) in height and with large purple flowers. The fruit, a brown capsule open at both ends, releases oval seeds.

Parts Used: The young shoots in spring, aerial parts at the beginning of flowering, in July.

Chemical Composition: Tannins, mucilages, pectin, potassium, beta-sitosterol, bioflavonoids.

Medicinal Properties: Antioxidant, immunostimulant, emollient, laxative, diuretic, dissolvent, nutritive, regenerating, protective, vulnerary.

Applications: The young shoots can be eaten in soup or steamed, or, in the case of diarrhea, a decoction. So as not to lose any of the plant properties, use a mother tincture: 1 part plants to 2 parts alcohol: take 10 drops, 2 times daily. It treats diarrhea and gastritis.

Epilobium augustifolium: skin disorders.

Epilobium parviflorum: prostate problems.

Anecdote: Although feminine in its bearing, attractive colors and production of thousands of seeds, it treats mostly problems relating to an imbalance in male functions.

PROSTATE DECOCTION

1 oz (30 g)	Tiny-flowered fireweed flowery tops
1 oz (30 g)	Mallow flowery tops
1 oz (30 g)	Wild thyme flowery tops
1 oz (30 g)	Nettle leaves
1 oz (30 g)	Dandelion roots
4 cups (1 liter)	Water

Combine all the fresh plants and place in the water. Simmer for 5 minutes. Infuse for 30 minutes, then strain. Drink the entire amount during the day. In the case of serious infection, extend this treatment for 1 to 2 months.

This decoction cleanses the kidneys and treats chronic infections of the prostate and bladder.

GOLDENROD

ARISTERACEAE FAMILY

Latin name: *Solidago virgaurea* (Europe) or *Solidago canadensis* (Canada)

Common names: Aaron's root, woundwort

History: In Europe during the 16th century, Arnaud de Villeneuve, an alchemist and physician, was the first to discuss the diuretic and vulnerary medicinal worth of goldenrod. The conquerors of the New World had brought it back with them by accident along with other plants. John Gerard said: "It is all the more precious because it is rare and it comes from afar, but a good number of local native plants are better, it is praised because that which comes from elsewhere and costs more, pleases women more." In 1636, Olivier de Serres, in *Théâtre de l'agriculture*, says that "goldenrod is a plant that, by its nature, is cold and very efficient in moderating the hot maladies of the liver and the kidneys, and in relieving the stomach that has fallen victim to the torments of diarrhea."

North American Indians used it as an

internal antidote to toxic alkaloids, and as a fomentation against rattlesnake bites, wounds and ulcers. Dr. Vogel used it as one of the main ingredients in his famous diuretic tincture. Danièle Laberge maintains that goldenrod is the most effective plant against allergies and that it restores the cellular integrity of all the mucous membranes.

Habitat: Sandy soils, rich in ancient alluvion, and sunny fallow lands.

Description: Herbaceous perennial plant 6 in to 3.3 ft (15 cm to 1 m) in height with thin, lanceolate leaves with 3 nerves. The hermaphrodite flowers have small, yellow flower heads.

Parts Used: The leaves before flow-

Goldenrod is an ally worth its weight in gold for reinforcing our immune system against disease.

143

ering, and the flowery tops, just before they completely flower, between mid-July and mid-August, depending on the variety and the region.

Chemical Composition: Mucilages, saponins, essential oil, glycosides, solidagalactones, inulin, acids, tannins.

Medicinal Properties: Antiuric, diuretic, astringent, antiseptic, antispasmodic, antitoxic, choleretic, immunostimulant, tonic, vulnerary.

Applications: In an herbal tea, or a decoction, the flowery top of the goldenrod is recommended for treating seasonal allergies of the pulmonary mucous membranes, and for treating chronic intestinal problems: 1 t (3 g) in 1 cup (250 ml). In the case of ulcerous colitis: 1 average plant (exposed parts) to 2 cups (500 ml) boiled water. This is also an effective parasiticide against pathogenic yeasts.

In a decoction: 4 t (12 g) in 4 cups (1 liter) water. Drink 4 cups (1 liter) daily. This is also an excellent diuretic treatment for water retention and uremia.

Warning: Some sensitive people are allergic to its pollen. Avoid consuming goldenrod if this is the case.

Anecdote: The elixir made from goldenrod flowers reinforces a sense of self in harmony with the collective consciousness.

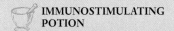
IMMUNOSTIMULATING POTION

¾ oz (20 g)	Fresh goldenrod flowers (dried: 10 g)
⅓ oz (10 g)	Fresh dandelion root (dried: 5 g)
⅓ oz (10 g)	Wild thyme leaves
4 cups (1 liter)	Water

*B*oil the plants in the water for 3 minutes. Infuse 10 minutes. Strain. Drink hot or cold during the day, between meals.

Diuretic and disinfecting cure of the mucous membranes and major organs: 7 to 15 days. It is recommended for those suffering from allergies, constipation, colitis and chronic pulmonary or kidney disease.

GRAPE VINE

AMPELIDACEAE FAMILY

Latin name: *Vitis vinifera*

Common names: Vine

History: In the Book of Genesis, the strange story appears where, for the first time, the vine is mentioned: Noah gets drunk on the fruit of the first grapevine grown by him, dances naked and ends up damning his son and his descendants.

In Ancient Greece, the grapevine was the symbol of civilization. The Ancient Greeks worshiped Dionysus, the god of the grapevine, wine and ecstatic delirium, who is also called *Bacchus* in Latin.

At the time of the Gauls in France, the dried leaves were used in powder form to treat cows suffering from dysentery. They were also used to prepare a hemostatic tonic for the veins, especially red grapevines, which recall the capillary and venous systems according to the signatures theory. In 1535, Jacques Cartier and his crew dropped anchor at the Île d'Orléans: they called it the Island of Bacchus because of the incredible number of wild vines, the "vine of the foxes" (*Vitis vulpina* or *Vitis viparia*) that could be found there.

In the 15th century in France, country doctors used the gummy and limpid sap, called "vine tears," pure or reduced to a resin, on superficial wounds and as an eye lotion. At the end of 18th century, German and British hygienists recommended the grape—Rabelais, the French physician and writer in the 16th century, called it the "heavenly meat"—as the sole ingredient in a depurative diet.

In Quebec, in 1889, Alfred Des Fossés published his *Traité sur la culture du raisin sauvage* (Treatise on the cultivation of wild grapes). But his project to grow wild grapevines never materialized.

Rice wrapped in a vine leaf soaked in vinegar or olive oil is a national Greek dish.

Habitat: Vineyards, of course, but also clay and siliceous fallow lands, sunny slopes, hedges and trellises.

Description: Shrub with more or less twisted stems bearing small, round, green branches adorned with large, alternating and palmlike leaves. The tiny flowers are grouped in a light green panicle. The fruit is a berry of variable color (from light green to deep blue depending on the variety) that contains between 5 and 10 seeds. A plant originally from good stock can live for 600 years!

A generous plant, the grapevine can cure us, nourish us or intoxicate us!

Parts Used: The sap that flows from the small branches in the spring, the flowers, leaves, raw berries and seeds.

Chemical Composition: Leaves, juice and small branches: flavonoids, tartaric salts, choline, inositol, beta-carotene, minerals (calcium, potassium), fiber, tannins, chlorophyll. Fruit: sugar, acids, pectin, pigments, vitamins A, B_1, B_2, B_{12} and C, ionized water (80%), trace elements. Seeds: anthocyanins, polyunsaturated oil.

Medicinal Properties: Astringent, cicatrizant, anti-inflammatory, antiseptic, antioxidant, regenerating, diuretic, lithotriptic, hypotensive, cardiotonic, laxative, nutritive, regenerating, vulnerary.

Applications: The sap can be used directly on suppurating wounds or diluted in the same volume of boiling water to treat eye infections.

In a decoction: boil the fresh or dried leaves (1 leaf in 1 cup [250 ml] water). They are diuretic, excellent against cellulite and diarrhea, but especially tonic for the capillaries in the legs or the uterus; when used in a sitzbath, or to bathe the hands or feet, the leaves are effective against circulatory blockages

good health and contains as many flavonoids and antioxidant polyphenols as the fermented juice. As for the wine, although it lightens the heart, its dependence has caused much misfortune. However, a glass of good-quality wine every day can be healthy.

The crushed pips are a formidable source of immunostimulating agents, and their cold-pressed oil is among the recommended sources of fat.

Anecdote: Just like the vine, the flower elixir (recommended by the famous Dr. Bach) is ideal for domineering personalities: it opens the mind to unselfishness and tolerance.

(hemorrhoids, varicose veins); in a poultice, they soothe headaches.

The grape represents one of the healthiest and most easily digested fruit. It makes it easier to tolerate fasting without suffering from hunger: it is, however, essential to choose organic fruit and, for sensitive stomachs, to spit out the pulp and pits, which act as a laxative and are indigestible.

Sulphur-free dried sultana raisins or currants soaked for several hours constitute a good pectoral: take before meals, 3 times daily.

Red grape juice without preservatives and unpasteurized is excellent for

SLIMMING HERBAL TEA	
3 t (10 g)	Vine leaves
3 t (10 g)	Common elder flowers
3 t (10 g)	Sapwood from the linden tree
6 cups (1.5 liters)	Water

*B*oil the plants for 5 minutes, infuse for 10 minutes. Drink all the liquid during the day, between meals.

To eliminate water retention and intercellular toxins, drink 3 to 4 cups (750 ml to 1 liter) daily, before meals, for 10 to 30 consecutive days.

GROUND IVY

Latin name: *Glecoma hederacea*

Common names: creeping charlie, gill run over, hedge maid, field balm, wild snakeroot

History: Physicians have been using ground ivy since Ancient Greek times. Galen said it was acrid, hot and biting, capable of curing all pulmonary problems. Dioscorides recommended its use in a 40-day cure against sciatica and osteoarthritis of the hips. At the beginning of our own time, the Vikings and Celts used it to clarify and preserve beer. John Gerard prescribed it against buzzing and ringing in the ears. Culpeper advocated it for treating a black eye, hematoma and other problems of this type. St. Hildegard advised drinking it in case of migraines and to wear crowns made from blanched whole plants. These crowns were also worn to ward off bad luck while dancing around the fires on the feast of St. John.

Habitat: Temperate zones around

the globe, moist areas located near gardens and on grasslands, rubble, rocky mounds and along dirt roads.

Description: A herbaceous perennial plant that grows 8 in to 20 in (20 cm to 50 cm) in height on a square stem bearing round, dentate leaves. The flowers are a purplish-blue, tending towards light mauve, for flowering can last 3 months or more, which is exceptional for a wildflower. The leaves give off the smell of camphor with a touch of citronella and peppermint.

Parts Used: Stems, flowers and leaves at the start of flowering, in May.

Chemical Composition: Wax, acid, choline, glucides, lipids, protein (glechomine), essential oil, lactone, bitter principle (marrubin), saponins, resin, tannins, vitamin C.

Medicinal Properties: Antiseptic,

Ground ivy represents warmth, femininity and the permanence of plant forces. It cleanses us and keeps us humble by keeping our feet on the ground.

fortifies the bronchial tubes and energizes all the gastrointestinal organs, the urinary system, and the genitals.

Ground ivy is also one of the great healing herbs: compresses made from a concentrated decoction are used to treat abscesses, wounds, cuts and bruises. An herbal tea cure (3 plants in 1 cup [250 ml] water) cleanses the blood and tissues of any toxic heavy metals such as cadmium, copper, lead and zinc: approx. 30 oz (1 liter) per day for 10 days or up to 3 months, depending on the seriousness of the poisoning. The dried plant, reduced to a powder, is a sternutator, ideal for headaches and sinusitis.

Anecdote: St. Hildegard maintained that if you rinse your head often with a decoction made from ground ivy, all head ailments will disappear... as well as those of the brain!

antispasmodic, astringent, bechic, cicatrizant, emollient, expectorant, stomachic, tonic, vulnerary.

Applications: The flowers can be eaten or used as a lovely garnish for salads. The whole plant can be used in preparing a mother tincture (50% saturated in 100% alcohol; take 15 drops, 3 times daily). It is also easy to dry, requiring less than 1 week. In a decoction and a hot herbal tea, ivy is especially good for treating nasal, throat and ear infections by disinfecting the mucous membranes and liquefying the mucus right down to the lungs. The ivy helps cleanse the lungs through expectoration. It also

HEALING OIL

1 ¾ oz (50 g)	Ground ivy, freshly dried
4 cups (1 liter)	Olive oil

Grind the ivy in a mortar or in a blender. Add the oil and mix. Macerate 1 month and carefully strain. Pour the oil into several small bottles (easier to use and less likely to go rancid).

Excellent for wounds, bruises and even muscular pain.

HAWTHORN

Latin name: *Craetaegus oxyacantha*

Common names: cheese tree, may-blossom, white thorn

History: Joseph of Arimathea (the one who buried Christ's body) and his family are credited with first bringing the hawthorn, originally from North Africa, to England. They considered it to be sacred, for the crown of thorns worn by Christ was made from it. It has been the symbol of defense and purity since Ancient Greece: the nuptial bedroom and the newborn's cradle were decorated with it to keep away evil spirits.

In the 18th century, the Irish physician K'Eogh and his French colleagues Huchard and Reilly elevated it to its cardiotonic status for controlling angina pectoris, arteriosclerosis, hypertension and palpitations. Dr. Vogel confirmed the gentle power of the flowers and leaves in a mother tincture (harmless even in an extended cure) as a substitute for digitalin. Dr. Binet calls it "heart valerian."

Habitat: Old fallow lands, abandoned grasslands and the edges of forests.

Description: Perennial shrub that grows 6.6 ft to 16.5 ft (2 m to 5 m) high and whose central trunk is subdivided into numerous slender branches that bear long thorns. The white flowers with a pink center grow in clusters. The bright red fruit has a central pit that contains the seeds.

Parts Used: All the young shoots taken from the ends of the branches, the flowers in early May, the leaves, the fruit and the bark.

Chemical Composition: Bioflavonoids, rutin, vitexin, organic acids, protein. Fruit: starch, polyphenols, sugars, mucilages, vitamin C. Leaves, bark and fruit: minerals (calcium, potassium, zinc, copper), coumarin.

Medicinal Properties: Antispasmodic, calming, antidiarrheic, astringent, regenerating, hypotensive, vasodilator, nutritive, a restorative febrifuge.

Applications: Using the young shoots, prepare a mother tincture (double the volume of alcohol): excellent against problems involving cardiac rhythm, hypertension and hyperactivity. Gently pick the flowers and dry them on

Its large concentration of antioxidants justifies a return to popularity at a time when many people are suffering from cardiovascular disease.

HEART-FRIENDLY TINCTURE

1 cup (60 g)	Hawthorn flowers
2 cups (500 ml)	Gin, brandy or, ideally, kirsch

Crush the flowers in a mortar. Pour in the alcohol and macerate for 1 month away from light. Strain.

Take 1 t (5 ml) in a little water every morning and evening before meals for 20 consecutive days to treat arrhythmia, hypertension and palpitations. To maintain the blood vessels in general, follow this same treatment at the start of each season.

fine paper. They calm the nervous system. Used fresh in a decoction or dried in an herbal tea: 1 flowery top in 1 cup (250 ml) water to treat anxiety, hot flashes due to menopause and palpitations. The mother tincture has the same effect: 30 flowery tops in 1 cup (250 ml) alcohol; take 20 drops, 3 times daily before meals or, in case of emergency, the normal dose.

In a tincture or an herbal tea, the leaves soothe circulatory problems and help the gentle yet beneficial vasodilatation of the cardiac muscle. They are also diuretic. The fruit can be eaten raw in

151

August and September. Dried in the shade or used in a mother tincture, the fruit is recommended for treating diarrhea or for fortifying the blood vessels: 5 berries in 1 cup (250 ml) liquid. In winter, the bark of the young branches is collected because of its fever-fighting virtues in a decoction: 1 t (5 g) bark in 2 cups (500 ml) boiled water for several minutes.

Anecdote: If the hawthorn was symbolic of love and birth in Antiquity, in England during the Middle Ages, it was associated with the plague, its smell recalling that of decomposing corpses.

152

HOP

CANNABINACEAE FAMILY

Latin name: *Humulus lupulus*

Common names: Common Hop

History: Chinese healers have known the hop for more than 2000 years: they used it against diarrhea, leprosy and even tuberculosis. It was in the Caucasus during the 11th century that hops were first used in the production of beer. This practice progressively spread throughout all of Europe, except in England where Henry VIII prohibited its use by decree. The belief that the hop caused melancholy was behind this prohibition that remained in effect for 2 centuries. The Italian physician, Pietro-Andrea Mattioli, adored the hop and used it as an appetizer, a depurative, a diuretic, a laxative, a febrifuge and a vermifuge. Dr. Lemery recommended it for treating liver and spleen ailments, for purifying the blood and for stimulating urination.

Habitat: Abandoned fences, walls and trellises and, of course, farms, all in full sun.

The hop is a narcotic plant that creates many victims. It should be used in herbal teas or to make relaxing pillows!

Description: A perennial climbing plant with solid stems. The male flowers are grouped in a lanceolate formation at the end of the small branches and the female flowers at the axil of the leaves. The fruit is the shape of cones or strobiles consisting of light, yellow-green scales filled with a yellowish, resinous powder called lupulin.

Parts Used: The young shoots in the spring, but especially the cones at the end of summer. They are also called "strobiles."

Chemical Composition: Lupulin, essential oil, bitter principles, pectin, resin, sugars, tannins, acids, phytoestrogens, vitamin C.

Medicinal Properties: Astringent, antiseptic, appetizer, stomachic, antispas-

a mother tincture. Combined with the same amount of valerian tincture, it acts as an occasional sleep medication: 30 drops, 30 minutes before bedtime. While beer is effectively appetite-inducing, diuretic, galactagogue, nutritive and relaxing, it can, unfortunately, also cause a dependency, for the hop is a member of the same family as cannabis. Caution! When ingested in large quantities, beer provokes bloating, nausea, diarrhea and impotence.

Warning: Hops contain a lot of estrogen and often trigger menstruation in female harvesters within a few days of picking. It also inhibits sexual desire in men. Limit consumption to an herbal tea and a beer!

modic, anaphrodisiac, diuretic, lithotriptic, emmenagogue, pro-estrogenic, hypotensive, cholesterol-reducing, sedative, soporific, sudorific, vermifuge.

Applications: In a quick decoction, fresh hop is calming, diuretic and hypotensive: prepare 3 cones in 1 cup (250 ml) water, 3 times daily. At bedtime, the dose can be doubled. In the case of insomnia, sew a small pouch to slide inside your pillow; hop reduces pain when applied hot on a tooth abscess or on an infected ear. Mrs. Grieve recommends an infusion combining hops, chamomile and poppy in a compress to eliminate all kinds of localized pain: neuralgia, rheumatism or external trauma.

Since hop cones lose 90% of their properties in 1 year, it is better to make

Anecdote: The floral elixir made from hops is excellent for individualists and materialists. It encourages teamwork and opens the mind to spiritual values.

SLEEP-INDUCING MINI-POUCH

1	Cotton or linen pouch, 2 ¾ in x ¾ in (5 cm x 2 cm)
2 ¾ oz (50 g)	Hop cones, dried
1 oz (30 g)	Catnip leaves, dried
¾ oz (20 g)	Linden flowers, dried

Combine the plants and insert into the cloth pouch.

Slide the pouch inside your pillow to induce inspiring dreams.

HORSERADISH

CRUCIFEREAE FAMILY

Latin name: *Cochlearia armoracia*

Common names: great raifort

History: Originally from Eastern Europe, horseradish is one of the five salty and holy plants consumed by Jews during Passover, the others being coriander, lettuce, common horehound and nettle. The Germans and the Slavs used it as a condiment, whence its nickname the "German mustard." In 1640, the English physician James Parkinson announced that this plant was reserved for German laborers and that it was too delicate for English stomachs! Contrary to Parkinson, Culpeper advised eating it as follows: "Grated, moist and hot, and applied in a fine cloth to the painful area affected by gout, a sprain or sciatica, and even for the swollen liver and spleen, it helps marvelously everywhere where the organs or tissues are congested." The Russians call it *hren* and drink it in a decoction with honey to cleanse the liver. They also use it to make a diuretic beer by combining it with juniper. Horseradish has long been included in

the *Codex* along with "antiscorbutic wine" and "blended horseradish syrup." The English adopted and used it against dyspepsia and chronic rheumatism.

The great herbalist Fritz Weiss maintains that horseradish is the most powerful antibiotic against skin, lung and bladder infections.

Habitat: Loose, moist garden soils rich in nitrogen, fields and ditches near cultivated land, always in full sun.

Description: Great herbaceous perennial with a stem that branches out and grows 20 in to 3.3 ft (50 cm to 1 m) high. The stem bears huge, light green leaves. The white flowers are clustered in a lanceolate formation. The taproot is fleshy and brown on the outside and white inside. Its flesh emits a spicy and sulphurous scent.

Parts Used: The flower in June and July, the root in autumn when the exposed parts have already withered. Ideally, wait until the second year.

This strong and fleshy root, unjustly underutilized, can help us regain our lost energy.

Chemical Composition: Glucosides, vitamin C, minerals (potassium, sulphur, calcium, magnesium, phosphorus, iron).

Medicinal Properties: Antibiotic, antiseptic, analgesic, aphrodisiac, revitalizing, appetizer, choleretic, bechic, expectorant, diuretic, anti-inflammatory, dissolvent, mucolytic, vermifuge, parasiticide.

Applications: The simplest way to consume horseradish is to cut a fine slice and to suck it gently without crunching; in this way, it gently releases its scent and helps to unplug the sinus in the case of allergies, a cold or sinusitis. Inhaling the juice, freshly grated and squeezed in a cloth, or the powder made from the root (which provokes sneezing), can quickly treat a frontal headache. Grated, horseradish acts as the base for a counterirritant poultice applied locally to a cold abscess, a torn muscle or neuralgia. In the case of bronchitis, place the poultice onto the back after moistening it with a little hot water for greater comfort.

For internal use: macerate pieces of horseradish root for a few hours (½ oz per cup, or 2 g). Reheat without boiling. Honey or the roots of elecampane, marsh mallow or licorice can also be added. Take 3 cups (750 ml) daily: excellent for clearing the lungs and intestines.

It can also be enjoyed on its own in a marinade, puréed or as seasoning.

Warning: Whether used internally or externally, horseradish can be very caustic and dilate the blood vessels. Follow the recommended dosage and rely on your common sense and your five senses to avoid taking an overdose.

Anecdote: According to the signatures theory, horseradish suits men lacking in vigor. My 70-year-old neighbor came for some horseradish for his father who is 90!

 HORSERADISH SYRUP (UNCOOKED)

2 cups (500 g)	Creamy, unpasteurized honey
8 oz (250 g)	Fresh horseradish root

*C*over the horseradish roots with honey. Cover with a lid that is not airtight to keep out insects. A syrup will form along the top by the end of 1 week, but remove the roots only after 1 month. For a 10-day or 20-day cure, take 1 t (5 ml), pure or diluted in water, 3 times daily before meals. This syrup is excellent for treating bronchitis, hoarseness, fatigue, anemia, arthritis and hepatic insufficiencies.

HORSETAIL

EQUISETACEAE FAMILY

Latin name: *Equisitum arvense*

Common names: cattail, joint grass, bottlebrush, shave grass, horse pipe

History: In 11 BCE, Pliny called it the "hair of the earth" and said: "Its nature is so marvelous that it merely had to be touched and it stopped the bleeding in patients." The Romans recommended its use as a tonic and general re-energizer. North American Indians relied on finding horsetail to help them locate large stretches of water; they also used it to treat the kidneys and venereal disease brought by the white man. Culpeper recommended it to treat inflammation of the genitals, to stop bleeding and to eliminate swelling.

Dr. Leclerc advises using horsetail to dress hemorrhoids and varicose ulcers. According to the Chinese, it is perfect for combating the hot ailments: hepatic headaches, acute fevers and infections. The Russians proved its effectiveness for draining lead from the blood: they have used it for centuries against water reten-

Horsetail represents the survival instinct and the power of experience. It helps to restructure priorities for a better future.

tion, even that caused by heart problems.

According to Dr. Louis Kervan, a revolutionary French biochemist, horsetail may be the best remineralizing plant and the only one that truly makes calcium, and even magnesium, biologically available. Moreover, several capsule producers have been inspired by his research.

Today, horsetail is recognized for its cancer-fighting virtues in cures involving baths, compresses and decoctions.

Habitat: Acidic, moist, and poorly drained clay soils, ditches, the edges of woods and swamps.

Description: A plant that grows 8 in to 24 in (20 cm to 60 cm) high, equipped with a sterile, green, channeled and hollow stem lacking both flowers and leaves. It reproduces, thanks to male sporiferous stems that sow spore dust around themselves, occasionally at some distance from the female plants.

Parts Used: The entire stem and its branches, at the beginning of summer.

Chemical Composition: Organic acids, vitamin C, starch, fiber, alkaloids, glucosides, minerals (silicon oxide: 40% of the plant).

Medicinal Properties: Antiseptic, antispasmodic, astringent, cicatrizant, antilithic, diuretic, emmenagogue, depurative, tonic, remineralizing, immunostimulant.

Applications: In a fairly concentrated decoction: 1 oz (30 g) of fresh plant (⅓ oz dried or 10 g) per 4 cups (1 liter) of water, in a cure for 10 days to 1 month: against allergies, aphthous disorders, arthritis, arteriosclerosis, asthma, hair loss, cystitis, diarrhea, edema, osteoporosis, eczema, gout, hyperacidity, excessive nervousness, soft nails, prostatitis, psoriasis, ulcers, rickets. In the case of an emergency, or in the case of serious hemorrhaging, double the quantity of plants and apply compresses.

In an herbal tea or mother tincture: 10 to 30 drops, 3 times daily before meals.

A sitzbath prepared using a decoction made from fresh horsetail is effective against lumbago, and osteophytes between vertebrae; footbaths regulate the problem of smelly, sweaty feet.

Warning: The toxicity of horsetail may be linked to the enzyme that concentrates inorganic nitrates and selenium in farmland. Avoid picking near cropland and pastureland treated with artificial fertilizer.

Anecdote: About 270 million years ago, horsetail had the same appearance and measured 33 ft (10 m) in height. Over many millennia, not only has it been used to cure humans, but also to polish wood, metal and copper!

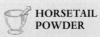

HORSETAIL POWDER

*H*eat the previously dried horsetail in a cast-iron frying pan at fairly high heat. Stir vigorously with a thick, wooden spoon (boxwood, olive) until a fine powder is obtained. Preserve in a glass jar.

This powder is very useful for stopping bleeding and skin suppurations. Diluted in a little water and taken internally, it soothes heartburn and even digestive hemorrhaging. Combined with flower pollen, it combats tumors.

INDIAN TOBACCO

Latin name: *Lobelia inflata*

Common names: lobelia, asthma weed, bladder pod, emetic herb, eyebright

History: Indian tobacco, originally from North America, got its name from botanist Matthias de l'Obel who was the first to identify the plant in the 16th century. North American Indians had been using it for years to induce vomiting in the case of food poisoning, as an antidote against alkaloids and, in small doses, as a means of treating venereal disease. They also smoked it for its calming effect.

The Quakers of New England were the first to export packages of dried Indian tobacco to England where it was used to treat asthma, convulsions and poisoning. Soon apothecaries began to grow Indian tobacco themselves. Dr. Thompson, a famous American doctor of the 19th century, increased the plant's

popularity by successfully treating many chronic sufferers of pulmonary or nervous diseases.

Indian tobacco appeared in the American *Codex* between 1820 and 1960. It can be found in many recipes for poultices, enemas, liniments, oils, pills and mother tincture blends. In 1949, Indian tobacco injections were used to revive newborns and the elderly suffering from

In order to use Indian tobacco intelligently in treatments, it pays to use good judgment and to be cautious, for it is a broncho- and vasodilator that works at the speed of light!

160

apnea or alkaloid poisoning or who were suffocating.

Health Canada (the federal Ministry of Health) has classified Indian tobacco as a drug or poison and prohibits its sale and use. Herbalists agree, however, that, in minimal doses and under proper supervision, this complementary remedy combined with a tonic can cure the worst heart, lung and nervous ailments.

Habitat: Fallow land, dry grasslands, clearings, poor pastureland, along the edges of forests and around ditches.

Description: An herbaceous annual with an erect stem that grows 16 in to 32 in (40 cm to 80 cm) high bearing alternating leaves. The abundant flowers are a pale blue with 5 joined, dark blue stamens. The fruit is a swollen capsule that contains up to 500 brown seeds that look like insect eggs.

Parts Used: Leaves, flowers and capsules.

Chemical Composition: Alkaloids (14 of them!), gums, resins, lipids, essential oil, lobelic acid.

Medicinal Properties: Antispasmodic, relaxing, emetic, expectorant, diuretic, sudorific, emmenagogue, oxytocic, broncho-dilating, counterirritant, astringent.

Applications: Indian tobacco is an extremely powerful and concentrated plant that has an immediate effect, even in very small doses: chewing one-half of a small leaf is enough to provoke severe salivation, or at the very least, to lead to

161

throat spasms and palpitations. It is important to follow traditional recipes. One or several of the Indian tobacco aerial parts can be added in a decoction or an antispasmodic or pectoral infusion: 1 g of the leaf in 1 cup (250 ml) or 1 capsule for 4 cups (1 liter) water.

Indian tobacco should be combined with gentler, complementary plants. For the lungs: mullein, coltsfoot and Indian tobacco leaves; against excessive nervousness: skullcap, valerian and Indian tobacco leaves.

In the interest of greater caution, effectiveness and speed, choose a mother tincture prepared in vinegar (25% plant, 100% vinegar): take 1 to 5 drops, 3 times daily. Indian tobacco is also very effective against localized friction, for example, on the sternum during an anxiety attack. Sometimes, Indian tobacco is an ingredient in salves used to treat allergic dermatoses such as eczema.

In some severe cases of asthma, Indian tobacco leaves can be smoked or even burned and the smoke inhaled.

Anecdote: The Indian shamans of North America used powdered Indian tobacco to make love potions. It was also used to keep thunderstorms away: the shamans would throw the powder into the air in the direction of the lightning. Indian tobacco floral elixir stimulates inner strength, restores tranquillity and balances the male libido.

SOS TINCTURE

4 t (20 g)	Fresh Indian tobacco capsules
1 t (5 g)	Ripe cayenne pepper
⅘ cup (200 ml)	Apple cider vinegar

Crush all the plants using a mortar or a food processor. Cover with vinegar in a glass jar. Macerate for 1 month away from light and stir regularly. Carefully strain.

This is a remedy to be used in case of emergency during an angina or asthma attack, broncho-spasms, anxiety attack or hysteria: use a very small dose of 3 to 5 drops diluted in a little water. It will take between 5 and 10 minutes to take effect once swallowed. Do not exceed 3, well-spaced doses over the course of the same day.

Latin name: *Eupatorium maculatum*

Common names: ague weed, gravel root, boneset, Indian sage, feverwort

History: The French name *eupatoire* is derived from the name of the Persian king Mithridates IV Eupator who "discovered" it in the 2nd century. He tested it on himself, and then used it in a compress on the wounds and contusions suffered by his soldiers. The Indians of South America used it to treat renal and urinary diseases, and also to combat swamp fever, whence the two English nicknames of Joe-pye weed and Indian sage.

In Holland, at the end of the 17th century, Joe-pye weed was used to treat jaundice and hepatic edema. Dr. Boerhaave prepared fomentations (salves, compresses, etc.) made from this plant against purulent ulcers. At the end of the 18th century, English physician William Withering recommended its use in treating food or toxic poisoning, even hemlock poisoning, because of its emetic and purgative effect.

At the beginning of the 20th century, the famous American physician Henry Sloan asserted that one small dose of Joe-pye weed cured him of malaria. From that moment on, Joe-pye weed has been included in the American *Codex* in tablet form, as an infusion and as a liquid extract. This plant saved many American lives during the typhoid epidemic between the First and Second World Wars.

Habitat: Moist areas, along streams, rivers, lakes and in ditches where it grows in vast colonies.

Description: Perennial plant approximately 3.3 feet (1 m) high, with a round stem bearing lanceolate, downy leaves, with softly dentated edges. The pale mauve flowers become double aigrets upon flowering.

Parts Used: All aerial parts at the start of flowering; less common is the use of the root, in fall.

Chemical Composition: Bioflavonoids, bitter principles, oleoresins, pyrrholizidine, acids, inulin, tannins, minerals (potassium, manganese, calcium, iron).

Medicinal Properties: Antibiotic, antiseptic, antispasmodic, calming, cicatrizant, astringent, diuretic, febrifuge,

Visible everywhere at summer's end, this powerful yet gentle plant is refreshing. It soothes all the organs that control movement affected by too much heat.

plant in oil or cook for some time in a double boiler. Solidify in animal fat or coconut oil. Excellent against additional bacterial skin infections.

In a decoction, the fall root is a powerful diuretic: 1 t in 1 cup (250 ml) water.

Warning: At doses higher than 1 T (15 ml) per cup (250 ml) for internal use, Joe-pye weed causes vomiting or intense diarrhea. Its vasodilating effect is impressive; paralysis and listlessness are signs of an overdose.

Anecdote: Joe-pye weed symbolizes duty and reason, in the image of Persian king Mithridates IV Eupator, its discoverer.

laxative, emetic, sudorific, purgative, tonic, immunostimulant.

Applications: The entire plant is used in a fresh decoction (1 t per cup [250 ml]). Both the infusion and the hot decoction are laxatives and purgatives, especially when taken in higher doses. The cold herbal tea is, on the other hand, astringent and reduces fevers. In a mother tincture, Joe-pye weed treats fever, biliary constipation and arthritic pain.

Joe-pye weed can also be used to prepare ointments and salves. Macerate the

DIURETIC DECOCTION	
1 oz (30 g)	Hemp agrimony, Joe-pye weed or gravelroot root
1 oz (30 g)	Plant glycerin
4 cups (1 liter)	Water

Submerge the plants in water. Boil at low heat for 20 minutes. Let cool and strain. Simmer with the glycerin and reduce by half. Chill.

In a cure: 1 T (15 ml) before meals for 3 weeks. Very effective against renal congestion, edema of the legs, water retention, fever and inflammatory rheumatism.

165

KELP

FUCACEAE FAMILY

Latin name: *Fucus vesiculosus*

Common names: bladderwrack, cutweed, sea-wrack

History: For thousands of years, kelp has been used in coastal areas to feed horses, heat homes, smoke fish, fertilize potato and cabbage fields and enrich pastureland. In 1750, English physician Dr. Russel discovered that kelp could be used to treat goiter (enlarged thyroid gland). He used the jelly made from the floats to make a medicated rub, and took coal made from kelp, which he referred to as *Aethiops vegetabilis*, to treat scrofula. In 1812, Bernard Courtois, a French chemist, was able to isolate iodine in kelp and make the connection with hypothyroidism. In 1862, in treating psoriasis with kelp, Dr. Duchesne-Duparc discovered its slimming properties. Thalassotherapy (the use of sea water for theraputic purposes) and beauty institutes know to whom they owe their success!

At the beginning of the 20th century,

Lord Leverhulme, owner of the Isle of Lewis in the Hebrides, distilled kelp to produce fuel alcohol, and the Danes use it to make paper.

Habitat: On rocks along the Atlantic and northern Mediterranean coasts.

Description: Crytogam or flowerless plant capable of reaching 6.6 ft (2 m) in length, with brown, rubbery fronds bearing round floats filled with a viscous jelly.

Parts Used: The entire plant.

Chemical Composition: Sugars, mucilage, minerals (potassium, sodium, calcium, chlorine, magnesium, sulphur, iodine), brown pigment, proteins, fats, growth hormones, all the vitamins.

Medicinal Properties: Slimming, lymphatic depurative, antiseptic, fights scrofula, emollient, laxative, nutritive, protective, detoxifying, thyroid tonic, general tonic, restorative, remineralizing.

Applications: For internal use, pick

Kelp contains all the necessary substances to sustain all forms of life.

Macerated, kelp is an excellent slimming lotion: dry the kelp in the sun. After chopping, macerate in 4 times its volume of vegetable oil and add a few drops of mint essential oil for its scent and to stimulate local blood circulation.

Capsules and tablets represent a worthwhile replacement: follow the manufacturer's suggested dosage and choose a pure and good-quality product.

Anecdote: Experiments performed at McGill University in Montreal proved that kelp is a powerful aid in draining radioactive heavy metals (barium, cadmium, cesium, plutonium, strontium).

SLIMMING POWDER

1 ⅓ oz (50 g)	Kelp powder
1 oz (30 g)	Marsh mallow
¾ oz (20 g)	Licorice powder

Combine all the ingredients and preserve in a glass jar away from light. Take 1 T (15 g) powder before meals, diluted in ½ cup (125 ml) warm water. This mixture fills the stomach, produces a loss of appetite and softens the digestive mucous membranes. It provokes weight loss and acts as a laxative and a tonic.

Caution: Do not consume any sugar, brewer's yeast or too much starch at the same time, for there is a risk of too much gas!

fresh, unpolluted kelp. Consume fresh or rehydrated (soak for 10 minutes): limit amount used to 1 T (15 g) per serving, finely chopped or in a salad. In a mother tincture: limit amount taken to 7 drops in the morning and at noon because of its stimulating effect. Kelp is a mild laxative and a general tonic; it treats chronic skin disorders such as eczema and psoriasis.

LINDEN

TILIACEAE FAMILY

Latin name: *Tilia americana* (North America) or *Tilia cordata* (Europe)

Common names: Lime tree, linn flower

History: The linden tree is one of the oldest trees in the world. It dates from the Eocene, at the start of the Tertiary epoch. It inspired a German legend: the Valkyrie may have dipped Siegfried's son in blood to render him invincible, but, because of a linden leaf that covered his heart, he died, struck in exactly that spot. St. Hildegard used it in rituals to drive away the plague.

During the German occupation, Professor Binet would prepare a nutritious gruel using linden leaves, oatmeal and buckwheat. The French are one of the biggest producers and consumers of linden (approximately 100 metric tons annually).

In *The Way of Herbs*, Michael Tierra talks about the linden as a "national panacea for nervous fatigue." He also reveals the results from experiments

Plant many of these
peaceful and purifying trees if you
want to control your nerves for
a long time to come!

carried out at the University of Chicago, supervised by 2 eminent pediatricians, Troisman and Hardy. They proved that children suffering from a serious flu, and simply treated with linden infusions, were cured faster—and without any side effects—than those who were treated with antibiotics.

Habitat: Cleared forest, fallow land and sunny, moist grassland.

Description: Slender tree capable of reaching 99 ft (30 m) in height and of living for up to 500 years. The leaves are bright green on top and silvery underneath. The pale yellow flowers have a heavy scent and bear 2 translucent wings or bracts.

Parts Used: The young leaves in spring, the flowers and bracts from late June to mid-July, and the sapwood or inner bark in late fall.

Chemical Composition: Bark: coumarin, tannins, polyphenols, potas-

bath: 1 oz (30 g) flower heads boiled in 8 cups (2 liters) water, infused and strained. This calms the nerves and relaxes the muscles. In a compress: 1 t (5 g) in 1 cup (250 ml) water: excellent for treating eye infections, and in a face lotion to soothe dry skin and treat brown spots.

The linden sapwood is recognized as one of the best aids in draining the gallbladder and as a good diuretic: boil 1 t (5 g) bark in 1 cup (250 ml) water for a few minutes. Macerate for several hours. Take 1 cup (250 ml) before each meal for 10 to 30 consecutive days.

Anecdote: It is only once the linden tree is 7 years old that it provides its best honey for bees, its best wood for the sculptor and its best perfume for women. And what about the dreams of those who sleep beneath its flowering branches on the summer solstice!

sium. Leaves: mucilages, quercetin, glucosides, chlorophyll, iron. Flowers: essential oil, alkaloid, acid.

Medicinal Properties: Antidepressant, euphoriant, calming, sedative, diuretic, lithotriptic, immunostimulant, febrifuge, vulnerary, regenerating.

Applications: The most pleasant way to consume linden is in the form of an infusion: 3 flowers in 1 cup (250 ml) hot water, with or without honey. Linden is excellent when taken during the day to treat anxiety and neurasthenia, and at night to relax and induce sleep. In a concentrated decoction in the

169

ABSORBING POWDER

*C*ompletely burn a small, well-dried linden log. Collect the charcoal and pound in a mortar until you obtain a fine powder.

In case of an overly acidic or nervous stomach, take before each meal or, in case of emergency, dilute 1 T (15 ml) in water. Use pure on an infected wound, an abscess or a hemorrhage.

LOOSESTRIFE

LYTHRACEAE FAMILY

Latin name: *Lythrum salicaria*

Common names: partyke, purple violet, purple willow

History: The Latin name is derived from *salix* or "willow," for it enjoys the company of this plant, and from *lythrum* meaning "blood," because of its color and hemostatic properties. Culpeper advised purple loosestrife in a decoction and for bathing the eyes to treat swelling due to infection or injury. He also said that it washes away dust and prevents blindness.

In the 18th century in Switzerland, purple loosestrife became famous, for it cured thousands of people during a typhoid epidemic. Contemporary French researchers, such as Dr. Jean Valnet, in his book *Phytothérapie*, confirm its effectiveness against bacillary diarrhea and cholera. In France, purple loosestrife is still used in syrup to treat allergic diarrhea among nursing infants.

Extremely invasive, loosestrife invaded Quebec in as little as 100 years.

Even if it is extremely invasive and a threat to many plant species, purple loosestrife cleans ditch water and our intestines.

The first campaign to eradicate this plant occurred in 1943 in the Lac-Saint-Pierre area. Today, environmental groups are continuing to battle this plant.

Habitat: Ditches, the clay soil of the banks of streams and rivers. Thanks to the proximity of water, its tremendous fertility and the lack of any herbivorous predator, loosestrife can quickly colonize whole areas.

Description: Herbaceous perennial 3.3 ft to 5 ft (1 m to 1.5 m) in height. The central stem is covered with short hairs. The leaves concentrated at the base of the plant become shorter towards the

top. The fuchsia-colored flowers are clustered in a spike. The fruit holds hundreds of tiny white seeds.

Parts Used: All the aerial parts of the plant, at the start of flowering. This takes place gradually, flower by flower, progressively advancing from the bottom to the top of the stem.

Chemical Composition: Salicarin, vitexin, mucilages, starches, pectin, iron, phytosterine, antibiotic, tannin.

Medicinal Properties: Antibiotic, antiseptic, astringent, antidiarrheic, febrifuge, hemostatic, regenerating, ophthalmic, viricidal, tonic, vulnerary.

Applications: Fresh, in a decoction, or dried, in an infusion (1 stem in 4 cups [1 liter] water), it treats epidemic diarrhea. Boiled (1 stem in 1 cup [250 ml] water), the plant is used to bathe infected eyes, hemorrhaging and suppu-

rating wounds. In powder form (1 pinch, or as required depending on the area to be treated), it stops nosebleeds, bleeding of the skin and the mucous membranes.

The mother tincture (50% plant, 100% alcohol [see page 43]) is useful in winter to treat colitis, fever or chronic catarrh: take 15 drops in warm water, 3 to 5 times daily.

It also produces a regenerative salve.

Anecdote: In Celtic folklore, purple loosestrife was believed to be the home of elves. Its floral elixir helps keep our minds alert and both feet on the ground, while protecting us from religious fanaticism.

SWEET VULNERARY SALVE

1 ⅓ oz (20 g)	Beeswax
3 oz (100 g)	Salted butter
3 oz (100 g)	Cane sugar
1 ⅓ oz (20 g)	Purple loosestrife flowers, dried and crushed
5	1 ⅔ oz (50 ml) amber-colored glass jars

*M*elt the wax, add the butter, sugar and loosestrife. Simmer at low heat for 15 minutes. Strain. Fill the jars and cool before sealing. Store in a cool place.

Astringent, antibiotic and cicatrizant, this salve treats suppurating wounds such as impetigo, weeping eczema and varicose ulcers.

MAIDENHAIR FERN

POLYPODIACEAE FAMILY

Latin name: *Adiantum pedatum*

Common names: five finger fern, rock fern

History: In his treatise *De Materia Medica*, Dioscorides described maidenhair fern as a "remarkable pectoral." Olivier de Serres, agriculture minister under French king Henry IV, noted: "Hair of Venus breaks the stone and gravel causes urination, staunches the flow of blood from the nose, cures ringworm and those who suffer from jaundice." Maidenhair fern enjoyed an increase in popularity thanks to the Jesuits of New France who saw the Indians use it to successfully treat serious pulmonary diseases. In 1761, Swedish writer Pehr Kalm, a disciple of Swedish botanist Carolus Linnaeus, told of the Indians who scoured the woods in search of maidenhair fern to fill entire boats destined for the court of Louis XVI, where it was very popular. One part of its Latin name stems from John Gerard's assertion that it could be used to treat venereal disease, whence the name *veneris*, which refers to a well-known variety, namely *Adiantum capillus veneris*. As for the word *capillus* (hair), there are two origins: the aerial shape of the leaves and the belief that this plant, when applied in lotion form, stimulated hair growth on the face and head. The French name recalls the city of Montpellier, for the city's botanical garden was the first to promote and intensively grow this plant, thanks to the support of the great botanist Lobelius. He treated asthma and whooping cough using maidenhair fern.

Habitat: Ancient deciduous forests with a thick humus, near caves and old rocks, often in out-of-the-way, somewhat mysterious places.

Description: A very elegant fern with light green fronds finely divided into orbicular blades. Also recognizable by its long reddish-brown petiole and fanlike shape.

Parts Used: The foliage, before seeds are formed in the fall.

Chemical Composition: Chlorophyll, vitamins A, C and E, capillarin, flavonoids, mucilages, tannins, sugars, terpenoids, minerals (iron, magnesium).

Medicinal Properties: Antiseptic, astringent, bechic, pectoral, depurative, oxygenating, laxative, regenerat-

A green remnant of ancient forests, maidenhair fern has shrunk considerably both in size and in number. It is important that this plant be preserved.

ing, refreshing, relaxing, tonic, remineralizing.

Applications: Since the properties of maidenhair fern are highly sensitive to time and heat, it needs to be used fresh in a poultice (raw and crushed), directly applied to a wound or scalded and infused—1 plant for 1 cup (250 ml) water—for several minutes for a topical poultice to treat eczema, suppurating infections and wounds. In the form of a hair lotion, it stimulates hair growth. In an herbal tea: 1 plant in 1 cup (250 ml) water, it is excellent in treating coughs and chronic skin disorders. In the case of poor blood circulation, take 3 cups (750 ml) daily. Given the rarity of the plant, a mother tincture is also a good choice as an effective concentrated preparation: ⅔ oz (20 g) in 1 cup (250 ml) alcohol. Take 20 drops, 3 times daily.

Anecdote: Maidenhair fern was a specialty of Café Procope in Munich in the 18th century. A combination of maidenhair fern, a strong black tea and milk, known as a "Bavarian," was served, sometimes to treat bronchitis, but more often to sober up drunks.

MAIDENHAIR FERN SYRUP

2 cups (40 g)	Fresh maidenhair fern leaves
4 cups (1 liter)	Water
2 cups (500 ml)	Unpasteurized honey

*B*oil the plant in the water for 3 minutes, cover and infuse for 3 hours. Strain the decoction, and then gently melt the honey, without bringing to a boil, for 5 minutes. Pour the mixture into a glass bottle. Store in the refrigerator and consume within 2 months at a rate of 1 to 2 T (15 to 30 ml) diluted in water, 3 times daily. Take in the event of chronic pulmonary disease, anemia or persistent skin disorders. This gentle treatment can be followed for 1 month without risk, by adding other, more caustic pectoral plants such as horseradish or wild thyme, but in small quantities.

MALLOW

Latin name: *Malva moschata*

Common names: cheeses, mouls

History: Pythagoras asserted that mallow tempered the passions and kept the mind in check while freeing the gut. Hippocrates recommended it for those who have bitter, salty saliva, who digest poorly and who feel a burning sensation when they urinate or have a bowel movement. Baptiste Platine de Cremone, a 15th century Italian chef and herbalist, advised its use for softening the stomach, curing gravel and dissolving kidney stones. In the 16th century, in Italy, it was called *omnimorbia*, meaning "cure-all." Around the same time, it was used as a rather peculiar type of pregnancy test: a woman had to urinate on the mallow flower on 3 consecutive mornings. If it wilted, the woman was pregnant!

Today, the Bedouins of the Sahara eat it to refresh the blood; the Gypsies

chew it and then spit it onto wounds. In Celtic countries, girls make crowns with mallow flowers to celebrate May Day, and many people plant it near their doorstep to invite the joy of life into their home.

Habitat: In the temperate climates in the West: pastureland, sunny grasslands, along the edges of cultivated land. Some species are able to survive in the Mauritanian desert as well as the Canadian tundra.

Description: An herbaceous plant 8 in to 20 in (20 cm to 50 cm) high. Its heliophilous flowers, shaped like lacy, pale pink or white tutus, appear in early June. The stem, lying flat or partially erect, is round and thick, and covered with small, soft hairs. The leaves are shaped differently depending on the

174

No matter whether its name is derived from the Latin *mal va* ("evil be gone!") or the Greek *malosso* ("that which softens") or the Hebrew *malakos* (tender), all of these are appropriate!

degree of maturity. The whitish roots are thick and fleshy. The fruit is shaped like a round, brown disk that resembles drained cheese, whence its name "little cheese" in rural France.

Parts Used: The leaves and flowers before they open fully, the roots, preferably in very late fall, just before the first frost.

Chemical Composition: Vitamins A, B and C, minerals (iron, potassium), mucilages, antioxidants, starches, sugars, asparagine, malvadin, fibers.

Medicinal Properties: Softening, emollient, calming, euphoriant, alterative, nutritive, laxative, lubricating, digestive, regenerating, pectoral, bechic, counterirritant, vulnerary.

Applications: The fresh leaves can be eaten (maximum 5 per serving) in a

salad. The flowers can also be used (10 per person) as a garnish: they stimulate digestion following a filling meal or in the case of chronic constipation. Mallow, a mucilaginous plant, is better able to release its active principles when it is eaten raw. Ideally, do not macerate the flowers or leaves for more than a few minutes in hot (but not boiling) water.

Quickly dry the flowers in the shade to avoid any loss of color or properties. The leaves take twice as long to dry. In winter they can be used to prepare an herbal tea or a decoction. In a mother tincture (50% plant, 100% alcohol, wine or vinegar), they keep all of their properties: take 20 drops, 3 times daily. The dried root in a decoction acts as laxative: 1 T in 1 cup (250 ml) water.

The raw, crushed plant can also be applied to wounds and to soften hard swellings. Macerated or in an herbal tea, mallow helps to loosen all the undesirable substances in the intestines, lungs and even the kidneys. It is also often used as a plant tampon. For example, in a laxative mixture that includes dandelion (more choleretic) and balsam fir (more drastic as an intestinal tonic), mallow will coat the mucous membrane to ease the elimination process.

Anecdote: In Ancient Greece, mallow was planted around sepulchers to ensure that the souls of the deceased rested in peace.

HORACE'S LIBERATING SALAD

1	Chicory plant
10	Small mallow plants (leaves and flowers)
20	Black olives
	Homemade vinaigrette

𝒫it the olives, wash and drain the plants. Toss everything with the vinaigrette and garnish with the mallow flowers.

Eat this salad at the start of the meal.

It gently cleanses all of the digestive tract, especially the liver and colon. Ideal after overeating!

176

MEADOWSWEET

Latin name: *Spirea ulmaria*

Common names: queen of the meadow

History: The Druids considered meadowsweet a sacred herb like mint and vervain; at the beginning of the first millennium, the Greeks and the Celts used it to scent their banquet halls, places of worship and homes. The Scandinavians and Slavs used it to flavor their beers and wines, especially their mead, whence its name "meadwort" (mead signifies honeyed water while wort refers to "plant").

Culpeper said that "the scent of meadowsweet makes the heart joyous and fills all the senses, especially its flowers boiled in white wine which cures even quartan fever and stops burning of the eyes and clears the vision." In the 18th century, it was revered for its analgesic and febrifuge virtues, and used to treat typhoid, dysentery, measles and smallpox. In 1838, the Italian chemist

The meadowsweet flower
is a powerful antidote for unhealthy
crystallization and promotes the
circulation of positive energy, whether
biochemical or subtle.

and pharmacist Raphael Piria noted the presence of salicylaldehyde in meadowsweet, and in 1853, the Alsatian chemist Charles Gerhardt was able to isolate acetylsalicylic acid. In 1890, the German chemist Felix Hoffman, a member of Friedrich Bayer's team, produced aspirin, whose name was taken from *spiraea*, the Latin name for meadowsweet.

Habitat: Moist grasslands, along the edges of ditches, rivers and non-stagnant swamps, in full sun.

Description: A perennial plant 24 in to 48 in (60 cm to 120 cm) high. It has red, very thin and erect stems, which bear creamy-white terminal flowers that give off an alcoholic scent. The leaves are reddish on top, silvery and hairy underneath and concentrated near the base of the plant.

Parts Used: The flowery tops, just before they fully bloom, towards the end of June or the beginning of July, and the leaves, before or after flowering.

Chemical Composition: Salicylic acid, aldehydes, essential oil, glycoside, polyphenols, ascorbic acid, coumarin, minerals (calcium, magnesium, potassium).

Medicinal Properties: Anticoagulant, dissolvent, antispasmodic, analgesic, astringent, cicatrizant, anti-infective, antiseptic, diuretic, antilithic agent, diaphoretic, febrifuge, immunostimulant, cardiotonic.

Applications: In an infusion (simmering water): 1 T (15 ml) in 1 cup (250 ml) water. Boil 3 to 6 cups (750 ml to 1.5 liters) per day: treats chronic pain, fever, migraine or arthritis attacks.

In a decoction (5 leaves in 1 cup [250 ml] water): for internal use against diarrhea. For external use against infected wounds and joint pains.

In a decoction for the bath (1 handful per 4 cups [1 liter] water), the flowers help lower fever; in a mother tincture (50% plant, 100% alcohol): take 20 drops, 3 to 4 times daily. It is analgesic with the same contraindications as those for aspirin (taking with anticoagulants, bleeding and Reye's syndrome).

A cure using meadowsweet flowers for 10 to 30 consecutive days has a powerful slimming effect and also fights water retention.

Anecdote: Meadowsweet has long been symbolic of success and sensual pleasure: in summer, it is among the flowers in a bride's bouquet. Queen Elizabeth I used to rub meadowsweet oil on her body before making love.

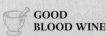

GOOD BLOOD WINE

1 cup (50 g)	Meadowsweet flowers
1 cup (25 g)	Sage
1 cup (25 g)	Parsley
approx. ½ cup (100 g)	Creamy, unpasteurized honey
4 cups (1 liter)	Tannic red wine

Chop the plants in a blender. Combine with the red wine and macerate and let stand for 1 month. Stir from time to time. Strain using cheesecloth and stir in the honey; dissolve well. Drink 1 oz (25 ml) before the two main meals to enrich the blood, reinforce the heart and combat postmenstrual anemia.

MOTHERWORT

ROSACEAE FAMILY

Latin name: *Leonorus cardiaca*

Common names: lion heart, throwwort, motherwomb

History: In China, around 500 B.C., during the Zhou dynasty, motherwort was used to regulate the menstrual cycle and female reproductive functions. It was also used to calm the nerves and regulate the heart. In the energetic Taoist language, it is referred to as bitter, spicy and refreshing. Dioscorides, in *De Materia Medica*, described it as cardiac. Culpeper said that it dissipates the "cold phlegm of melancholy that oppresses the heart."

The Eclectics prescribed it as a tranquilizer. Today, Ukrainian healers, the "znakaris," recommend its use against arteriosclerosis, hypertension, epilepsy, hysteria, insomnia, diarrhea and gastritis, not to mention menstrual pain and difficult childbirth.

Habitat: Rubble, near stables where the soil is rich in nitrates, alongside ditches, in among hedges, preferably on moist, shady, uncultivated land.

Description: A perennial plant that can reach 5 ft (1.5 m) in height. It has a central, square stem and dentated leaves that grow perpendicular to the stem. The pale pink flowers with dark red spots are bilabiate. The plant is also able to reproduce by way of its root, whence its English name of "motherwomb."

Parts Used: The flowery tops and the fresh leaves.

Chemical Composition: Alkaloids, glycosides, essential oil, acids, tannins, calcium chloride.

Medicinal Properties: Anti-inflammatory, antitumoral, antidiarrheic, antispasmodic, emmenagogue, oxytocic, hypotensive, cardiotonic, calming, sedative, nervous and uterine tonic.

Applications: Prepare the herbal tea from a fresh or dried plant, using 1 whole adult plant for 4 cups (1 liter) water that has been quickly boiled.

In a mother tincture, take 10 to 15 drops, 3 to 6 times daily.

Motherwort soothes hormonal fluctuations, premenstrual syndrome, and hot flashes and insomnia due to menopause. It is not recommended in the case of uterine hemorrhaging or in the event of pregnancy. However, it can help immensely during childbirth. Motherwort makes the contractions

Motherwort is an ordinary plant, but truly effective in treating the heart and the nerves. It reintroduces a physical and psychic balance, especially in women.

**HARMONIZING
MOTHER TINCTURE**

| 1 cup (250 ml) | Spirits (60%–90% alcohol content): brandy, gin, vodka |
| 1 oz (30 g) | Fresh motherwort leaves |

*C*ombine all the ingredients and let stand in a glass jar away from light for 1 month. Strain.

Take 10 drops at a time, 3 times daily for acute cases. The treatment can be extended for up to 3 consecutive months. The tincture has a bitter taste, but it works quickly and effectively. For use against anxiety attacks, hysteria, gastritis and heart palpitations.

more effective, for it tonifies the uterus. It also prevents postpartum hemorrhaging. Motherwort is an aphrodisiac for women, for it regulates hormone levels. Men won't complain!

Anecdote: According to Nicholas Culpeper, astrologist and herbalist, "Not only does it expel retained urine or accumulated menses but it also helps she who is to deliver her child at the right moment."

181

ASTERACEAE FAMILY

Latin name: *Hieracium pilosella*

Common names: mouse ear, hawkweed

History: Mouse-eared hawkweed owes its French name *épervière* to the popular belief that sparrowhawks (*éperviers*) rub the eyes of their young with this plant in order to cure eye infections, and that they eat it to sharpen their eyesight. St. Hildegard viewed it as a tonic for the heart. According to Culpeper, the fresh, crushed leaves applied in a poultice close any wound; the powder works wonders against ulcers, especially those of the mouth.

During the 18th century, the *Dictionnaire de Trévoux*, written by the Jesuits, maintained that it is detersive and vulnerary, and recommended its use against jaundice, water retention, ulcers, phthisis and tuberculosis.

Experiments carried out in France at the beginning of the last century proved

that mouse-eared hawkweed fights brucellosis and epizooty in cattle. Dr. Leclerc and other eminent French phytotherapists confirm the plant's hypotensive and choleretic qualities.

Habitat: Poor, limestone or siliceous soils, abandoned fallow land.

Description: Small perennial herb with bright yellow flowers that resemble dandelion flowers. The fruit is a cylindrical achene. The entire plant is covered with a fine, whitish down, especially the leaves that grow in a rosette at the base of the plant. Orange hawkweed is very similar to this plant and often grows nearby, especially in North America.

Parts Used: All the aerial parts, in particular, the flowery tops at the start

Mouse-eared hawkweed is little known for its draining virtues. It is ideal for getting rid of organic waste and for cleansing the arteries.

of flowering, in the middle of summer.

Chemical Composition: Cafeic acid, beta-carotene, flavonoids, essential oil, oxycoumarin, pigment, minerals (potassium, sulphur), bitter principles, tannins.

Medicinal Properties: Antibiotic, antidiarrheic, anticoagulant, antiseptic, antifungal, antiuric, bechic, cholagogue, choleretic, diuretic, lithotriptic, febrifuge, sudorific, hemostatic, astringent, hypotensive, cholesterol-lowering, tonic, vermifuge.

Applications: In a decoction: ½ cup (20 g) fresh plant in 4 cups (1 liter) water. Drink the entire amount during the day with a little honey to treat infectious pulmonary disorders, in particular, whooping cough.

In a mother tincture (50% saturated), in an intensive cure: take 20 drops, 6 times daily for 3 consecutive days, with lots of distilled or demineralized water.

The leaves can be dried and reduced to a powder: apply to hemorrhages and suppurating wounds.

Anecdote: Olivier de Serres advised rubbing the blade of a knife or a sword with hawkweed latex to slice wood and iron more effectively.

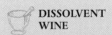

DISSOLVENT WINE

1 cup (60 g)	Fresh mouse-eared hawkweed flowers and stems
2 cups (500 ml)	White wine
1	Opaque glass jar

Combine the hawkweed and the wine in a blender and crush for 20 seconds. Macerate for 1 month away from light. Carefully strain.

Take 1 t (5 ml), 6 times daily, diluted in pineapple juice, for the mixture is bitter. Effectively treats atherosclerosis, fever, bronchitis, small kidney stones and gallstones.

183

MUGWORT

ASTERACEAE FAMILY

Latin name: *Artemisia vulgaris*

Common names: felon herb, naughty man, sailor's tobacco, witch herb

History: Hippocrates often mentions mugwort for its ability to cleanse the uterus after childbirth or in the case of hemorrhaging or difficult menstrual periods. During the Middle Ages, Russian physicians used it against epilepsy, while the Mongols massaged it into their calves to prevent cramping and muscle fatigue caused by horseback riding for long periods of time. In China, mugwort is the main ingredient in a moxa or "cone of fire" used in acupuncture, as it concentrates heat on one point. Chinese medicine treats malaria with annual wormwood, a variety close to mugwort; recent American experiments confirm its antimalarial effect. Beginning in the Middle Ages, in all Northern European countries, on the feast day of St. John, dancers would leap

Mugwort is a powerful depurative, especially good at cleansing the blood. Its strong and honest personality helps us to focus and reassures us in our choices.

around a fire wearing a crown made from mugwort to protect them from disease during the coming year. Avid walkers tuck mugwort into their shoes to protect against blisters, heat and pain.

Habitat: Mugwort grows in dense, highly visible colonies in full sun, along paths and ditches, among rubble and ruins.

Description: Perennial plant 5 ft (1.5 m) in height, supported by erect, ramose stems that turn a reddish color when they reach maturity. The deeply indented leaves are dark green on top, downy and silver underneath. The flower heads are a strange greenish-yellow. The hermaphrodite flowers bloom from July to October. The fruit contains a lot of tiny gray seeds.

Parts Used: The entire plant, especially the leaves.

Chemical Composition: Tannins, vitamins A, B_1 and B_2, minerals (calcium, potassium, iron), mucilages, resin, essential oils, flavonoids, inulin, lactones, thujone.

Medicinal Properties: Appetizer, digestive, anticonvulsant, antispasmodic, astringent, regenerating, choleretic, depurative, emmenagogue, oxytocic, cardiotonic, tonic, adregenic, parasiticide, vermifuge.

Applications: The fresh plant can be chopped and used in spring soups and

vinegar, and strained; it can be used for 2 to 3 years to treat irregular menstrual periods, anemia, fatigue, diarrhea and worms. In an herbal tea, combined with more aromatic plants with compatible properties, it stimulates the appetite, is an emmenagogue, a tonic or a vermifuge: ⅓ oz (10 g) in 4 cups (1 liter) water. Mugwort bouquets strewn about the floor chase away fleas.

Anecdote: The French name *armoise* is taken from Artemis (Greek goddess) or Diana (Roman goddess) who represents the emancipated woman. This plant helps fortify, cleanse and tone the female organs. This is why it is also called the "witch's herb."

PROTECTIVE AMULET

Purple velvet: 1 rectangle 4 in x 2 in (10 cm x 5 cm)

Freshly picked mugwort that has been dried: approx. 5 g.

Sew a small pouch and fill it with the dried mugwort. Carry it in a pocket to protect against all sorts of bad external influences and slide it into your pillow to encourage revelatory dreams.

salads, combined with other young leaves of such plants as watercress, plantain, chickweed or violet. In a poultice: use ⅓ oz (10 g) crushed leaves to treat abscesses, boils, bites and wounds, including those that are infected. In a mother tincture: ¾ oz (20 g) leaves in approx. ½ cup (100 ml) alcohol, wine or

Latin name: *Verbascum thapsus*

Common names: Adam's flannel, Aaron's rod, beggar's blanket, shepherd's club, fluffweed, hare's beard, velvet dock

History: Dioscorides said of mullein: "A decoction made from this helps those who are exhausted, spasmodic, and worn-out, and against old coughs, and by rinsing the mouth, it lessens a toothache."

The Romans, who referred to mullein as *candellaria*, used it to make candles for night expeditions by dipping them in pitch, and Roman women used the flowers to dye their hair lighter. St. Hildegard swore by mullein for curing aphonia (the loss of voice caused by disease) among her fellow nuns. John Gerard maintained that the old English of Kent gave it to their cows suffering from a cough, and that all asthmatic Irish grew mullein in their gardens for

its antihistaminic properties. The mullein flower has been one of the ingredients in the famous blend of the 7 pectorals described in the French *Codex* for centuries. Germans have long been producing vulnerary and antiseptic oil for use against otitis (ear infections) and suppurating infections.

Habitat: Vacant lots, rubble and uncultivated and rocky fallow land where it often grows in colonies.

186

This great, gold and silver woolly taper is attractive and reassuring. Caution! It needs to be carefully strained. Its toxic seeds should only be used for propagating this species.

Description: Plant between 3.3 ft and 6.6 ft (1 m and 2 m) in height (at 2 years), with a sturdy, round, hairy central stem. Adorned with large, oval, silvery leaves with a cottony texture. The oily, yellow flowers form a tight spike. They open in the morning and die in the evening after pollination.

Parts Used: The leaves, in the spring in the second year, the flowers in August, and less commonly, the roots in fall.

Chemical Composition: Mucilages, bioflavonoids, rutin, saponins, aucubin, essential oil, pigments.

Medicinal Properties: Softening, emollient, antihistaminic, antioxidant, antiseptic, astringent, cicatrizant, vulnerary, depurative, remineralizing, expectorant, mucolytic.

Applications: The freshly cooked leaves can be crushed one by one and applied as is to a wound or hemorrhage, or on hemorrhoids. They can also be dried and used to produce a vulnerary oil or ointment: excellent against chilblain, contusions and hemorrhoids. For internal use, strain using fine gauze to avoid contact with the irritating hairs. The flowers, when prepared in a quick decoction (1 t [5 ml] for 1 cup [250 ml] water), or combined with other pectoral plants such as mallow or elecampane, soothe chronic bronchial irritations. For asthma, allergies and stubborn bronchitis, drink 3 cups (750 ml) daily for 7 days.

Anecdote: Witches used mullein to make torches for the Sabbath. To ward off demons, the superstitious carried a mullein leaf with them at Halloween and monks grew it around their monasteries.

GERMAN BACTERICIDAL OIL

1 cup (40 g)	Mullein flowers
2 cups (500 ml)	Olive oil
2 t (10 ml)	Benzoin or myrrh tincture
1	Green glass jar

Quickly crush the flowers in a mortar. Combine all the ingredients and macerate in a green jar near a fire or in a window for 21 days. Strain using a fine cotton cloth. Place in the ear in case of otitis or an infected pinna (part of the inner ear), or apply in the case of eczema, ringworm or mycosis.

188

NETTLE

URTICACEAE FAMILY

Latin name: *Urtica dioica*

Common names: stinging nettle

History: Julius Caesar's troops rubbed their bodies with nettle to warm themselves during northern campaigns. The Roman writer Caius Petronius maintained that a man's virility improved when he was whipped with nettle branches below the kidneys and the belly button. For centuries, rheumatics were also whipped to expel the sickness.

According to John Gerard, nettle is a marvelous antidote against poisonous plants and, when cooked with myrrh, it becomes a powerful diuretic. Albertus Magnus, a 15th century herbalist and alchemist, asserted that, by dipping the hand in a nettle decoction, then in a stream, huge numbers of fish would swim nearer (a tip for fishers!). Nettle has a powerful magical aura: it was one of the herbs capable of chasing away demons, and it was used to bless swords and billhooks before the ritual harvest. In the 16th century in France, great quantities of nettle herbal tea were drunk, a trend started by Marie Antoinette's physician.

Pregnant Native-American women drank nestle herbal tea to strengthen their babies, their uterus and their blood. In the medical treatise *King's America Dispensatory*, the Eclectics advised using it as a diuretic and to treat cystitis and urinary incontinence. They claimed it was astringent and hemostatic, and recommended it in a decoction made from the fresh plant for use against eczema, diarrhea and hemorrhoids. Recent research conducted in Germany, Japan and the United States confirms its effectiveness against benign hypertrophy of the prostate.

Habitat: Soils rich in clay, old, composted manure piles near stables, near gardens, abandoned houses and debris and, of course, near fields where manure has been spread.

Description: An herbaceous perennial 20 in (50 cm) high with a solid, square stem and dentated leaves covered in prickly hairs. The flowers are greenish in color and clustered at the axis of the leaves, on the upper part of the stem.

The nettle stings, but if it did not defend itself in this way, it would have disappeared from the planet a long time ago. A natural remedy is always close at hand: crushed sheep sorrel, curled dock or plantain quickly soothes its stings.

Parts Used: The entire plant, especially the leaves before flowering in May and June.

Chemical Composition: Carbohydrates, proteins, chlorophyll, vitamins A and C, minerals (iron, silica, potassium), ammonia, gallic and formic acid, indole group, serotonin, lecithin, enzymes, mucilages.

Medicinal Properties: Antibiotic, antiallergic, antirheumatic, antiseptic, antidiabetic, combats gout, depurative, fortifying, galactagogue, nutritive, hypoglycemic, tonic, vermifuge, counterirritant.

Applications: Pick the nettle flowers 1 month before flowering; always wear gardening gloves and use pruning shears. The very young leaves are eaten in soup, in a quiche, or puréed, or even in a decoction to cleanse the blood.

In an herbal tea: 3 leaves in 1 cup (250 ml) water: to fortify the blood, fight anemia, and the demineralization of young children and breast-feeding mothers. Since it has a neutral taste, honey can be added to sweeten the flavor.

In a mother tincture (50% plant, 100% alcohol, wine or vinegar): take 7 to 15 drops, 3 times daily. This is excellent against severe allergies, rheumatism, major fatigue and anemia.

In an inhalation: 1 t (5 g) nettle leaves, 1 t (5 g) balsam shoots in 2 cups (500 ml) water. In the event of an asthma attack, inhale the steam in a container with a spout or over a bowl, with the lower part of the face wrapped in a towel.

An herbal tea made from nettle and horsetail, and a little lemon juice or vinegar, can be used as a rinse for dry or lifeless hair.

Anecdote: "If only people knew its many uses: when it is young, nettle is a good vegetable, adult its stems can be used to make ropes and a very strong fabric! In forage, it causes hens to lay eggs and cows to produce more calves, and its seeds make a horse's coat shine. Its boiled root produces a beautiful golden tint. Decidedly, nettle offers much for the little it demands!"

—VICTOR HUGO,
Les Misérables

HEALTHY-BLOOD HERBAL TEA

1	Plantain leaf
2	Nettle leaves
3	Mint leaves
1 cup (250 ml)	Water

*B*oil the plants for 3 minutes. Infuse. Drink hot before breakfast and lunch to enrich the blood, drain the kidneys and treat allergies or prostate problems. If the plants are dry and the water has evaporated, extend the treatment for 1 month and double the dosage.

OAK

FAGACEAE FAMILY

Latin name: *Quercus alba*

Common names: gospel tree, tanners bark

History: The botanical name *quercus* comes from the Celt words *quer* (good) and *cuez* (tree), and the common name of *chen* (beautiful). The Celts once considered the oak a holy symbol: on the sixth lunar day in December, the Druids harvested mistletoe with a gold billhook and announced the new year with cries of: "To mistletoe, the new year." For many years, the acorn was used to produce flour for the peasants. Today, some Berber tribes still use it to make a nutritious gruel called *racahout*. The Ancient Greeks associated the oak with Zeus because of its strength and power, while the Romans associated it with Jupiter. The tradition of celebrating rituals in the shade of the oak tree continued after the introduction of Christianity, from which it got its

Jean de la Fontaine spoke
of this magnificent tree in his fable
The Oak and the Reed: "The one whose
head was in the heavens and whose
feet touched the kingdom of
the dead."

English nickname "the prayer tree" or gospel tree.

The Goths considered the oak a symbol of strength and triumph: the expression "strong as an oak" is deeply entrenched in popular memory. The anonymous healers of the Middle Ages and the Renaissance used the leaves and the bark internally against diarrhea, hemorrhaging, tuberculosis and rickets; externally in a poultice to treat oozing wounds, in powder form to stop nosebleeds, and as a talc to stop hemorrhaging.

The bark was often combined with iron salt to dye fabrics black and, to a certain degree everywhere in the world, to tan hides. Oak wood is one of the most prized raw materials for building ships, furniture, house frames and railroad trestles. Oak was a natural resource highly coveted by settlers. In the space of 200 years, the French and the English completely plundered thousands of acres of white oak in southern Quebec.

Habitat: Open clearings or grasslands near mixed deciduous forests.

Description: An imposing tree capable of reaching 99 ft (30 m) in height and 33 ft (10 m) around, and of living for 1000 years. Its grayish bark is smooth; its wood is pale brown, hard and heavy with a dense grain. The leaves are

Chemical Composition: Bark: gallic acid, tannins, minerals (calcium, iron, potassium). Leaves: vitamins A, C and E, chlorophyll, mucilages, carbohydrates. Fruit: starches, sugars, tannins, calcium oxalate.

Medicinal Properties: Antidiarrheic, astringent, aphrodisiac, fortifying, febrifuge, immunostimulant, hemostatic, antihemorrhagic, nutritive, restorative, tonic, remineralizing.

Applications: The buds are used to make a mother tincture in alcohol (1 part buds to 10 parts alcohol). At a rate of 20 drops before each meal, it combats impotence, low blood pressure and general physical and mental fatigue. The young dried leaves are drunk in a decoction: 1 leaf for 1 cup (250 ml) water to stimulate biliary flow, cleanse the spleen and regenerate irritated bowels.

The outer bark and sapwood are harvested from a tree that is at least 7 years old. The bark is cut into pieces before being boiled for a few minutes. Use in a 10-day cure at a rate of 1 oz (30 g) per 4 cups (1 liter) water: use internally to treat copper, lead or mercury poisoning, and bloody diarrhea. Use externally in a compress against anal or vaginal infections, leukorrhea, hemorrhoids and all other abnormal skin suppurations.

Warning: Absorbing too much oak bark can lead to serious constipation. Avoid cooking in a cast-iron saucepan, as the tannins become toxic for the kidneys when exposed to the iron.

divided into several rounded lobes. The fruit is a smooth acorn, caramel-colored at maturity, and topped with a sculpted cup that covers a quarter of the fruit. A healthy, 25-year-old oak tree can produce up to 25,000 acorns. Its roots have a wide spread.

Parts Used: The buds and young leaves in early spring, the acorns in fall, and, at the end of winter, the outer bark and the sapwood (inner bark).

Anecdote: According to Dr. Bach, oak in a floral elixir helps to balance the excesses of those who don't know when to stop, even when they are sick or overworked. Highly recommended in these difficult times!

 ACORN COFFEE

*P*ick the fruit once it is mature, shell and dry after finely chopping and covering with cheesecloth. Finely grind in a coffee grinder. Complete drying by quickly frying the ground coffee in a dry frying pan. Store in a glass jar. Prepare acorn coffee in the same way as coffee infused in a Bodum coffeemaker (1 t [5 ml] per cup) to derive the greatest benefits from its astringent, tonic and remineralizing properties.

PENNYROYAL

LAMIACEAE FAMILY

Latin name: *Mentha pulegium* (Europe) or *Hedeoma pulegioides* (North America)

Common names: squaw mint, stinking balm, tickweed

History: Pliny called this plant *Pulegium*, for it drove away fleas (*pullex* in Latin) and ticks. The Romans, like the Greeks, took into account Dioscorides's advice and used it as a digestive after their feasts, as a nerve stimulant and also to calm hysteria in women, which he associated with menstrual pain. North American Indians used it to keep mosquitoes away and offered it in a decoction during childbirth. According to John Gerard, pennyroyal dipped in infected water acts as a disinfectant; when used to make a crown and placed on the head, it treated pain, confusion and vertigo. The herbal tea with honey cleanses the lungs and clarifies the humors of the chest. Culpeper recommended inhaling pennyroyal vinegar to revive a person suffering from syncope,

Let's hope that this marvelous, wild and aromatic plant with innumerable qualities will once again be restored to favor!

rubbing pennyroyal ash on the gums to strengthen them and applying a poultice to dissolve skin blotches. In the 19th century, pennyroyal was recorded in the American *Codex* as a powerful digestive, an emmenagogue and a general stimulant. However, from 1916 on, it was listed as abortifacient, irritating and toxic. This paradox is due to the confusion surrounding the effects of the plant and those of the essential oil. In 1980, Dr. Norman Farnsworth, a pharmacist in Illinois, proved that it would take 75 gallons (300 liters) of herbal tea to reach the same level toxicity contained in 1 T (15 ml) of essential oil!

Habitat: The edges of forests, clay soils, moist and shady areas.

Description: A small annual with a woody stem adorned with many small oblong and very aromatic leaves. The small brown root has many fine roots to anchor the plant.

Parts Used: The stems with the leaves, picked at the end of summer, at the start of flowering.

Chemical Composition: Essential oil rich in pulegone, chlorophyll, minerals (calcium, potassium).

Medicinal Properties: Antiseptic, antispasmodic, aphrodisiac, diuretic, carminative, digestive, emmenagogue, oxytocic, insect repellent, parasiticide, tonic, nervine.

Applications: Use against intestinal gas, fungal disorders or difficult menstrual periods. Fresh, in a decoction or in a concentrated herbal tea: 1 leafy stem for 2 cups (500 ml) water daily for 3 to 10 days. In a mother tincture (25% plant, 100% alcohol): 5 to 10 drops, 2 to 3 times daily in a cure lasting 3 to 10 days.

When used to make a simple crown, pennyroyal soothes headaches. Hanging in a bouquet or sprinkled (reduce to a fine powder) on strategic spots, it repels insects and rodents.

In addition to being antiseptic and antifungal in the case of a wound, the medicinal wine is also a joint and muscle antispasmodic.

Warning: Pennyroyal essential oil is toxic when used internally: several women have died due to an overdose. Moreover, the plant itself can be

abortive and stimulating. Never take at night or in the case of severe hypertension.

Anecdote: The Ancient Greeks used pennyroyal during rituals seeking Demeter's favor (the goddess of harvests), and the dead were washed with a pennyroyal decoction to help the soul escape from the body.

CULPEPER'S MENTHOLATED VINEGAR

| 1 cups (500 ml) | Apple cider vinegar |
| 1 cup (30 g) | Pennyroyal |

In a blender or using a knife, chop the leaves and stem of the plant. Place in a tinted glass jar. Cover with vinegar. Macerate for 1 month, shaking the jar regularly. Strain using cheesecloth and store in a cool place away from light.

This vinegar will keep for 1 year: it soothes all kinds of localized pain, burns, stomach cramps, tendonitis, sprains and neuralgia. It is also used as an antiseptic on infected wounds and as insect repellent. In the case of an open wound, dilute it in 5 times its volume of boiling water.

PEPPERMINT

LAMIACEAE FAMILY

Latin name: *Mentha piperita*

Common names: None

History: Peppermint may have originated in Asia Minor; the Babylonians were distilling it 500 years before Christ to produce a concentrated digestive. Its name comes from Greek mythology: while cavorting with Pluto, the nymph Mentha is interrupted by Persephone, Pluto's wife. Upon catching the two lovers, Persephone changed Mentha into wild mint. In Dioscorides's and Pliny's time, the Greeks and Romans drank a mint herbal tea and placed a few branches in jars of fresh milk to help preserve it better. Pliny said "mint revives the spirit"; he had bouquets of mint placed in the room of the ill. Culpeper noted, "It was apt to disperse the winds of the stomach, to soothe colic in infants, to eliminate monthly pains in women, cure infected wounds and rabid dog bites." The Eclectics prescribed mint for headaches, flu, stomachache and recurring fevers such as malaria.

197

Mint is the most famous medicinal plant in the world, yet we continue to underestimate and misuse it despite its many qualities.

Recent research in Germany and Russia has proven its antacid and cholagogue virtues. Many stomach remedies sold in pharmacies contain peppermint. In Europe, it is common to drink mint-flavored alcohol as a digestive.

Habitat: On the banks of streams and rivers, ditches and wet fallow land.

Description: Peppermint grows from 12 in to 20 in (30 cm to 50 cm) high and has a square, purplish stem. The leaves are dentated. The lilac-colored flowers grow in terminal spikes. The roots consist of whitish runners that allow the plant to quickly spread.

Parts Used: The leaves are picked before the plant flowers. It is, however, easier to cut the entire plant and to dry it in a bouquet or spread out on a rack.

Chemical Composition: Chlorophyll, vitamins A and C, minerals (iron, magnesium), essential oil rich in menthol and terpenes, aromatic and analgesic principles, alcohols, aldehydes, tannins, bitter principles, flavonoids.

Medicinal Properties: Antiseptic, bactericidal, analgesic, anti-inflammatory, aphrodisiac, euphoriant, carminative, digestive, cholagogue, choleretic, refreshing, tonic, pectoral, vasodilating.

Applications: Fresh mint leaves are added to tabbouleh, (a Middle Eastern salad made with semolina), to cucumbers and cream salad, and to a salad made with duck gizzard. Lamb and wild game go particularly well with mint. The raw peppermint leaves are also effective when chewed or pounded to treat insect bites. In a poultice, mint can be used to treat headaches, muscle cramps and spasms, and rheumatic pain.

Peppermint oil, when used in a topical massage, acts as a vasodilator: when applied quickly, it prevents bruises and ecchymoses from appearing. It also treats insect bites. Avoid the mucous membranes. In the case of muscle pain, dilute to 20% in a good vegetable oil.

For internal use, do not consume more than 3 drops of essential oil at a time.

When prepared whole (1 plant in 1 cup [250 ml] water), in a decoction to be inhaled, it clears the respiratory tract; when taken as a drink, it treats problems of the alimentary system: colic, constipation, gastritis, intestinal gas and indigestion. In an herbal tea, at a rate of 3 leaves for 1 cup (250 ml) water, peppermint acts as an excellent general tonic that stimulates blood circulation and the heart. Avoid drinking it at night.

Warning: Avoid exceeding the

REFRESHING ANALGESIC OIL

| 1 ½ cup (40 g) | Well-dried peppermint |
| 2 cups (500 ml) | First, cold-pressed olive oil |

Combine the 2 ingredients in a bottle or glass jar. Store away from light for 1 month and shake every 2 to 3 days. Strain.

Use in the case of pain, headaches, intestinal or muscle cramps: by massaging or by applying a topical compress depending on the area requiring treatment.

Can be kept for 1 year away from light.

prescribed dosage for the essential oil. Keep out of the reach of children. Do not combine the peppermint leaf with aloe, cinnamon and resins in general: this will result in an extreme purgative and stupefying effect.

Anecdote: If Culpeper blamed it for impure dreams and nocturnal emissions, the Ancient Greeks revered it and drank it as a love potion, a tradition still practiced by modern-day Russians.

199

PLANTAIN

PLANTAGINACEAE FAMILY

Latin name: *Plantago major*

Common names: black jack, lamb-stongue, kembs, quinquenervia

History: Dioscorides and Galen praised the plantain's cicatrizant, ophthalmic and vulnerary virtues. Pliny noted that it cured no less than 24 different illnesses. In her treatise *Maladies des femmes avant et après l'accouchement*, Trotula, a healer and midwife, advised using plantain to treat uterine hemorrhages and insisted that it can restore "the very essence of a woman" to the extent that it could give a woman the appearance of being a virgin. For many years in England, plantain seeds were sold for sowing on local hills to grow plants and feed sheep. During the Renaissance, French physicians took the boiled root and used it to treat intermittent fevers; they also produced an eyewash from the soaked seeds, a wash that is still used today. Father Kneipp noted: "The plantain seals open wounds as if sown with a gold thread, for just as gold does not allow rust, so too the plantain

does not allow infection or decayed flesh!"

In Quebec, Dr. Aldéi Lanthier, a generalist and phytotherapist, supports the notion that plantain increases the ability of blood to coagulate and greatly helps hemophiliacs, those suffering from enteritis, and even tuberculosis, by promoting the regeneration of the capillaries and mucous membranes. The plantain seed (of the *Plantago psyllium*) is currently very popular, for it is one of

This common plant is very strong: its nervures have even been used to weave garments.

the best mucilaginous and non-irritating laxatives.

Habitat: Uncultivated land near human habitation, poor soil, along paths, in full sun.

Description: Perennial herb 8 in to 16 in (20 cm to 40 cm) in height. The green leaves are attached to the same base. The tiny green flowers that adorn the central stems eventually change into seeds.

Parts Used: The leaves in spring and summer, the mature seeds in fall.

Chemical Composition: Leaves: chlorophyll, vitamins A, C and E, luteolin, pro-progesterone, scutellarin, flavonoids, mucilages, pectin, iridoids, acids, minerals (iron, magnesium, potassium). Seeds: cellulose, fiber, proteins, mucilages, sugars, silica.

Medicinal Properties: Antiseptic, analgesic, astringent, hemostatic, bechic, pectoral, emollient, laxative, ophthalmic, regenerating, nutritive and revitalizing, cicatrizant and vulnerary.

Applications: The crushed or chewed leaves are used against insect bites, wounds and all kinds of infections. In a decoction, in an herbal tea or in a mother tincture: treats blood disorders (anemia, low blood pressure, hemophilia), recurring infections, and all acute and chronic pulmonary conditions.

The seeds act like a sponge or broom for the mucous membranes, especially the intestines. Soak the seeds in 10 times their volume of water. Macerate for 1 month (unless they are ground first) to allow them to swell. To prepare an eye lotion, strain the mixture well.

Anecdote: In Quebec, the Indians called it "the white man's foot," for it was the settlers who brought it with them along with grain seeds, and in France it is referred to as "flea's herb" because of the resemblance between the seeds and this insect.

REVITALIZING GREEN JUICE

3 cups (180 g)	Fresh plantain leaves
1 cups (250 ml)	Pure liquid honey
1	Opaque glass bottle

Crush the leaves in a food processor, drain and squeeze in cheesecloth. Combine 1 cup (250 ml) of the green juice with the honey and simmer for 10 minutes at low heat, stirring regularly. Let cool and pour into the opaque bottle.

Take this nectar 1 spoonful at a time like a syrup to treat a cough; also use it to treat a sore throat, anemia, fatigue and eczema: 1 T (15 ml), 3 times daily.

PROSTRATE KNOTWEED

Latin name: *Polygonum aviculare*

Common names: allseed, hogweed, ninety knot, pigweed, sparrow tongue

History: Birds everywhere have enjoyed eating knotweed seeds since time immemorial, whence its name in French *renouée des oiseaux* (birds' knot-grass). Dioscorides and Pliny called it *sanguinaria*, for they used it against hemorrhages.

In 16th century England, a popular belief that Shakespeare recalls in *A Midsummer Night's Dream* held that eating knotweed prevents children and small animals from growing. At the same time, it was used to treat anorexic and dyspeptic pigs.

In an illustrated treatise dated 1710, Salmon, a Scottish herbalist of the 17th century, described it as being "effective against bleeding and kidney leakages, it cools wounds and cleanses old suppurating ulcers, its decoction cures diarrhea and its balm reinforces the joints and makes the nerves and tendons more

flexible, it also cures gout if taken correctly morning and night."

According to Dr. Valnet, prostrate knotweed controls blood sugar levels in diabetics. Dr. Leclerc maintains that it treats arthritis and combats hyperacidity.

Habitat: Dry, rocky paths, roadsides, and semi-wild, untreated lawns.

Description: Small annual semi-repent plant, 4 in to 20 in (10 cm to 50 cm) high with small lanceolate leaves. The flowers have small white or pink petals.

202

Knotweed, evident in fields everywhere but little known, hides numerous virtues that only the little birds know!

Parts Used: The aerial parts, picked in June and July, rarely the root, sometimes the seeds in the fall.

Chemical Composition: Sugar, starches, anthraquinones, acids, minerals (calcium, silica), rutin, saponins, vitamins C and K, chlorophyll.

Medicinal Properties: Antidiabetic, hypoglycemic, antilithic agent, astringent, dissolvent, cathartic, laxative, diuretic, hemostatic, regenerating, remineralizing, antirheumatic, vasodilating, vulnerary.

Applications: The whole knotweed plant can be applied raw, rinsed and crushed, directly to a recent wound, or it can be wrapped in gauze. In a concentrated decoction and in a compress, it stops bleeding and cleans the infection; when repeated several times throughout the day, it promotes scarring of the tissues: ⅓ oz (10 g) in 1 cup (250 ml) boiling water.

Used internally, in a decoction (quickly heated, but infused for a long time), 1 ¼ oz (20 g) in 4 cups (1 liter) water. Drink during the day to treat water retention, gout, kidney stones and arthritis. It can be combined with an aromatic plant such as mint or an emollient plant such as mallow to improve the taste and get the best results.

In a mother tincture, knotweed is rich in bioflavonoids, sugars and vitamins.

The plant with its seeds is nutritious, hypoglycemic and remineralizing: 1 t (5 g) in 1 cup (250 ml) water.

Anecdote: The Chinese have revered the prostrate knotweed (bian xu) for more than 2000 years. They use the liquid to provoke urination and they eat it in the form of a paste to stop diarrhea.

 DR. LECLERC'S BONE-BUILDING TINCTURE

⅓ oz (10 g)	Knotweed
⅓ oz (10 g)	Horsetail
3 oz (100 ml)	Spirits (40 or 60 proof)

Crush the plants in a mortar or food processor. Combine with the alcohol and macerate for 3 weeks. Strain.

Take 20 drops, 3 times daily in water or juice: effective against excessive nervousness, digestive and blood hyperacidity, arthritis, rheumatism, fibromyalgia, osteoporosis and spasmophilia. In the most severe cases, follow a specific dietary regimen, take concentrated supplements and consult a qualified therapist.

QUITCH GRASS

Latin name: *Agropyron repens*

Common names: couch grass, dog grass, quick grass

History: As is the case with many medicinal plants, it is animals, in particular dogs, which showed man how to eat quitch grass, for herbivores eat it systematically in the spring to purify their blood or to treat food poisoning. The ancient Babylonians made alcohol by fermenting the quitch grass roots in juniper honey and yeast. Dioscorides recommended its use against "opaque and infrequent" urine and Pliny advised its use to treat urinary calculi and bladder ulcers. During times of famine and war, quitch grass was mixed with chestnut flour in Europe, and with purple heart to make a nutritious and easily digestible bread in the United States. For centuries, and until very recently in rural areas, people made brooms, brushes and woven baskets from dried quitch grass rhizomes. Fabric was combed using quitch grass leaves to

achieve a beautiful, subtle gray-green effect.

Currently, the Japanese include quitch grass leaves in their "nutriceuticals" or functional foods (food supplements) because they are rich in chlorophyll, sugar and available vitamins.

Habitat: Temperate zones in both hemispheres, the loose, fertilized soil of lawns and truck farms, in full sun. Quitch grass is public enemy number one of all farmers!

Description: Green, perennial herb with long, sharp leaves. Its whitish flowers are clustered in a spike. The pinkish-white roots end in a sharp, tapered point capable of piercing those of its competi-

---

The tonic acidity of
quitch grass is refreshing, and it
chases away old and false
obsessions!

204

tors. Quitch grass is so rich in growth hormones that it only takes one root to revive a plant that can spread over approx. 100 sq ft (10 m^2) in one year!

Parts Used: The leaf before flowering and the root in fall (or at any time in case of emergency).

Chemical Composition: Leaves: chlorophyll, iron, vitamins A, C and E, sugars. Rhizomes: antibiotic principles, glucosides, saponins, potassium and silica.

Medicinal Properties: Antilithic agent, cholagogue, blood depurative, refreshing, remineralizing, diuretic, febrifuge, vermifuge.

Applications: The boiled rhizome is used to combat jaundice, weakness and biliary lithiasis. Boil 1 oz for 4 cups water (30 g per liter). Drink 1 cup (250 ml) of the warm liquid before each meal. In the case of cystitis and urinary lithiasis, add the same amount of mallow flowers and bedstraw leaves. Quitch grass leaves in a decoction (a fresh plant if possible) or even the fresh-squeezed juice of the raw plant constitute a marvelous skin and mucous membrane cicatrizant. Taken in the form of an anal injection, it treats hemorrhoids. Quitch grass juice is an excellent tonic.

In a springtime cure against chronic catarrhs due to constipation and congestion of the lymph, drink 6 cups (1500 ml) of decoction made from the leaves before meals for a period of 15 days to cleanse vital filters and fluids.

Anecdote: In China, quitch grass symbolizes perseverance against adversity, for it is very difficult to eradicate.

 RESTORATIVE PLANT COFFEE

In equal parts:

Dried and ground quitch grass roots

Dried and ground dandelion roots

Roasted and ground barley grains

Grind the 3 ingredients separately and combine. Pour into a glass jar, stored away from light.

Prepare an infusion by filtering the grounds in a coffee filter. Since it is diuretic and tonic, it is better to drink it only in the morning and at noon.

Latin name: *Rubus idaeus*

Common names: hindberry, raspbis

History: According to Dioscorides, the raspberry originated at Mount Ida, in Crete, whence its names "Mount Ida bramble" and *Rubus idaeus*. The great English herbalist Mrs. Grieve recommends a cold herbal tea or enema made using raspberry leaves to immediately soothe diarrhea and stomachache in children. In 1941, the British medical journal *Lancet* confirmed that the raspberry leaf contains an effective uterine relaxant principle. Since then, raspberry has been included in many perinatal herbal medications. The Chinese use it to treat the liver and spleen, to tonify female genital organs, to regulate menstruation and to ease childbirth.

Habitat: Scorched forests, where wood is harvested, the edge of forests and moist vacant lots.

206

Description: Perennial shrub 3.3 ft to 6.6 ft (1 m to 2 m) high with purple, woody stems covered with small prickles. The leaves are dark green on top

Don't ignore the leaves
of this well-known fruit: they repair
and remineralize.

and whitish underneath. The whitish flowers are corymbiforme. The red fruit has a delicious scent and taste.

Parts Used: The stem leaves in the second year, before flowering; the fruit in July.

Chemical Composition: Leaves: flavonoids, tannins, minerals (calcium, magnesium, manganese, potassium), acids, pectin, mucilages. Fruit: sugar, acids, vitamins A, B and E, proteins, fibers, pigment.

Medicinal Properties: Antiscorbutic, anti-inflammatory, astringent, antiseptic, depurative, diuretic, decongestant, deobstruent, febrifuge, sudorific, ophthalmic, regenerating, remineralizing, oxytocic, uterine tonic.

Applications: To preserve the restorative principles of the leaves, use

pregnancy to combat morning sickness, colds or bleeding. Light infusion: 1 leaf in 1 cup (250 ml) water in the early stages of pregnancy (3 leaves in the last month) tonifies the uterine muscles.

Raspberries are very nutritious and rich in antioxidants. They must be chewed well so as not to irritate sensitive bowels.

Anecdote: According to contemporary American herbalists, raspberry leaves have two other virtues that have been overlooked: combined with ginger, they treat all kinds of nausea, and, with a pinch of cayenne, they promote blood circulation in the feet and hands.

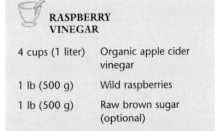

RASPBERRY VINEGAR

4 cups (1 liter)	Organic apple cider vinegar
1 lb (500 g)	Wild raspberries
1 lb (500 g)	Raw brown sugar (optional)
1 or 2	Opaque bottles

Crush the raspberries with a pestle and macerate in the vinegar for 10 days. Carefully strain. Simmer the liquid at low heat and dissolve the sugar. Let cool, bottle, seal and store in a cool place. This rosé-colored vinegar is effective, whether pure or diluted, in treating flu, diarrhea, fatigue or even a drop in blood pressure.

In a cure, take 3 T (45 ml), 3 times daily.

them fresh, in a quick decoction, or dried in the shade on whole branches before putting them in bags for the winter. Raspberry leaf decoction is an effective vaginal douche against leukorrhea: 6 leaves in 1 cup (250 ml) boiling water.

The herbal tea soothes all the mucous membranes and helps regenerate irritated tissues due to excess acidity or infection. Pregnant women can drink raspberry tea regularly throughout their

RED CLOVER

FABACEAE FAMILY

Latin name: *Trifolium pratense*

Common names: trefoil, cow grass, cleaver grass

History: Red clover is the preferred forage of herbivores. At the beginning of the first millennium, the Celts instinctively planted it on grassland, unaware that the plant proteins completed one another. During a famine, the Irish mixed it with wheaten flour to make bread. The Russians have traditionally used it in a poultice on burns and abscesses, and to soothe eye inflammations. They also applied it (boiled and salted leaves) in a compress to relieve headaches. They gave the floral mother tincture to delicate children and women suffering from uterine hemorrhaging.

At the turn of the 20th century, Jethro Kloss, the great American healer, maintained that red clover is one of the greatest gifts from heaven, for, he said, "It is a marvelous blood depurative and formidable remedy for leprosy, pellagra and malignant tumors." Red clover is,

essentially, one of the basic ingredients in the Indian tea marketed under the name "Essiac" or "Floressence" which is said to have cured hundreds of cancer patients in Ontario in the 1950s.

Recent laboratory experiments have shown the contraceptive virtues of red clover due to the plant's high concentration of estrogen. Therefore, it represents an interesting substitute for synthetic hormones.

Red clover sprouts are eaten in a salad; their sweet and grassy taste is very refreshing.

Habitat: Grasslands, sunny, acidic and moist fallow land, alongside fertile fields and gardens.

Description: A small plant 8 in to 16 in (20 cm to 40 cm) high with an erect and branching stem. The flowers are either pink or purple. The oval leaves, which grow in groups of 3, are green with white spots in the middle.

Parts Used: The flowers from early June until the end of August. Pick only those that are completely pink and have a regular flower head. The whole plant is used externally.

Chemical Composition: Sugars, coumarin, tannins, proteins, essential oil, estrogens, minerals (calcium, iron, potassium, magnesium, manganese).

Medicinal Properties: Alterative, depurative, anticoagulant, astringent,

The flower of the red clover picked on the night of a full moon and offered to one's lover is a measure of one's fidelity, and it promotes fertility!

the lymph, the blood and the kidneys in the case of cystitis, eczema or fatigue due to infection or glandular imbalance.

In a mother tincture (50% plant, 100% alcohol): take 20 drops before breakfast and at noon.

In an herbal tea and a decoction: 3 flowers in 1 cup (250 ml) water. Drink up to 4 cups (1 liter) per day between meals to purify the lymph and the blood, and stimulate blood circulation in general.

A topical lotion (with a decoction of ⅓ oz [10 g] in 1 cup [250 ml]) can be used to treat abscesses, cysts and infected wounds. The salve is also effective.

calming, sedative, contraceptive, diuretic, deobstruent, emmenagogue, pro-estrogenic, expectorant, mucolytic, immunostimulant.

Applications: Usually only the red clover flower is used as a depurative of

Anecdote: The elixir made from red clover flowers suits people suffering from agoraphobia and who feel alienated from others. During a catastrophe, it prevents collective hysteria.

INDIAN TEA OR ESSIAC

3 oz (90 g)	Red clover flowers
3 oz (90 g)	Wood sorrel flowers
3 oz (90 g)	Common burdock root
1 oz (30 g)	Kelp
1 oz (30 g)	Slippery elm powder
1 oz (30 g)	Canada thistle head

Combine all the plants.

Boil 1 t (5 ml) of the mixture in 1 cup (250 ml) water for 5 minutes. Drink 3 cups (750 ml) per day for 1 to 3 months. This is the closest recipe to the original famous North American Indian tea used to fight cancer. It is also an excellent lymphatic and blood depurative.

ROSEHIP

Latin name: *Rosa eglanteria*

Common names: dog rose, sweet brier, wild rose

History: Roses have always symbolized love, joy and beauty. The Romans depicted Venus with a crown of roses. In his *Natural History*, Pliny tells of the boiled rosehip root that cured rabies, and of its fermented fruit that produced a highly energizing wine. St. Hildegard of Bingen used it as a basic plant for treating most illnesses. According to Culpeper, the fruit of the rosehip is a formidable restorative for those suffering from chronic catarrhs and even tuberculosis; the dried and diluted pulp breaks down gravel in the bladder. In France, beginning in the 16th century, "rose" vinegar could be found in every medicine cabinet: this tincture made from rose petals in vinegar was used to treat heatstroke, burns and headaches, not to mention fainting. In Spain, mothers have been producing a paste made from the crushed seeds for a long time. Taken

210

Rosehip is the ancestor of the queen of flowers. Its fruit remains one of the best tonics for the immune system that nature has ever produced.

on an empty stomach for several consecutive days, it is an excellent vermifuge. In India, as in Turkey, rosehip is still consumed on a daily basis in yogurts or a rose lassi and rose jelly to cure delicate intestines, or simply for pleasure.

After the discovery of vitamin C in 1930, it was proven that the rosehip fruit contained a large quantity (500 mg to 800 mg per 100 g). Since then, it has been included in a number of supplements.

Habitat: Fallow land, shrub hedges and the edge of forests and along roadsides.

Description: Climbing perennial shrub that grows 3.3 ft to 6.6 ft (1 m to 2 m) high, and consisting of reddish branches covered with thorns and pale pink flowers. The oval leaves are shiny and dentated. The orange-red fruit is filled with numerous yellowish seeds. At the end of the stem there is a strange orange mass: this protuberance is the bedegar, resulting from the sting of a relative of the bee, the mossyrose gall wasp.

Parts Used: The flowers towards the end of June, the fruit and the bedegar in mid-fall.

Chemical Composition: Vitamins A, B_1, B_2, B_3, C and K, bioflavonoids, polyphenols, essential oil, vanillin (flowers and leaves), pectin.

Medicinal Properties: Antidiarrheic, depurative, antioxidant, restorative, anti-infective, antiseptic, astringent, regenerating, diuretic, lithotriptic, febrifuge, sudorific, ophthalmic, bactericidal, stimulating, tonic, vermifuge, parasiticide, vulnerary, cicatrizant.

Applications: By immediately placing the rosehip petals in alcohol, a mother tincture is produced that can be used pure or diluted as a cicatrizing lotion or a facial tonic, against rosacea and oily skin. The petals can also be eaten raw in a salad and used to garnish drinks or desserts: this is the most recommended way to prepare them, for cooking destroys the vitamin C. In an herbal tea, they are calming, astringent and euphoriant.

The bedegar can be dried or boiled just like the ripe fruit, or drunk in a decoction: ideal against the flu, diarrhea and general fatigue. In this case, take 3 cups (750 ml) at a rate of 3 bedegars or pieces of fruit in 1 cup (250 ml) water. The mother tincture in alcohol remains the most recommended way to prepare the bedegar (see the recipe below): take ½ t (2.5 ml), 2 to 3 times daily.

In an herbal tea, the dried leaves are astringent for the intestines. They can replace tobacco.

Anecdote: According to Dr. Bach, drinking the elixir or contemplating the rosehip flower brings back joy and the will to live. It is ideal for people who are depressed, ill or sad, or who tend to let themselves go.

LIQUID VITAMIN C

1 cup (250 ml)	60% alcohol content
½ cup (125 g)	Ripe rosehip fruit
	Honey (optional)

*C*rush the fruit using a knife, mortar or food processor, cover with the alcohol and macerate for 1 month. Strain.

For use against the flu or as an antiseptic: ½ t (2.5 ml) in ½ cup (125 ml) water or fruit juice, 2 to 3 times daily (with or without honey).

211

SHEPHERD'S PURSE

CRUCIFERAE FAMILY

Latin name: *Capsella bursa-pastoris*

Common names: cocowort, shepherd's heart, pepper grass, pickpocket, poor man's pharmacy, witch's pouches

History: Shepherd's purse got its name from its resemblance to the triangular, flat pouch carried by shepherds. Moreover, it was the shepherds who noticed that the sheep and cows ate huge quantities of the plant to repair the uterus after giving birth.

Dioscorides, followed by Tragus (Hieronymus Bock), used shepherd's purse to treat abnormal female hemorrhaging. For many years, North American Indians combined the seeds with the roots, rich in starch, to make bread. In the spring, they ate the young leaves for their purifying and revitalizing benefits.

In the Middle Ages, the plant once again became very famous thanks to an Italian herbalist, Count Mattei, who made it the main ingredient in his "elec-

Few plants possess greater
virtues than this one and few are
less known.

CULPEPER,
Complete Herbal

tric fluid": it was effective against all kinds of bleeding, especially that found in urine. According to Culpeper, shepherd's purse stops bleeding both internally and externally; applied to the wrist and the area around the ankles, it reduces fever and jaundice, and its pure sap applied to the ear eliminates buzzing and acute pain.

During the First and Second World Wars, shepherd's purse was used as a hemostatic and an oxytocic remedy in the event of a difficult childbirth.

The renowned Dr. Leclerc often recommended it for treating hemophilia, metrorrhagia and menstrual blood clots. Dr. Vogel, as well as many North American herbalists, marketed the alcoholature to treat these disorders.

Habitat: Garden paths, poor fallow land and arid soil where it grows in colonies and in full sun, and along paths.

Description: An annual 20 in (50 cm) high with erect, round and divided stems. The leaves grow in a rosette at the base of the plant. The small, white flowers are corymbiforme; they have the 4 petals typical of Cruciferae. The heart-shaped fruit contains numerous small, oval seeds.

Parts Used: Leaves, flowers and siliquae picked when the plant is still green, and the flowers mid-summer.

Chemical Composition: Bioflavo-

noids, acetylcholine, choline, compound sulphurized acids, saponins, minerals (potassium, calcium), chymosin (digestive enzyme), amino acids.

Medicinal Properties: Antispasmodic, calming, diuretic, lithotriptic, emmenagogue, uterine tonic, febrifuge, sudorific, hemostatic, cicatrizant, hypotensive, anticoagulant, vulnerary, astringent.

Applications: Shepherd's purse is most effective when it is raw and fresh. The young leaves with a radish taste can be eaten in a salad or steamed. In a quick decoction: 1 plant for 1 cup (250 ml) water, revitalizes the blood at the end of winter. In the case of demineralization, hemorrhaging, diarrhea and osteoporosis, a one-month cure can easily be carried out. In a compress or a poultice (3 chopped plants in a quick decoction, strained or unstrained), shepherd's purse cures wounds or oozing skin dis-

orders. The mother tincture (double the volume of alcohol or wine) is very useful in treating hemorrhages (especially uterine), renal lithiases and cystitis: 30 drops in ½ cup (150 ml) water, 3 times daily.

As for the fruit, once it has been dried, it can be used as a spicy seasoning for cooking.

Warning: Since shepherd's purse is a coagulant and an oxytocin, avoid using it if there is a history of phlebitis, thrombosis, and in the case of pregnancy.

Anecdote: This small, fertile Cruciferae annually produces 64,000 seeds per plant. It symbolizes femininity, even if the alchemists dedicated it to Saturn, the master of time.

REVITALIZING SPRING SALAD

In equal parts:

Shepherd's purse leaves

Plantain leaves

Sheep sorrel leaves

Chickweed leaves

Daisy leaves

Homemade vinaigrette

*W*ash and spin-dry the plants. Season to taste.

Eat as quickly as possible once the plants have been picked.

SLIPPERY ELM

ULMACEAE FAMILY

Latin name: *Ulmus rubra*

Common names: Indian elm, red elm

History: North American Indians used slippery elm powder for thousands of years against all sorts of skin disorders: eczema, impetigo, scrofula and ulcers. In the 15th century in France, Iran and Italy, it was used to wash wounds and infected eyes, and to treat contusions. A viscous liquid called "slippery elm water" was drawn from the galls (an excrescence on the leaves) of the slippery elm. Culpeper also maintained "it cleanses the skin and makes it clear."

In the United States, the Eclectics recommended a decoction made from slippery elm powder for small children who are always hungry or who suffer from colitis: it is best used as an enema combined with milk, sugar and even a little olive oil. Around the same time, the sale of sticks longer than 4 in (10 cm)

and made from the bark was prohibited because many women used them to abort their fetuses, resulting in hemorrhaging and infection. The slippery elm powder—pharmacists referred to it as *Cortex ulmus*—is still recorded in several major pharmaceutical *Codices*. It remains one of the most effective and gentle emollients for regenerating the skin and the digestive and pulmonary mucous membranes.

Habitat: Very thin arable layers of soil, poor grassland, the edge of woods, limestone fallow land where no other tree can compete.

Description: Large, umbrella-shaped tree capable of reaching 99 ft (30 m) in height. The very thick bark cracks with age in long, vertical scaly ribs. Its rough and dentated leaves have fine nervures.

Besides its regenerating virtues, slippery elm is a satisfying food substitute with few calories, making it ideal for all bulimics, those dieting and insatiable nursing infants.

Parts Used: The inner bark or sapwood, starting in the 10th year, the leaves of the young trees, and the flowers less frequently.

Chemical Composition: Starches, sugars, mucilages, coumarins, tannins, minerals (potassium, calcium), resinous gum, ulmic acid.

Medicinal Properties: Astringent, cicatrizant, calming, refreshing, diuretic, dissolvent, emollient, expectorant, laxative, depurative, nutritive, restorative, tonic, vulnerary.

Applications: The inner bark, the most important part of the tree, is collected in the following way: select an elm that is at least 10 years old, cut out a rectangle without, however, peeling all the way around so as not to injure the tree—ideally, apply a clay poultice to regenerate the tree. The bark of a healthy elm will fold when pressure is applied. Remove the outer bark. Cut the inner bark into small pieces and dry in the shade for at least 2 weeks. Finely grate and reduce to a powder using a coffee grinder: the finer the powder, the more powerful its effect on ulcers, digestive ulcers, aerophagia or anorexia. The active principles are soluble in warm or cold water: combine the powder with 4 times its volume of water and stir well. Excellent against all sorts of digestive inflammations.

In an infusion, when combined with comfrey, slippery elm treats ulcers; with angelica, it eliminates intestinal gas; and with loosestrife, it stops diarrhea.

Applied externally, powder-based poultices, combined with antibiotic herbs such as burdock or wild thyme, are marvelous against bacterial infections.

In the case of an anal infection, use a water solution or an herbal tea: ⅘ cup (200 ml) with 1 t (5 g) powder, strained and lukewarm, and combined with chamomile, catnip or oak bark. To prepare an enema, increase the amount used to ¾ oz (20 g) slippery elm powder.

ANTI-ULCER DECOCTION

⅓ oz (10 g)	Catnip leaves
⅓ oz (10 g)	Comfrey leaves
⅓ oz (10 g)	Slippery elm powder
2 cups (500 ml)	Water

*I*nfuse the plants in the boiling water for 10 minutes. Strain and let cool to lukewarm; combine the slippery elm powder in the teapot. Allow to swell for 10 minutes.

Take small sips between meals or during a crisis.

In a paste (with 6 T [100 ml] water), it can be applied to all kinds of skin ulcerations.

This decoction treats ulcers, as well as the painful attacks of ulcerous colitis and acute diarrhea.

Note: do not be put off by the slippery elm's sticky texture and fenugreek taste. Its aromatic mucilages can perform miracles!

Anecdote: Dr. Bach recommended drinking a slippery elm floral elixir to people overwhelmed by too many heavy responsibilities, and who did not feel up to handling them.

216

ST. JOHN'S WORT

HYPERICACEAE FAMILY

Latin name: *Hypericum perforatum*

Common names: klamath weed

History: Its Latin name *Hypericum* comes from the Greek *hyper* and *eikon* meaning "more powerful than an icon." Indeed, St. John's wort had the reputation of keeping bad spirits away. Pliny prescribed it macerated in wine to treat snakebite, and Dioscorides recommended an herbal tea that was emmenagogue, febrifuge and diuretic, and could fight sciatica. John Gerard recommended it for treating bleeding (wounds or blood in the urine and stool). The Greeks, Romans, and later, the Christians attributed a special power to the plant, believing it was capable of protecting them from disaster and bad luck. Culpeper also recommended its use to cure wounds and lumps, and, when used internally, to stop spitting phlegm and blood.

The first white settlers to arrive in America used St. John's wort against diarrhea, fever, wounds and snakebite.

St. John's wort, consisting of a thousands points of light, is a beneficial balm for the wounds of the soul and the body.

Beginning in the 19th century, it was used as a basic remedy in homeopathy for treating asthma, diarrhea, hemorrhoids and some paralyzing neuralgia.

In 1988, researchers at the New York University noticed its powerful immunostimulant virtues, in particular, against AIDS. German researchers noted that the oil had, without a doubt, antibiotic qualities capable of treating very serious wounds and burns.

In 1995 and 1996, Drs. E. Ernst and K. Linde proved that St. John's wort acted as an antidepressant, tempered but constant, after 2 months. It deserves its new nickname "natural Prozac."

Habitat: Sunny, well-drained, limestone soils throughout the northern hemisphere.

Description: An herbaceous perennial 8 in to 32 in (20 cm to 80 cm) high and consisting of several stems. The leaves are dotted with a multitude of tiny holes. The flowers in corymbiforme are a bright yellow. The fruit is a capsule with three chambers filled with numerous black seeds.

Parts Used: The flowers, the day they open and before they are pollinated, and the leaves.

Chemical Composition: Active principles (hypericin, pseudohypericin), bioflavonoids, sugars, essential oil, pigments, acids.

Medicinal Properties: Antidepressant, antispasmodic, astringent, cicatrizant, antiviral, analgesic, emollient, cholagogue, depurative, diuretic, hemostatic, regenerating, vulnerary.

Applications: With the flowers barely open, prepare a tranquilizing or immunostimulating mother tincture and floral elixir, or an analgesic oil, the only one based on fresh flowers. St. John's wort mother tincture can be added to a calming mixture to treat nerves, pain, insomnia and even depression. Follow the treatment for one month to obtain convincing results.

Take 10 drops in the morning and night, and 20 drops at bedtime of the following mixture:

- 40% St. John's wort mother tincture
- 40% linden mother tincture
- 20% valerian mother tincture

In a decoction (1 whole St. John's wort plant with 1 cup [250 ml] water), St. John's wort treats diarrhea and circulatory disorders. In the case of a viral illness, take 1 t (3 g) of the chopped plant in 1 cup (250 ml) water, 3 times daily. Standardized St. John's wort extracts are used, in particular to treat depression and chronic viral illnesses. It is not recommended for people taking antidepressants, antihistamines or tranquilizers.

Warning: To pick, wear gloves: fair-skinned people can develop spots. Avoid consuming beer, chocolate, camembert, sliced meats and red wine. These foods contain tyramine, a dangerous substance when combined with St. John's wort.

Anecdote: An old magic custom was to throw branches of fresh or dried St. John's wort into the fire while calling out to the spirits of light to watch over the house and its inhabitants.

ST. JOHN'S OIL

2 cups (500 ml)	Olive oil
1 ½ oz (50 g)	St. John's wort flowers
1	Colored glass jar (blue, brown or green)

Harvest the St. John's wort flowers on a dry and sunny day. Put them in the jar and cover with the oil. Store away from light; stir regularly. Macerate for 2 months and strain by wringing in cheesecloth.

This oil treats minor burns, contusions, neuralgia and rheumatism. It soothes all sorts of internal and external pain. To preserve longer, add 5% lavender essential oil.

TANSY

Latin name: *Tanacetum vulgare*

Common names: button

History: Its name comes from the Greek *athanaton*, which means "immortal." Tansy is able to keep for a long time when dried, and it prevents meat from rotting. This plant also had the reputation of prolonging life and was one of the herbs included in a mixture used to embalm the dead. It is one of the bitter herbs eaten with unleavened bread during the Passover celebration, a custom that was continued by the first monks of the Roman Catholic Church who ate tansy cake at the end of Lent. John Gerard asserted "a cake made with young tansy leaves in the spring is pleasant to the taste and good for the stomach and, moreover, eliminates the bad humors."

Benedictine monks immortalized this plant through the famous bitter tonic liqueur Benedictine. Tansy was included in the French *Codex* for a long time as an excellent vermifuge. The

220

This powerful aromatic flower, in small amounts, is very effective at correcting the results of our excesses.

contemporary physician and herbalist David Hoffman advised using it in a light decoction against gout, intestinal gas, hysteria and jaundice.

Habitat: Sandy, limestone soils, uncultivated land in full sun where tansy grows in colonies, and along paths and roadsides.

Description: A perennial herb 3.3 ft (1 m) high with a light green and pinkish central stem, and featherlike leaves. The bright yellow flowers grow to form a flower head.

Parts Used: The leaves and the flowers at the very beginning of flowering.

Chemical Composition: Tannin,

bitter principle, essential oil, thujone, proteins, nutritive sugars, acids.

Medicinal Properties: Bitter, appetizer, antiputrid, antiseptic, carminative, cholagogue, diuretic, febrifuge, emmenagogue, antispasmodic, nervine, tonic, vermifuge, antifungal.

Applications: Flowering tansies last a long time in a bouquet. In an herbal tea: 1 dried flower bud in 1 cup (250 ml) water, it treats flatulence, hepatic insufficiency, fungus and disorders involving intestinal parasites. In a mother tincture in alcohol: a very aromatic aperitif or digestive liqueur that should be consumed using a dropper given its high essential oil content, which is potentially toxic: 10 drops, 3 times daily over a period of 30 days.

Add a few leaflets to a meat dish to help digestion or to preserve the meat longer.

In a decoction, poultice or compress, the fresh flowers and leaves treat fungal infections of the skin and the mucous membranes: 1 whole flowery top in 1 cup (250 ml) boiling water.

Warning: Tansy essential oil is very toxic and prohibited in many countries.

More than ⅓ oz (10 g) of the plant can lead to abortion, convulsions and stupor. Restrict use of this plant to occasional cures and follow the recommended dosage.

Anecdote: Tansy, symbolic of renewal, represents that which is eternally female: Gaia, Venus or Mary. Women healers of long ago offered it in recognition of their women friends, their mother or their women teachers.

SIMPLIFIED BENEDICTINE

1 ⅓ oz (50 g)	Tansy flowers
4 cups (1 liter)	Brandy
1 cup (250 g)	Cane sugar
1	Glass jar

Finely chop the fresh flowers. Put them in the jar and cover with the brandy. Store away from light for 1 month. Carefully strain. Add the sugar and shake to dilute it.

Consume this liqueur as an aperitif before meals, or as a digestive after meals or a diuretic at a rate of 1 t (15 ml) diluted in 1 cup (250 ml) water, 2 times daily, for no more than 10 consecutive days.

221

VALERIAN

Latin name: *Valeriana officinalis*

Common names: all-heal, garden valerian, fu, setwall

History: Dioscorides and Galen both gave valerian the name "phu" or "fou," evoking its rather dubious smell. Moreover, they considered it to be a panacea for all problems associated with the nervous system. Its Latin name, which appeared in the 11th century, comes from *valere*, meaning "valuable" or "of great value." In 1450, Saladinus d'Ascoli, a master at the Salerno school, declared, "if you want to calm bellicose men who are fighting for nothing, give them valerian juice to drink."

North American Indians snorted valerian powder to calm epileptic seizures; valerian became popular once again in the 16th century after the Italian physician Fabius Calumna testified in his work *Phytobasanos* that it had cured epilepsy.

Valerian intoxicates cats and even rats. It has already been used as bait in England where it is grown and con-sumed in large quantities. Since the Middle Ages, valerian, in combination with other spices, has been used to kill mites in cupboards.

In the 19th century, Samuel Thompson, as did many of his herbalist colleagues, recognized it as the best-known tranquilizer.

Habitat: Moist, swampy areas, moist copses and clearings where it grows in colonies, in full sun.

Description: Perennial plant 32 in to 4 ft (80 cm to 1.2 m) high, with a round stem bearing large leaves composed of dentated and deeply indented leaflets. The flowers are a beautiful pale pink. The strong-smelling roots are black on the outside and whitish on the inside.

Parts Used: The leaves in early summer, the flowers in mid-summer, the roots in the fall, preferably once the plant is at least 2 years old.

Chemical Composition: Essential oil, organic acids, alkaloids, tannins, choline, bitter sap, albumin, resins, monoterpenes.

Medicinal Properties: Anticonvulsant, antispasmodic, calming, relaxant, digestive, vermifuge, febrifuge, immunostimulant, hypnotic, nervine, tonic, revitalizing.

Applications: The young, tender leaves are eaten in a salad or used in a poultice on wounds and localized pain:

This pretty pink flower is
a precious ally: it helps find a certain
peace and tranquility.

1 oz (25 g) chopped leaves quickly boiled in 1 cup (250 ml) water. In an elixir (5 drops, 3 times daily for 10 to 30 days) or pulverized in an organic preparation, the flowers stimulate growth, protect from the cold and attract earthworms. The fresh root is an effective antispasmodic and relaxant: macerate 1 t (3 g) of rootlets in 1 cup (250 ml) water for 1 hour. During the day, it helps combat anxiety, nerve and muscle spasms, and worms. Taken at bedtime, it helps you fall asleep faster and brings on pleasant dreams. In case sleep does not come easily because of time changes, take ½ t (3 g) of the powder diluted in ⅓ cup (100 ml) water for 10 consecutive nights, 1 hour before bed.

Warning: In a strong dosage, valerian can become irritating, indigestible or stupefying.

Anecdote: To attract a woman, a man must make a magic pouch that holds cayenne pepper, patchouli and valerian root: he must pick the valerian in the nude and stand on one foot as he says the name of the sought-after woman. . . .

PLANT VALIUM

1 ⅓ oz (50 g)	Fresh roots, washed and dried for 2 hours in the sun
⅘ cup (200 ml)	Acidic white wine

Crush the roots in a food processor and combine with the wine. Macerate for 1 month. Strain.

In the case of hypertension or nervousness: 10 drops, taken in the morning on an empty stomach. Repeat as needed at noon and again in the evening.

To treat spasms or insomnia: 20 drops, 20 minutes before bed.

VIOLET

Latin name: *Viola canadensis* (Canada), *Viola odorata* (France)

Common names: sweet violet, heart's ease, jump up, trinity violet, butterfly violet

History: The violet was revered in Ancient Greece; it symbolized Venus, the flower of love, and was placed under the hats of brides and laid on the coffins of young women. Hippocrates prescribed its use to treat skin indurations and pulmonary blockages. According to St. Hildegard, the violet leaf dissolves malignant tumors, in particular, those of the skin and large colon.

John Gerard advised using it on suppurating wounds and even in an enema, for, he said, "Its gentle, moist freshness reduces excess heat."

René Laennec, French physician and inventor of the stethoscope, regularly imbibed an anti-flu cocktail: a violet flower infusion with a drop of brandy.

An anonymous poem written at the Salerno school illustrates this antiviral quality:

> To dissipate drunkenness and cure a
>   migraine,
> The lowly violet remains sovereign,
> From a heavy head it lifts the crush-
>   ing weight,
> Of a vicious cold it does liberate.

In England, crystallized violet petals have been enjoyed for a long time. The nuns in Flavigny, France, make candies from them; violets are grown extensively in Grasse, France, the capital of French perfume. The violet symbolizes sweetness, simplicity and modesty. Napoleon, however, made it his imperial emblem. This discreet little flower is still listed in the *British Pharmacopeia* as an anticancer agent especially effective against throat and skin cancers. North American Indians have always revered the violet, and the great herbalist Susun Weed regularly praises it for its virtues.

Habitat: Moist, shady grasslands, the edge of forests and clay soils.

Description: Small perennial plant 2 in to 8 in (5 cm to 20 cm) high with heart-shaped leaves and violet-colored flowers. There are also yellow and white flowers.

Parts Used: The flowers in early spring, the leaves in summer, the root in fall.

Chemical Composition: Flowers:

The heart-shaped leaf of
this young flirtatious plant conceals
a great protective power, and its root
has a purifying effect.

glucosides, essential oil. Leaves: mucilages, saponin, salicylic acid. Roots: alkaloid.

Medicinal Properties: Alterative, depurative, nutritive, immunostimulant, antiseptic, regenerating, emollient, vulnerary, laxative, restorative, antiallergic, expectorant, calming, euphoriant.

Applications: The flowers can be eaten raw in a salad, as a dessert garnish or dried in a pectoral herbal tea.

The mother tincture (only the flowers or with the leaves: 50% plant, 100% alcohol) is recommended against cancer. The frozen and crushed leaves are more effective than the dried ones.

The brushed, washed and dried roots (1 hour in the sun and 1 week in the shade) can be used in a concentrated decoction (1 t [5 g] in approximately ⅓ cup [150 ml] water) in the case of food or alkaloid poisoning.

In the case of poisoning, a mother tincture made from the roots will provoke vomiting.

Anecdote: Before their orgies, the Romans made violet crowns to delay drunkenness and herbal teas to cure hangovers the next day.

ORIENTAL VIOLET SYRUP

1 cup (125 g)	Violet flowers
2 cups (500 ml)	Water
2 cups (500 ml)	Honey
1 oz (30 ml)	Gin

*B*ring the water to a boil. Add the violets and combine. Infuse overnight in a non-metallic container. Strain and add the honey. Simmer for 10 minutes at low heat. Let cool and pour into glass bottles or jars. Add the gin to preserve the mixture. The syrup can be kept for 3 months in a cool place: excellent on crepes, cakes and sherbet. It soothes the throat and intestines.

WALNUT

Latin name: *Juglans regia*

Common names: Jupiter's nuts, tree of evil

History: The edible walnut, which undoubtedly originated in Asia Minor, owes its botanical name to the Greek *Ju glans* or "Jupiter's glans." Jupiter is believed to have created walnuts when the gods lived on earth among mortals. According to Culpeper, walnut leaves combined with onion, a little honey and salt neutralize all the poisons of venomous animals.

The walnut was grown primarily because of its nuts. France is one of the biggest producers; the *appellation contrôlée* "European walnut" dates from 1938. Its wood is used in carpentry. Its leaves and husk are still used commercially for medicinal and cosmetic purposes (tanning oil). Even its shells are included in insulating materials.

Professor Binet proved that walnut leaves have an effective bactericidal action on smut disease pustules and on the scrofula of tuberculosis. Dr. Max Tetau, the creator of gemmotherapy, asserts that walnut blossoms are effective against stomach ulcers, anxiety, and impotence. North American Indians used them to treat parasitical disorders of the skin and as a purgative in the case of jaundice.

Contemporary American herbalists consider the native walnut leaf to be the best fungicide, vermifuge and antiparasitical agent (external and internal use). They advise the inner bark of the butternut tree as the only laxative to be used by pregnant women.

Habitat: The European walnut (*Juglans regia*) is grown in temperate regions, in sunny orchards where the trees have room to grow. In North America, the butternut tree (*Juglans cinerea*) and the walnut (*Juglans negra*) grow in old deciduous forests or near fallow land that has been fertilized by cows.

Description: A tree that grows 66 ft to 99 ft (20 m to 30 m) high and can live for up to 300 years. The bark is smooth and grayish. The deciduous leaves are coated with resin. The oval fruit is a drupe consisting of a thick pericarp called the "husk." It opens upon reaching maturity to release the shell that contains the nut.

Parts Used: The leaves in July,

These great and admirable trees are useful and precious. It is time to rediscover them and to help propagate them for future generations.

before the fruit appears, and the nut-meat that, ideally, has been left to ripen in the nut until December.

Chemical Composition: Leaves and husk: tannin, vitamins C and E, organic acids, minerals (iron, potassium, iodine), naphtoquinones and proteins. Nut: an oil rich in essential fatty acids, proteins, sugars, vitamins A, B_1, B_2 and PP, minerals (copper, iron, phosphorus, sulphur, zinc).

Medicinal Properties: Antiseptic, astringent, antidiabetic, hypoglycemic, blood and lymphatic depurative, fungicidal, tonic, stomachic, vermifuge.

Applications: The boiled leaves can be used in a poultice or a lotion in the case of infectious skin disorders such as fungus, herpes, weeping eczema and

---

STOMACHIC LIQUEUR

10 oz (300 g)	Green husk (in August)
4 cups (1 liter)	Brandy or spirits (60 proof)
1 cup (250 g)	Brown cane sugar

Finely chop the husk. Macerate for 1 month in the alcohol away from light. Carefully strain. Add the sugar, shaking well.

Consume 1 T to 2 T (15 ml to 30 ml), pure or diluted in water: excellent for treating lack of appetite, indigestion and ulcers.

---

psoriasis. They are effective against dandruff (last rinse water). In a concentrated decoction, 1 oz (20 g) leaves in 4 cups (1 liter) water and macerated for a few hours: drink 3 cups per day before meals to treat invasive yeast infections, stomach hyperacidity, poor digestion of fats and chronic skin diseases.

The macerated green husk (50% husk, 100% vinegar or alcohol) is an interesting anti-infective for use in mouthwashes and for gargling; simply diluted in water or in an herbal tea, it acts as a disinfecting lotion.

The nuts are very nutritious and, taken a rate of 3 T (50 g) for 3 consecutive nights, for example, in a salad, they represent an excellent vermifuge. They are also famous for being a male aphrodisiac. The oil of the fresh nut used in a topical rub fights dandruff and promotes hair growth.

Warning: Avoid eating rancid nuts, as they are very toxic, and avoid any nuts if you are suffering from hepatic problems. If using the husk of the nut in a cure, brush your teeth with bicarbonate soda, for the tannins darken the teeth.

Anecdote: According to popular belief, the walnut represents the sun and the male sex organ, and its fruit increases virility. Carry a walnut around to strengthen the heart and ward off rheumatism.

WATERCRESS

CRUCIFERAE FAMILY

Latin name: *Nasturtium officinale*

Common names: scurvy grass

History: Hippocrates recommended watercress as an expectorant, and Dioscorides, his countryman, suggested its use as an aphrodisiac. Roman soldiers regularly consumed this plant to be strong and courageous; they always grew it near their training camps. During the Middle Ages, the physicians at the Salerno school said, "Take watercress and rub your hair with it. This remedy will increase the strength of your hair, and make you grow more of it."

Given its high iron, iodine, sulphur and vitamin C content, watercress is the unequaled champion of salads!

Women of the upper classes, obsessed with the whiteness of their skin, regularly applied the sap of the watercress to their faces in the form of an alcoholized tincture diluted in blueberry and orange blossom water. In the 16th century, the French surgeon Ambroise Paré advised its use to treat scabies, and his contemporary, Thierry Lesplaigney, prescribed watercress for sciatica and headaches. Drs. Joseph Récamier (9th century) and Herni Leclerc (20th century) both recommended it and used it against bronchitis, general fatigue, diabetes and even tuberculosis, preferably taken daily in a salad.

Habitat: In streams and small rivers, always in clear, running water.

Description: Perennial which takes root in mud by way of strong nodes. The leaves are shiny and green. The small white flowers have cross-shaped petals and bloom from the outer edge towards the center. The seeds reside by

the dozens in a clove or long and delicate, cylindrical siliqua.

Parts Used: The leaves and stems, before flowering.

Warning: In areas where sheep are raised, caution is required, for watercress can be home to the eggs or larvae of the liver fluke, a formidable hepatic parasite. Soak the watercress in a water and 10% vinegar solution for a few minutes. Rinse several times.

Chemical Composition: Vitamins A, B, C, E and PP, minerals (iron, phosphorus, manganese, copper, sulphur, calcium [200 mg per 100 g], iodine), chlorophyll, bitter principle, allyl sulphocyanide.

Medicinal Properties: Antioxidant, immunostimulant, appetizer, stomachic, depurative, revitalizing, antianemic, antiscorbutic, expectorant, mucolytic, hypoglycemic, febrifuge, sudorific, antiseptic, diuretic, bactericidal, vermifuge, remineralizing, hair growth stimulant, nicotine antidote.

Applications: The green leaves can be eaten raw: they are depurative, nutritious and revitalizing. They can also be drunk in a freshly squeezed juice prepared in a juice extractor and combined with carrot or beet juice in order to sweeten it. Watercress soup is delicious.

The sap extracted from the crushed plant is used on an infected wound or as a tonic and bleach to lighten brown spots and freckles when directly applied to the face using a cotton pad.

In a poultice (the whole plant, slightly crushed): on abscesses, adenitis or closed cysts to help them heal. In a mother tincture for use in the winter: against fever, fatigue and vitamin defi-

ciency. If there is enough room in your garden, install a watercress bed and allow a gentle stream of water to flow through it. One small planting can provide an invigorating cocktail for years to come.

Anecdote: Watercress helps withdraw from nicotine, for it repairs the damage caused to the blood and the brain. In Ancient Greece, it was seen as an antidote for stupidity!

REVITALIZING SALAD

1	Bunch of washed and rinsed watercress
¼	Finely chopped fennel bulb
2	Grated carrots
VINAIGRETTE	
2 T (30 ml)	Olive oil
1 T (15 ml)	Lemon juice
1 pinch	Salt
1 pinch	Pepper
1 clove	Garlic
1 t (5 ml)	Dijon mustard

Combine all the ingredients in a salad bowl. Prepare the vinaigrette and pour over the salad. Eat this salad preferably at the start of the meal.

WHITE BIRCH

BETULACEAE FAMILY

Latin name: *Betula alba*

Common names: canoe birch, sweet birch

History: The word "birch" originates from the Celt word *berchta*, which means, "shining." It was dedicated to the mother goddess. From the 1st to the 10th centuries, all the Nordic peoples, from the Sami to the Vikings and the Siberians, revered this tree. For the North American Indians the birch became essential, not only as medicine but also for heating and as a raw material. The Chippewa primarily used the sap to purify themselves, the Huron used the leaves to treat the joints and the kidneys, and the Montagnais harvested the bark to cure skin diseases. They whipped themselves and burned the leaves in their sweat lodges. They also used it during healing rituals. St. Hildegard recommended the flowers and catkins be used in a poultice to treat wounds. Pietro-Andrea Mattioli called birch "the nephritic tree of Europe."

The great vigor of birch is evident as much in its luminous appearance as in its highly therapeutic use.

Today, the Russians produce *nastoika* (a mother tincture) by placing the buds in vodka, and they absorb the calcined bark to treat bloating and food poisoning. The Japanese recently began marketing birch sap in handy small bottles, in keeping with the trend of food remedies called nutriceuticals or functional foods.

Habitat: Young, moist forests, with adequate space and light to thrive.

Description: Slender tree capable of reaching 99 ft (30 m) high and of living 200 years. It has a whitish, smooth trunk, striated with red lines. The fine, papery bark can be stripped in long, flexible horizontal strips. The top of the leaf is green and shiny. The flowers consist of cylindrical catkins that release powdery yellow pollen. The brown roots are hard and deep.

Parts Used: In early spring, the birch sap, then the blossoms, catkins and flowers, and the leaves in summer and the bark in winter.

Chemical Composition: Leaves: acids, vitamins A, C and E, bioflavonoids, chlorophyll, saponins. Bark: essential oil rich in methyl salicylate, tar, resin, tannins, minerals (calcium, phosphorus, potassium, sodium).

Medicinal Properties: Antiseptic, antifungal, choleretic, lipotropic, cicatrizant, regenerating, blood and

lymphatic depurative, diuretic, lithotriptic, febrifuge, sudorific, remineralizing, tonic.

Applications: Many Nordic people carry out cures in the spring using birch water to cleanse the lymph, the blood and the kidneys: for about 10 days, drink 1 cup (250 ml) birch water, 2 times daily.

The buds (from the varieties *pubescens* and *verrucosa*) are recommended for treating skin disorders, while the flowers and catkins in a poultice can treat infected wounds: 5 catkins or flowers in 1 cup (250 ml) boiling water.

The fresh birch leaves are crushed and used in refreshing poultices in the case of burns or infected wounds. The young and shiny leaves can be prepared in a diuretic herbal tea for internal use: 3 cups (750 ml) daily at 5 leaves per 1 cup (250 ml) water.

The outer bark can be used as a hemostatic bandage; when applied as a band around the head, it is effective against headaches. Cures involving a decoction made from the sapwood or inner bark can be carried out to treat chronic skin disorders. The tar or a concentrate made from the bark heated to a very high temperature is used in dermatology against some parasitoses, dandruff and baldness. Birch essential oil is often sold as a substitute for that extracted from wintergreen (similar concentrations of methyl salicylate). It is used externally as an analgesic in concentrations of 10% vegetable oil. The birch produces a type of shell-shaped fungus on the outside of its bark that is rich in phosphorus and that glows in the night. North American Indians, just like the Chinese, used it in a moxa. A moxa is a stick of mugwort used in traditional Chinese medicine, which is burned when it comes in contact with the skin; its effects are similar to those of acupuncture.

Anecdote: The floral elixir of birch eliminates our animalistic and egotistical side. Its keywords are communication, empathy and support.

REVEALING BATH

2 lb (1 kg)	Fresh leaves
16 cups (4 liters)	Water
1	Cotton or linen bag or pillowcase

Bring the water to a boil. During this time, place the leaves in the fabric pouch, then seal tightly. Immerse the bag in the water and boil for 10 minutes. Let cool slightly. Fill the bathtub half full, pour in the concentrated liquid and sit in the tub. Place the pouch on the shoulders and rub the upper part of the body with the sticky sap while carefully listening to your body. Step out of the bath in the case of palpitations or, in some cases, before falling asleep. The Russians, fans of hydrotherapy, advise taking this bath for 30 consecutive days to cure joint or dermatological diseases.

237

WILD CARROT

Latin name: *Daucus carota*

Common names: bee's nest plant, bird's nest, root, Queen Anne's lace

History: Galen gave this plant its Latin name in 200 B.C. Pliny called it *Pastinaca gallica* ("of France"), as it was apparently consumed the most in France, and cultivation of this plant had already begun as people tried to improve both its taste and its texture. Culpeper said that Mercury dominated the carrot, and that it could prevent flatulence, induce urination, break kidney stones and flush them out.

Jean Valnet proved scientifically that the root of the cultivated or wild carrot, raw, grated and applied in a poultice, prevents wrinkles, promotes scarring and relieves pain, even in the case of burns or deep wounds. Professor Léon Binet, as well as researchers at the Academy of Sciences in Minsk, recommend bathing jaundiced babies in a decoction made from wild carrot root.

Habitat: Dry and rocky soil, rubble,

Wild carrot is one of the best plants for draining the excesses of both the mind and body.

along ditches. Heliophilous (sun-loving plant), it avoids shady areas.

Description: The wild carrot differs from the garden variety in that it has a tuberous root. It flowers in its second year. The slightly hairy and striated central stem produces white flowers, sometimes tinged with pink that curl up before producing flat green seeds.

Warning: Ensure that you can correctly identify wild carrot. Do not confuse it with its dangerous cousin, spotted water hemlock, or with wild parsnip (see chapter 7, on toxic plants). Its foliage contains psoralens and can provoke blotching among people who are extremely sensitive to this plant.

Parts Used: The flowers and seeds at the end of summer, the roots in fall or early spring.

Chemical Composition: Starches, sugars, beta-carotene, essential oil, proteins, minerals (iron, potassium, copper, iodine), tonics, plant growth regulators, dye element.

239

Medicinal Properties: Antioxidant, cicatrizant, carminative, laxative, digestive, diuretic, emmenagogue, galactagogue, nutritive, remineralizing, ophthalmic, vermifuge, parasiticide.

Applications: In a floral elixir (3 pure drops placed under the tongue, 3 to 5 times daily), the carrot fortifies eyesight and stimulates other physical, mental

carrots are just one of the miracle remedies applied at this famous spa town.

The well-brushed root can be eaten raw or cooked. It treats water retention and intestinal parasites, promotes good digestion of proteins and also fights constipation. In the fall, when the root is often tough and woody, it is consumed in the form of a diuretic decoction; in the spring, it is consumed in a vermifuge decoction. The juice extracted from the root is an excellent laxative. It also treats anemia and jaundice.

Warning: Do not consume in the early stages of pregnancy.

Anecdote: Recent experiments have shown that wild carrot seeds have the same effect as the morning-after pill.

and spiritual capacities. It offers surprising results for some spiritual illnesses otherwise difficult to treat.

The freshly crushed wild carrot seeds can be used in many cooked or boiled dishes, using just ½ t (2.5 g) in 1 cup (250 ml) water: an excellent diuretic, eliminates gas, and increases the amount of breast milk. Take 3 times daily, between feedings.

Steamed carrots consumed over several consecutive days represent a marvelous gastrointestinal regulator. Vichy

CARMINATIVE DECOCTION

4 cups (1 liter)	Water
3 T (15 g)	Carrot seeds
1	Glass or terra-cotta teapot

*B*ring the water to a boil and pour onto the seeds in the teapot. Infuse with the lid on for at least 30 minutes. Drink 3 to 4 cups (750 ml to 1 liter) daily, between meals, in the case of flatulence, water retention and rheumatism. Excellent for babies who are not getting enough milk. Breast-feeding babies will also benefit from its goodness.

WILD GINGER

ARISTOLOCHIACEAE FAMILY

Latin name: *Asarum canadense* or *Asarum europaeum*

Common names: coltsfoot, Indian ginger, snakeroot

History: Before America was discovered, wild ginger powder was already being used as an emetic, until the beginning of the 13th century when ipecacuanha replaced it. However, Saint-Ange powder, a famous witch's remedy based on wild ginger, which was secretly distributed in Paris during the Inquisition, saved many lives thanks to its emetic effect. It was seen as evil because of the hellebore and toad powder included among its ingredients. Wild ginger was also the main ingredient in the sternutatory powder in the French *Codex*; it was then called "head powder." North American Indians administered this powder during a long and painful childbirth to strengthen the nervous system and to induce contractions, properties confirmed by the physicians at the American Physic Medical School.

As the *Dictionnaire des plantes qui guérissent* (*Larousse Book of Plants That Heal*) reveals, the Russians used wild ginger as an emetic and antidote in the case of drunkenness, whence its nickname "cabaret," and as an antidote for poisonous mushrooms.

Habitat: Old deciduous forests with a thick humus, acidic soils and the shady edge of forest where it spreads in colonies. It flowers from May to July.

Description: A magnificent, small perennial plant with dark green cordate or heart-shaped leaves. Its single purple flower is bell-shaped. The plant is hermaphrodite, but survives thanks to its light green and highly aromatic repent rhizome, which sometimes grows several yards long.

Parts Used: The rhizome early in the spring and fall, and the leaves.

Chemical Composition: Bitter principle, resin, aristolochic acid, starches, camphor, mucilages, alkaloid.

Medicinal Properties: Antispasmodic, analgesic, aromatic, appetizer, deodorizing, disinfectant, diuretic, sudorific, emmenagogue, oxytocic, sternutator, immunostimulant, stomachic, antiputrid, antitoxic emetic.

Applications: In the summer, drink decoctions made from the leaves: 1 leaf

Wild ginger is one of the most aromatic plants that grows in northern regions. Long used as a perfume base, it counterbalances all our excesses!

for 1 cup (250 ml) water. Excellent for cleansing the blood, fortifying the heart and purifying the lungs. It can also be dried, but it loses many of its virtues.

The same applies to the rhizome, which is more effective when fresh. After drying, it barely remains active for 6 months. However, the aromatic roots can be used to produce a potpourri or cloth sachets for closets, for wild ginger is deodorizing. It also keeps mites and other pests away. Chewing a piece of wild ginger root the size of a match head leaves the breath scented for hours on end. Concentrated and macerated in good-quality oil, the root makes a pleasant and powerful analgesic oil. Grated and dried, it acts as an effective sneezing powder against migraines due to rhinitis or to a blocked sinus.

Used externally, the alcohol-based mother tincture can be used as a perfume. Applied internally, it induces appetite and acts as a digestive: between 5 and 10 drops maximum. By tripling the diluted dosage in hot water or milk, it becomes an excellent emetic.

The decoction (50% plant, 100% water) acts as an antiseptic compress in the case of a wound or fungal dermato-

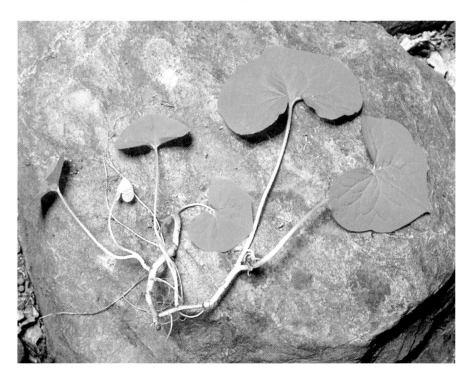

sis, or even as a revitalizing tonic for the face.

Warning: Avoid high dosages and extended cures if taking anticoagulants, suffering from anorexia, gastritis, colitis or diarrhea, and in the early stages of pregnancy.

Anecdote: North American Indians used it as a contraceptive in the second part of their cycle. Its contents and its scent invite amorous excesses.

POISON ANTIDOTE POTION

1 cup (250 ml)	Whole milk
1 t (5 g)	Wild ginger (rhizome)

Boil the wild ginger in the milk for 3 minutes. Drink the liquid as hot as possible in large sips. Effective against alkaloid, medication, alcohol and mushroom poisoning.

WILD PANSY
VIOLACEAE FAMILY

Latin name: *Viola tricolor*

Common names: heart's ease, Johnny jumper, stepmother

History: Hippocrates recommended wild pansy against headaches and migraines, while Dioscorides advised it for treating stomach hyperacidity. It gets its name from François Quesnay, physician to Louis XV, who made it the emblem of his coat of arms. John Gerard declared it was very effective against fevers and convulsions in children, for treating skin and lung disorders.

In the United States, the Eclectics viewed it as a powerful skin regenerator. In France in the 17th century, *syrop violae* was used frequently for its emollient and pectoral virtues. It is traditionally recognized as a powerful remedy for treating rheumatoid arthritis, gout and rheumatism in general, provided that it is used in an extended cure.

Habitat: Vacant lots, fallow fields and along cultivated garden borders, loose soil rich in nitrates. All areas where it grows must be in full sun.

Description: A plant that grows 6 in to 12 in (15 cm to 30 cm) high and consists of a central stem from which several secondary stems act as long petioles. The flowers always come in 3 basic colors: purple around the outside, bright yellow towards the bottom, pale yellow towards the top. The sun-loving flower closes up in inclement weather. The oval leaves are attached in threes to the secondary stems by way of an axil.

In *A Midsummer Night's Dream*, Shakespeare devoted a few lines to the wild pansy:

> *Yet mark'd I where the*
> *bolt of Cupid fell: It fell upon a*
> *little western flower,*
> *Before milk-white, now purple*
> *with love's wound: And maidens*
> *call it 'love-in-idleness'.*

Parts Used: The whole plant, but especially the flowers.

Chemical Composition: Glucoside, saponins, methyl salicylate, mucilages, pectins, violaquercetin, violanine, bitter principle (violine), tannins, minerals (magnesium, potassium), vitamin C.

Medicinal Properties: Antiseptic, antihistaminic, depurative, cicatrizant, diuretic, antiuric, emollient, laxative, febrifuge, diaphoretic, regenerating, vulnerary.

Applications: Usually only the flowers are eaten raw in a salad or used to decorate cakes. In an herbal tea or a cold maceration consisting of 3 flowers in 1 cup (250 ml) water, they cure fevers. The light herbal tea made from the flowers (1 g per cup) can be added to the baby bottle: it treats scald head, constipation or fever due to teething. It also purifies the blood and the milk of young mothers, but causes urine to smell like cat's pee!

chronic illness or a cure the season changes: 3 cups (750 ml) daily, preferably before each meal.

Anecdote: Absorbing the floral elixir made from wild pansies, or simply looking at the plant, protects the immune system from viral attacks and activates the right hemisphere of the brain where intuition and creativity reside.

REGENERATING MILK

3	Fresh wild pansy plants
or	
4 T (5 g)	Dried plant
1 cup (250 ml)	Fresh milk

$\mathcal{D}$ip the plant in the milk and bring to a boil. Macerate for 20 minutes. Strain and apply unadulterated to the areas to be treated, 2 to 3 times daily. This milk will only keep for 3 days in the refrigerator: marvelous against scald head, sores, pimples and infected wounds.

The entire, fresh plant in a decoction (1 plant for 2 cups [500 ml] water) is a depurative (blood and skin). To prepare a poultice, take ½ cup (125 ml) herbal tea and ½ lb [250 g] of clay: apply to acne, cysts, eczema or infected wounds. Sometimes, simple compresses are the most practical.

Take a decoction (1 t for 1 cup [250 ml water]) made from the burdock root, comfrey leaves and wild pansy leaves in a continuous treatment in the case of

WILD STRAWBERRY

ROSACEAE FAMILY

Latin name: *Fragaria vesca*

Common names: strawberry

History: Strawberry seeds have been found on the sites of prehistoric lakeside cities. Its Latin name *fragaria* ("perfume") evokes its fragrance. North American Indians have used strawberry flowers as a tonic for the nervous system, and against stomach and skin ulcers, and the fruit to treat scurvy and kidney stones. Linnaeus, the great Swedish botanist of the 18th century, regularly treated his own attacks of gout by carrying out a strawberry cure. Professor Binet recommended strawberries for treating anemics, and the strawberry leaves for children suffering from rickets and the elderly who were demineralized. Until recently, wild strawberry could be purchased in all the pharmacies in North America as Dr. Fowley's concentrated syrup made from strawberry roots, the remedy for diarrhea!

Habitat: Permeable, slightly acidic

This marvelous plant sweet
is the most appreciated fruit in
the world and the richest in
antioxidant principles!

---

and shady soils on the edge of forests and thickets.

Description: Small perennial plant with an orange-colored, semi-repent cylindrical rhizome. The trifoliate and dentated leaves are dark green on top, grayish and slightly hairy underneath. The whitish flowers produce a round, red fruit bearing oval, brown seeds.

Parts Used: The leaves fairly early in the spring, the flowers in May, the fruit in summer, and the rhizomes in the fall.

Chemical Composition: Leaves and roots: tannins, potassium, flavonoids. Fruit: sugars, fructose, levulose, sorbitol, acids, glucoside, minerals (iron, bromine, iodine, magnesium, silica), beta-carotene, vitamin C, water, pectin.

Medicinal Properties: Astringent, antiseptic, antiscorbutic, fortifying, diuretic, lithotriptic, depurative, dissolvent, laxative, purgative, regenerating, remineralizing.

Applications: The young fresh leaves can be used in a soup or decoction: 1 whole plant in 1 cup (250 ml) water to treat diarrhea and hyperacidity, to remineralize and to calm the nerves and muscle spasms.

The root, not recommended as often in an extended cure because of the high concentration of tannins, has a similar effect.

The best method is to eat the raw

fruit. People with sensitive intestines should crunch the seeds. Strawberries keep their flavor and their properties well when macerated in wine or spirits and, surprisingly, their scent after being dried in a dehydrator. Brushing the teeth with strawberry pulp whitens them, and chewing the root fortifies the gums.

248

Anecdote: An elixir made from strawberry flowers suits those who have a delicate disposition, and hypersensitive, pimply, blotchy-skinned and over-emotional adolescents. Strawberry water promises an abundance of joy, fantasy and pleasure.

 STRAWBERRY SPREAD

1 cup (250 g)	Wild or cultivated strawberries
½ cup (125 g)	Pure honey

Combine the two ingredients in a food processor and freeze the resulting mixture in an ice cube tray. Serve as a spread or dessert garnish. This is also an excellent remedy for treating burns and swelling, and for preparing an economical "shot of radiance" beauty mask.

WILD THYME

Latin name: *Thymus serpyllum*

Common names: mother of thyme, serpyllum

History: The French name *serpolet* is derived from the Greek word *serpyllum*, meaning "creeping." This designation allows it to be distinguished from common thyme. The Romans used it to fight melancholy (bath, fumigation, infusion). During the Middle Ages, it symbolized courage; several Crusades took it as their emblem and carried dried wild thyme to keep away the plague. Culpeper described it as being excellent against nervous disorders, for fortifying the lungs, increasing endurance and eliminating intestinal gas. He also advised it be used to make a pillow to chase away nightmares.

In 1718, the German chemist Gaspar Neumann isolated camphor from thyme to create thymol, the substance responsible for the antiseptic effect of thyme. This inspired the American war surgeon Joseph Lister to produce a mouthwash based on thymol, which is

This darling of wild rabbits is a doctor of the meadows. It would be wise to remember this!

still used today.

Recent research has proven that thyme helps to detoxify and even put someone off alcohol altogether.

The gland located at the base of the neck, the thymus, was called this because of its resemblance to the plant and its function as a guardian angel of the immune system.

Habitat: Rocky, clay soils, dry fallow land, heavily frequented areas, hills, mountains and along the seacoast.

Description: Semi-repent perennial plant with a square stem and light purple flowers. It emits an acrid scent.

Parts Used: All the aerial parts before flowering, in June or July depending on the area.

Chemical Composition: Tannins, essential oil consisting of cavacrol,

cymol, pinene and thymol, resin, saponins, minerals (iron, copper).

Medicinal Properties: Antispasmodic, analgesic, deodorizing, disinfectant, digestive, antiputrid, immunostimulant, antihistaminic, pectoral, mucolytic, tonic, relaxant.

Applications: In a vinegar- or brandy-based mother tincture (30 drops in 1 cup [250 ml] boiling water): apply to infected wounds. It can also be taken internally to treat digestive problems, the start of the flu, pulmonary infection, and to treat the aftereffects of any excesses: 20 drops at a time in ⅓ cup (100 ml) water, 3 to 5 times daily.

In an infusion, fresh or dried wild thyme is a good anti-flu pectoral and tonic; with honey, it soothes irritated mucous membranes: 1 t (5 g) of the fresh or ¾ t (3 g) of the dried plant in 1 cup (250 ml) water.

Add a few leaves to dishes that are difficult to digest.

Anecdote: The Gauls decorated their tombs with wild thyme to preserve the memory of the dead.

ANTISEPTIC AND DIGESTIVE TINCTURE

20 stems or 1 cup	Wild thyme
1 cup (60 g)	Peppermint
½ cup (125 g)	Wild or foreign ginger
4 cups (1 liter)	Spirits 40 or 60 proof (gin, brandy, vodka)

Trim, cut and chop the plants. Put them in a jar and cover with the alcohol. Macerate for 1 month away from light, shaking regularly. Carefully strain.

Ideal for treating colic, indigestion, intestinal cramps and headaches: 30 drops at a time in ½ cup (125 ml) water, up to 4 times daily.

In a poultice or a compress, pure or diluted, on infected wounds, against muscle spasms and joint pain. Scented and capable of killing germs, it can even be used as a breath-freshening mouthwash.

SALICACEAE FAMILY

Latin name: *Salix alba*

Common names: pussy willow, salicin willow, white, withy

History: In Europe more than 5000 years ago, inhabitants of lakeside cities used willow to treat swamp fever. If, for the Egyptians, it symbolized joy, for the Hebrews it personified the pain of exile, especially weeping willow, which can be commonly found near the Nile River. Moreover, it was used to build the cradle in which Moses slept. According to Dioscorides, willow catkins were just the right thing for stopping the "ardors of Venus"; the Salerno school confirms: "Its infused flower extinguishes the impure flame that lights lustfulness." Three centuries later, in his *Histoire générale des plantes* (General History of Plants), Dalechamps added: "The leaves when drunk cool those who are too hot in the game of love."

Doctors Cazin and Leclerc confirmed that the willow bark has febrifuge virtues similar to those of cinchona. In 1828, the French chemists Buchner and

These magnificent trees quietly calm physical and moral pain.

Leroux extracted salicin from willow to prepare a concentrated analgesic. But it was an Italian, Raphael Piria, who, 10 years later, isolated salicylic acid from meadowsweet, a bog plant with similar virtues. In 1972, German researchers Hovel and Steinegger proved that willow extract acted slower than aspirin, but 30% longer.

Habitat: Moist areas near ponds, lakes, rivers and swamps, and wet grasslands.

Description: Tree capable of reaching 99 ft (30 m) in height, covered with

251

a silver bark that grows thicker with age. In the spring, it produces catkins with golden pistils. The lanceolate leaves are light green on top and whitish underneath.

Parts Used: The catkins in early spring, the young leaves in June. The bark is removed only from a tree aged 2 to 5 years, preferably in late fall.

Chemical Composition: Salicin, glycosides, flavonoids, tannins, minerals (calcium, potassium), vitamin C, coumarin, oestradiol.

Medicinal Properties: Anaphrodisiac, calming, analgesic, anti-inflammatory, antacid, astringent, appetizer, dissolvent, diuretic, febrifuge, sudorific, hemostatic, regenerating, stomachic, antispasmodic, vermifuge, fungicidal.

Applications: In a mother tincture (50% saturated) in alcohol or wine, the catkins calm obsessive sexual ardor: take 20 drops, 3 times daily.

In an herbal tea, the dried leaves are diuretic and more effective when combined with common elder or meadowsweet.

Dry the inner bark for at least 3 months. Store in a non-airtight jar to encourage the water and some irritating principles to evaporate. Taken repeatedly in the form of a mother tincture or a fresh or dried decoction (20 drops, 3 to 5 times daily), it is recommended against all kinds of acute pain and inflammation (fever, migraines, etc.).

Anecdote: The willow floral elixir encourages acceptance, forgiveness and appreciation.

CHASE-AWAY-YOUR-PAIN APERITIF

3 cups (750 ml)	Sweet white wine (Alsatian Muscat, Muscadet)
3 T (50 g)	Willow bark, dried and crushed

*M*acerate the bark in the wine for 1 month. Strain.

Drink 2 T (30 ml), 3 times daily, before meals, pure or diluted, in the case of hepatic migraines, stomachache or rheumatism attacks.

253

WOOD SORREL

Latin name: *Oxalis acetosella*

Common names: fairy bell, cuckoo's meat, hallelujah, surell, wood sour

History: Its French name *oxalide* comes from the Greek *oxys*, which means "acid" and the Latin *acetosella*, which signifies "vinegar salt." Wood sorrel, in particular, its three joined leaves, were chosen by St. Patrick as the emblem of Ireland, the shamrock.

The painters of the Renaissance drew it to represent the Trinity: Fra Angelico often incorporated it in his paintings. Mrs. Grieve, in *The Modern Herbal*, maintains that Nordic people ate it in salad and in soup. Today, Russians use it to treat catarrhs, fever, hemorrhages and urinary infections. According to John Gerard, wood sorrel is better than sheep sorrel. Raw, it brings back an appetite and tonifies weak and sick stomachs. Apothecaries have long produced salts of lemon by evaporating the wood sorrel sap: 6 lb (3 kg) of sap pro-

duce 2 oz (60 g) of crystals consisting of a combination of citric and oxalic acids. The sap is excellent for treating catarrhs, fever and hemorrhaging.

Habitat: Moist, shady areas with sandy, acidic soil, including fields and forests.

Description: Small perennial hermaphrodite plant that grows in tufts and often in colonies. The delicate green heart-shaped leaves grow in groups of three. The flowers, consisting of five petals, are yellow in North America (the *stricta* variety), and white with pink veins in Europe (the *acetosella* variety).

Parts Used: The entire plant, but especially the leaves and flowers, from spring until the first frost.

254

Just like the ancient sages, children adore wood sorrel. What they know instinctively is not wrong: the plant's acidity deeply cleanses the body.

Chemical Composition: Chlorophyll, bioflavonoids, vitamin C, minerals (iron), oxalic acid, potassium bioxalate, beta-carotene, hormones.

Medicinal Properties: Appetizer, digestive, antiscorbutic, tonic, cholagogue, choleretic, diuretic, depurative, hemostatic, vulnerary, tonic, remineralizing.

Applications: During the summer, as a source of vitamins and tonic acids for the immune system, eat it in a salad, vegetable dip or cold sauce to accompany meats or fish that are difficult to digest. To make lemonade, chop the leaves and sweeten: 1 oz (30 g) leaves in 4 cups (1 liter) water. With 2 cups (500 g) cane sugar in 4 cups (1 liter) water:

allow fermenting for 24 hours at 68°F (20°C), then strain. Keep refrigerated for 8 days. This drink is refreshing, stomachic and tonic.

Reduced to gruel and a poultice, it is used to treat lumps, wounds, burns and even brown spots, and malignant skin tumors.

To ensure its virtues remain intact, prepare a vinegar-, wine- or alcohol-based mother tincture.

Warning: Avoid wood sorrel cures in the case of gout, urinary lithiasis and demineralization. Also avoid using it if you have worms. It appears that it causes the worms to gain weight!

Anecdote: Wood sorrel is also called "hallelujah" because it flowers in the spring, around the time of Easter, and "cuckoo's meat," for this bird is crazy about it and starts singing from the time of the plant's first flowering!

COLD SAUCE

1 cup (20 g)	Fresh wood sorrel leaves
1 clove	Garlic
½ cup (125 ml)	Sour cream
3 leaves	Basil
To taste	Salt, pepper

Combine all the ingredients in a blender; serve fresh with beef, salmon, asparagus or raw vegetables.

WOUNDWORT

Latin name: *Prunella vulgaris*

Common names: self heal, blue curts, heal-all, heart of the earth

History: During the Middle Ages, monks always carried this hemostatic plant with them when they left on a crusade. John Gerard confirms that, with the bugle plant, its closest relative, it is one of the best antihemorrhagic plants, even more effective in a decoction when combined half-and-half with old red wine and used as a compress on wounds. According to the signatures theory, woundwort resembles the larynx: it treats sore throats and problems involving the voice.

Woundwort is once again gaining popularity in the United States where it is used in numerous "subtle" (psychotherapeutic) remedies based on floral elixirs to stimulate all the self-healing processes.

Habitat: Moist and sunny grasslands, footpaths and on the edge of forests.

Description: Perennial plant 4 inches

to 12 inches (10 cm to 30 cm) high with a square stem bearing oblong and median leaves. The purple flowers alternatively bloom in the form of a spur with two protuberant lips.

Parts Used: All the visible parts of the plant.

Chemical Composition: Carbohydrates, acids, minerals (calcium, magnesium, potassium, copper), tannins, bitter principles, essential oils, vitamins B^1, C and K.

Medicinal Properties: Antibiotic, antiseptic, antitumoral, regenerating, cicatrizant, hemostatic, cordial, nutritive, diuretic, hypotensive, hypoglycemic, depurative, refreshing.

Applications: The small flowers can be eaten raw in a salad (20 flowery tops). Applying the raw and chewed plant stops hemorrhaging and treats skin infections and all types of sore throat.

256

This pretty plant,
full of life, fights excess heat
and acidity. It soothes irritations,
literally and figuratively.

The herbal tea, based on a mother tincture, is excellent for all the mucous membranes. In a decoction or herbal tea, woundwort cures benign fevers, diarrhea, hemorrhoids and even nephritis by repeating the following dosage: 5 flowery tops in 1 cup (250 ml) water before each meal. In a cerate or ointment, it is cicatrizant, hemostatic and regenerating.

Anecdote: Woundwort floral elixir is taken during a cure or while fasting to erase all the old physical and mental wounds. It helps to make some real changes and facilitates self-healing.

 SORE THROAT HERBAL TEA

5	Woundwort flowers, fresh or dried
1 t (5 ml)	Creamy honey
2 cups (250 ml)	Water
1 pinch	Salt (optional)

Simmer the fresh plant in the water, otherwise pour the water onto the dried plant and infuse for 5 minutes. Add the honey once the liquid has cooled in order to preserve the enzymes. Drink, taking small sips.

In the case of a purulent infection, add a pinch of sea salt and gargle. Spit out the herbal tea.

ASTERACEAE FAMILY

Latin name: *Achillea millefolium*

Common names: thousand weed, bad man's plaything

History: Achilles, a Homeric hero, treated his injured soldiers with this herb, whence the name *achillea*. The centaur Chiron, who was a physician, and Venus, the goddess of love and plants, recommended the plant to him. Until the 19th century, all soldiers used it to promote scarring. It was then given the name "soldier's woundwort."

For more than a thousand years, the Swedes called it "field hop" and added it to their beer. The Poles used it to preserve their wine, and many Nordic peoples add the leaves to their spring purgative salad.

In Quebec, yarrow has been the most popular and most widely used plant for over 3 centuries to treat fever.

258

Yarrow has a powerful aura. It represents protection against evil and those who want to do us harm, strength in the face of adversity, and a purity of intent. It can be grown around the house, kept in a handy bouquet or, even better, regularly absorbed in a floral elixir.

It has also been successfully used in gynecology: in his *Traité des plantes usuelles* (Treatise on common plants), the famous Dr. Cazin described it as indispensable for stopping abnormal uterine hemorrhaging, for regulating menstruation, for treating, varicose veins caused by a pelvic imbalance, and following childbirth.

Habitat: Commonly found throughout the northern hemisphere, in fields, meadows, along roadsides and embankments. It likes warm temperatures, light and relative dryness.

Description: Perennial plant 12 inches to 24 inches (30 cm to 60 cm) high. Its single, central stem is topped by an umbellate consisting of several white flowers with a yellow center. Its leaves are delicately dentated and emit, just like the rest of the plant, a camphorated and sweet scent.

Parts Used: The flowery tops from June to October. Check thoroughly before picking, for aphids love its nectar.

Chemical Composition: Essential oils, glucoside, tannins, minerals (calcium, potassium, phosphorus).

Medicinal Properties: Appetizer, digestive, vermifuge, antiseptic, cicatrizant, febrifuge and tonic.

Applications: In the event of an intense fever or painful hot flash (menopause), drink a cold infusion: 1

flowery top in 1 cup (250 ml) water. To promote the scarring of wounds, apply a compress. To stop bleeding, prepare a more concentrated decoction: 3 plants boiled in 1 cup (250 ml) water for 3 minutes, and strained.

Anecdote: The Chinese still use dried yarrow stems today as a rod for deciphering the sacred oracle of *I Ching* (*Book of Changes*). Slavic popular tradition tells of the custom of plugging a nostril with a yarrow flower and singing:

> *Yarrow, by your powerful white breath, tell me how*
> *Much my love may love me, make my nose bleed now!*

 A STOMACH-FRIENDLY WINE

2 cups (120 g)	Yarrow flowers
6 cups (1 ½ liters)	Dry white wine

Crush the flowers in a mortar or an electric blender. Let stand for 1 month in a glass jar away from light, then strain.

Bitter yet healthy for digestion, fighting stomach cramps and flatulence. As an aperitif or a digestive, take 1 T (15 ml).

259

CHAPTER 5

Common Illnesses and Their Plant Remedies

*Remedies come along, then one by one they are abandoned,
but the healing power of Nature is forever.*
—DR. HERBERT SHELTON

Abscess: Common burdock, avens, woundwort, chamomile, bedstraw, ground ivy, mallow, St. John's wort, mullein, chickweed, black mustard, slippery elm, plantain, figwort, red clover, violet.

Acidity: Chamomile, oak, comfrey, raspberry, nettle, wild pansy, dandelion, horsetail, red clover.

Acne: Yarrow, elecampane, common burdock, comfrey, raspberry, bedstraw, mint, chickweed, nettle, wild pansy, dandelion, plantain, wild thyme, red clover, common speedwell, violet.

Allergies: Yarrow, mugwort, elecampane, burdock, woundwort, quitch grass, rosehip, raspberry, ground ivy, mallow, chickweed, nettle, sheep sorrel, wild thyme, common elder, red clover, goldenrod.

Anemia: Angelica, mugwort, maidenhair fern, quitch grass, comfrey, watercress, rosehip, barberry, raspberry, mint, nettle, curled dock, wild pansy, dandelion, red clover, violet.

Arthritis: Yarrow, burdock, avens, white birch, shepherd's purse, bearberry, catnip, chokecherry, quitch grass, comprey, fireweed, Joe-pye weed, raspberry, common ash, bedstraw, common juniper, St. John's wort, nettle, mouse-eared hawkweed, dandelion, horsetail, willow, common elder, red clover, goldenrod.

Asthenia (fatigue): Angelica, male fern, oak, chicory, comfrey, watercress, rosehip, barberry, juniper, ground ivy, mint, chickweed, nettle, sheep sorrel, curled dock, wild thyme, common elder, red clover, violet.

Asthma: Elecampane, burdock, shepherd's purse, woundwort, maidenhair fern, catnip, comfrey, rosehip, ground ivy, Indian tobacco, mallow, mullein, slippery elm, nettle, curled dock, dandelion, plantain, balsam, common elder, red clover, coltsfoot, valerian, common speedwell, violet.

Atherosclerosis: Yarrow, hawthorn, elecampane, birch, shepherd's purse, chamomile, maidenhair fern, celandine, chicory, quitch grass, rosehip, barberry, common ash, bedstraw, mallow, chickweed, nettle, wood sorrel, wild pansy, poplar, mouse-eared hawkweed, dandelion, plantain, horsetail.

Athlete's foot. *See* Fungus, yeast, athlete's foot

Bronchitis: Elecampane, woundwort, maidenhair fern, catnip, quitch grass, ground ivy, Indian tobacco, mallow, mint, mullein, mustard, slippery elm, nettle, horseradish, wild thyme, coltsfoot, goldenrod, violet.

Burn: Agrimony, elecampane, burdock, woundwort, chamomile, maidenhair fern, comfrey, bedstraw, mallow, St. John's wort, slippery elm, wild pansy, plantain, wild thyme, coltsfoot, violet.

Bursitis: Yarrow, burdock, birch, bearberry, chokecherry, chicory, quitch grass, comfrey, rosehip, ash, bedstraw, mallow, slippery elm, nettle, wood sorrel, dandelion, meadowsweet, bramble, willow, common elder, red clover, valerian, goldenrod.

Cancer: Agrimony, elecampane, burdock, woundwort, maidenhair fern, celandine, comfrey, watercress, rosehip, raspberry, bedstraw, ground ivy, mallow, St. John's wort, chickweed, nettle, wood sorrel, wild pansy, plantain, wild thyme, common elder, red clover, common speedwell, violet.

Conjunctivitis: Yarrow, mugwort, shepherd's purse, woundwort, chamomile, oak, celandine, comfrey, rosehip, eyebright, strawberry, bedstraw, mallow, mullein, nettle, wild pansy, plantain, meadowsweet, linden, red clover, common speedwell, violet.

Constipation: Yarrow, agrimony, Joe-pye weed, chamomile, celandine, chicory, bearbind, mallow, mint, mullein, slippery elm, curled dock, dandelion, plantain, balsam, linden, valerian, violet.

Cut or wound: Yarrow, mugwort, elecampane, burdock, shepherd's purse, woundwort, white oak, comfrey, strawberry, raspberry, alfalfa, mallow, St. John's wort, mullein, chickweed, slippery elm, plantain, horsetail, red clover, common speedwell, violet.

Cystitis: Avens, birch, bearberry, chokecherry, chicory, quitch grass, rosehip, ash, bedstraw, juniper, ground ivy, mallow, nettle, mouse-eared hawkweed, dandelion, horsetail, meadowsweet, balsam, common elder, linden, red clover, goldenrod.

Decalcification, osteoporosis: Yarrow, motherwort, shepherd's purse, chamomile, maidenhair fern, oak, comfrey, watercress, strawberry, raspberry, dewberry, nettle, dandelion, cinquefoil, horsetail, red clover, coltsfoot.

Depression: Angelica, mugwort, hawthorn, woundwort, chamomile, catnip, chicory, barberry, Indian tobacco, mint, St. John's wort, curled dock, pansy, balsam, linden, valerian.

Diabetes: Agrimony, burdock, woundwort, bearberry, maidenhair fern, chicory, quitch grass, watercress, rosehip, Joe-pye weed, strawberry, bedstraw, juniper, mallow, blueberry, slippery elm, pansy, mouse-eared hawkweed, dandelion, horsetail, common elder, clover, common speedwell, violet.

Diarrhea: Yarrow, agrimony, mugwort, shepherd's purse, woundwort, bearberry, catnip, oak, comfrey, eyebright, strawberry, raspberry, mallow, blueberry, elm, cinquefoil, loosestrife, coltsfoot.

Dyspepsia, gas: Angelica, wild ginger, chamomile, wild carrot, chicory, comfrey, barberry, juniper, mallow, mint, slippery elm, curled dock, dandelion, horsetail, tansy, violet.

Eczema, psoriasis: Yarrow, motherwort, mugwort, burdock, birch, woundwort, chamomile, maidenhair fern, celandine, oak, comfrey, watercress, barberry, raspberry, bedstraw, ground ivy, Indian tobacco, mallow, St. John's wort, mullein, chickweed, nettle, pansy, figwort, wild thyme, clover, valerian, violet.

Flu: Yarrow, angelica, elecampane, avens, birch, woundwort, chamomile, maidenhair fern, rosehip, ground ivy, Indian tobacco, mallow, mint, mustard, nettle, plantain, meadowsweet, balsam, elder, linden, clover, coltsfoot, violet.

Food Poisoning: Yarrow, mugwort, wild ginger, chamomile, celandine, oak, barberry, Indian tobacco, mallow, mustard, slippery elm, sorrel, plantain, balsam, clover, speedwell, violet.

Fungus, yeast, athlete's foot: Mugwort, elecampane, burdock, celandine, oak, comfrey, rosehip, bedstraw, ground ivy, Indian tobacco, walnut, curled dock, horsetail, balsam, figwort, wild thyme, tansy, valerian, violet.

Gas. *See* Dyspepsia

Heart Failure: Motherwort, hawthorn, shepherd's purse, chamomile, maidenhair fern, quitch grass, watercress, rosehip, barberry, raspberry, ash, bedstraw, Indian tobacco, nettle, pansy, willow, elder, linden, clover, valerian.

Hemorrhage: Yarrow, agrimony, mugwort, shepherd's purse, oak, comfrey, strawberry, raspberry, chickweed, plantain, cinquefoil, horsetail, loosestrife, coltsfoot.

Hemorrhoid: Yarrow, agrimony, mugwort, burdock, shepherd's purse, woundwort, oak, comfrey, watercress, male fern, strawberry, raspberry, ground ivy, mullein, elm, plantain, balsam, grape vine.

Hepatitis: Yarrow, agrimony, mugwort, burdock, woundwort, chamomile, common thistle, celandine, chicory, watercress, rosehip, barberry, Joe-pye weed, peppermint, blueberry, evening primrose, wood sorrel, wild pansy, dandelion, wild thyme, tansy, red clover, goldenrod, speedwell, violet.

Herpes zoster: Yarrow, agrimony, mugwort, burdock, birch, maidenhair fern, catnip, celandine, comfrey, watercress, raspberry, bedstraw, gooseberry, mallow, chickweed, nettle, pansy, dandelion, plantain, figwort, red clover, coltsfoot, valerian, violet.

Hypoglycemia: Burdock, fern, chicory, quitch grass, rosehip, barberry, strawberry, raspberry, juniper, mallow, sweet clover, mint, chickweed, curled dock, pansy, dandelion, wild thyme, common elder, red clover.

Insomnia: Motherwort, hawthorn, shepherd's purse, chamomile, catnip, raspberry, hop, Indian tobacco, St. John's wort, balsam, linden, valerian.

Intestinal worms: Mugwort, elecampane, celandine, quitch grass, rosehip, male fern, bearbind, mustard, walnut, balsam, figwort, wild thyme, tansy, valerian.

Menopause: Yarrow, angelica, mugwort, hawthorn, chamomile, catnip, rosehip, barberry, raspberry, juniper, hop, Indian tobacco, mallow, mint, St. John's wort, nettle, curled dock, meadowsweet, red clover, valerian.

Migraine: Yarrow, hawthorn, shepherd's purse, chamomile, maidenhair fern, catnip, celandine, chicory, rosehip, barberry, raspberry, hop, Labrador tea, ground ivy, Indian tobacco, mint, dandelion, meadowsweet, common elder, valerian.

Nephritis: Yarrow, mugwort, elecampane, avens, birch, shepherd's purse, maidenhair fern, chokecherry, quitch grass, watercress, Joe-pye weed, ash, bedstraw, juniper, hop, nettle, mouse-eared hawkweed, dandelion, horsetail, meadowsweet, wild thyme, common elder, linden, red clover, goldenrod.

Nervousness: Angelica, mugwort, hawthorn, shepherd's purse, woundwort, chamomile, catnip, watercress, comfrey, rosehip, juniper, hop, Indian tobacco, St. John's wort, nettle, curled dock, willow, linden, valerian.

Obesity: Angelica, burdock, bearberry, chokecherry, chicory, quitch grass, watercress, rosehip, barberry, bedstraw, juniper, gooseberry, bearbind, mallow, mint, chickweed, blueberry, slippery elm, pansy, hawkweed, plantain, horsetail, meadowsweet, balsam, willow, common elder, linden, red clover, goldenrod, common speedwell.

Osteoporosis. *See* Decalcification, osteoporosis

Otitis: Yarrow, wild ginger, elecampane, chamomile, celandine, ground ivy, Indian tobacco, St. John's wort, mullein, plantain, balsam, wild thyme, common elder, linden.

Palpitations: Motherwort, mugwort, hawthorn, shepherd's purse, catnip, watercress, rosehip, strawberry, raspberry, mallow, St. John's wort, nettle, pansy, dandelion, horsetail, meadowsweet, balsam, linden, red clover, valerian.

Premenstrual syndrome: Yarrow, mugwort, chamomile, catnip, raspberry, hop, bearbind, mallow, mint, nettle, curled dock, dandelion, balsam, willow, linden, valerian.

Psoriasis. *See* Eczema, psoriasis

Wound. *See* Cut or wound

Yeast. *See* Fungus, yeast, athlete's foot

CHAPTER 6

Principle Properties of Wild Medicinal Plants

Follow the praiseworthy and healthy custom of the Ancients,
choose familiar remedies from your gardens and fields, the same ones your
ancestors used, grown in the same air and land as you, the same ones you
will be able to use fresh in all their vigour, without having to walk
very far or to languish while waiting for them.

—ANTOINE MIZAUD
16TH CENTURY FRENCH PHYSICIAN

Acidifying: Produces an acidic reaction leading to a drop in the pH level to below 7, particularly in the mucous membranes and organic liquids, which has an anticoagulant, antiseptic and stimulating effect on the lymphatic and blood circulatory systems.

Barberry, grape, raspberry, rosehip, strawberry, Watercress, wood sorrel.

Alkalinizing: Neutralizes acidic substances of the circulatory, digestive and nervous systems by raising the pH level to above 7; facilitates remineralization.

Birch, blueberry, chamomile, cinquefoil, comfrey, curled dock, dandelion, horsetail, linden, loosestrife, mugwort, mullein, nettle, oak, raspberry, red clover, shepherd's purse, strawberry, willow, yarrow.

Alterative (drains, cleanses): Allows a deep cleansing of the body by expelling toxins.

Ash, balsam, bedstraw, burdock, chickweed, chicory, common elder, dandelion, elecampane, ground ivy, maidenhair fern, mugwort, nettle, quitch grass, red clover, violet, watercress, wild pansy, wild thyme, yarrow.

Analgesic: Reduces, soothes or eliminates pain.

Locally: yarrow, angelica, wild ginger, mint, plantain, tansy.

Through neuro-sensorial centers: catnip, chamomile, cinquefoil, hawthorn, hop, linden, meadowsweet, mugwort, shepherd's purse, St. John's wort, valerian, willow, woundwort, yarrow.

Antidiarrheic: Acts on the irritated intestinal mucous membrane thanks to its absorbent, antacid, astringent and antiseptic properties.

Agrimony, blueberry, catnip, cinquefoil, comfrey, hawthorn, mugwort, oak, raspberry, shepherd's purse, strawberry, woundwort.

Antiphlogistic: Combats local or general inflammation and eliminates abscesses, swelling, boils and edema.

Balsam, burdock, celandine, chickweed, comfrey, elm, Joe-pye weed, linden, mallow, slippery plantain, St. John's wort, violet, wild ginger, watercress.

Antirheumatic: Soothes chronic or temporary inflammatory joint disorders by reducing localized congestion and by helping drain abnormal local crystallization.

Ash, avens, bedstraw, birch, bearberry, burdock, chickweed, chicory, common elder, common juniper, common speedwell, goldenrod, hawthorn, hawkweed, horsetail, Joe-pye weed, linden, mouse-eared meadowsweet, quitch grass, red clover, wild pansy, wild thyme.

Antiscorbutic: Adds vitamin C and its cofactors to food, often present in synergistic form in medicinal plants.

Balsam, barberry, chickweed, chokecherry, common elder, hawthorn, horseradish, maidenhair fern, pansy, plantain, raspberry, rosehip, strawberry, violet, watercress.

Antiseptic: Fights, prevents or neutralizes an infection by stopping pathogenic microorganisms from multiplying.

Balsam, barberry, burdock, celandine, comfrey, elecampane, figwort, mint, mugwort, plantain, rosehip, tansy, watercress, violet, wild ginger, wild thyme, yarrow,.

Antispasmodic: Fights the pain and spasms caused by a localized traumatism and transmitted by the nervous system.

Balsam, catnip, chamomile, hop, Indian tobacco, linden, meadowsweet, mint, motherwort, mugwort, shepherd's purse, St. John's wort, valerian, willow.

Antitoxic: Helps the organism eliminate and neutralize all kinds of toxic substances.

Agrimony, bearberry, burdock, chickweed, comfrey, common elder, common speedwell, dandelion, ground ivy, horseradish, Indian tobacco, nettle, oak, quitch grass, red clover, slippery elm, tansy, violet, watercress, wild ginger, wild pansy, woundwort, yarrow.

Appetitizer: Stimulates the appetite center in the brain and also the juices of the upper digestive tract.

Angelica, celandine, chickweed, hop, mint, mouse-eared hawkweed, mugwort, rosehip, watercress, wild ginger, wood sorrel, yarrow.

Aphrodisiac: Stimulates sexual desire by way of the endocrine, circulatory and neurological tracts.

Angelica, barberry, dandelion, chamomile, goldenrod, hop, rosehip, horseradish, juniper, mint, nettle, red clover, tansy, valerian, wild ginger, watercress, wild thyme, wood sorrel.

Astringent: Tightens and regenerates tissue, a useful function in the case of diarrhea, bleeding, enuresis or various wounds.

Agrimony, avens, bearberry, blueberry, birch, comfrey, coltsfoot, cinquefoil, horsetail, loosestrife, mugwort, mullein, oak, raspberry, strawberry, walnut, yarrow.

Balsamic: Aromatic resinous substances that disinfect and soothe the respiratory mucous membranes.

Balsam, juniper, slippery elm, walnut.

Bechic: Soothes coughing and the irritation of the respiratory tract.
Balsam, catnip, coltsfoot, comfrey, elecampane, fern, ground ivy, horse-radish, Indian tobacco, mallow, slippery elm, violet.

Bitter: A pronounced taste in the mouth. Bitter plants stimulate the production of digestive juices, promote an appetite and assist assimilation and good intestinal transit.
Dandelion, burdock, celandine, chamomile, chicory, common thistle, curled dock, goldenrod, ground ivy, Joe-pye weed, linden, mouse-eared hawkweed, mugwort, tansy, walnut, willow, yarrow.

Cardiotonic: Increases the regularity, tonus and vascularization of the heart muscle.
Barberry, Indian tobacco, horseradish, motherwort, raspberry, red clover, rosehip, shepherd's purse, watercress, willow, wild pansy, wild thyme.

Carminative: Prevents intestinal gas and encourages its expulsion.
Angelica, balsam, catnip, chicory, dandelion, juniper, mint, tansy, walnut, wild carrot, wild ginger, wild thyme.

Cathartic: Stimulates intestinal peristalsis (waves of muscle contractions) and acts as a purgative.
Balsam, barberry, bearbind, celandine, chamomile, chicory, chokecherry, dandelion, Joe-pye weed, mallow, mint, violet.

Cholagogue: Stimulates liver function and helps evacuate bile.
Agrimony, balsam, barberry, bedstraw, chamomile, celandine, chicory, coltsfoot, dandelion, goldenrod, mint, mouse-eared hawkweed, mugwort, quitch grass, tansy, watercress, yarrow.

Choleretic: Stimulates biliary secretions in the intestinal tracts.
Barberry, celandine, chamomile, chicory, dandelion, meadowsweet, mint, tansy, yarrow.

Cholesterolytic: Partially or totally dissolves aggregates of bad cholesterol (LDL).
Barberry, bedstraw, celandine, chickweed, common speedwell, dande-

lion, elecampane, mint, mouse-eared hawkweed, mugwort, red clover, watercress, yarrow, .

Depurative: Purifies the body by facilitating the elimination of waste or organic toxins, generally from the lymph, skin and blood.
Ash, avens, barberry, birch, burdock, chickweed, common elder, curled dock, figwort, ground ivy, maidenhair fern, mint, mugwort, quitch grass, raspberry, red clover, rosehip, strawberry, violet, watercress, wild pansy, wild thyme.

Digestive: Aids the entire digestive process.
Angelica, carrot, catnip, celandine, chamomile, chicory, hop, juniper, mint, mugwort, raspberry, slippery elm, tansy, walnut, wild thyme, yarrow.

Dissolvent: Prevents the formation of and helps dissolve calculi, lithiases, biliary or kidney stones.
For the gallbladder: agrimony, barberry, celandine, chamomile, dandelion, hop, mint, mouse-eared hawkweed, quitch grass, tansy, yarrow.
For the kidneys and bladder: bearberry, bedstraw, birch, chickweed, chicory, chokecherry, dandelion, goldenrod, hop, horsetail, Joe-pye weed, juniper, linden, meadowsweet, mouse-eared hawkweed, nettle, quitch grass, red clover, rosehip, willow.

Diuretic: Promotes urination.
Angelica, avens, bearberry, bedstraw, birch, chicory, chokecherry, common elder, common speedwell, dandelion, goldenrod, ground ivy, horsetail, Joe-pye weed, linden, meadowsweet, mouse-eared hawkweed, nettle, quitch grass, rosehip, wild thyme.

Emetic: Induces vomiting.
celandine, chamomile, Indian tobacco, violet, wild ginger.

Emmenagogue: Induces and regulates menstruation.
Angelica, celandine, chamomile, motherwort, mugwort, pennyroyal, raspberry, red clover, skullcap, tansy.

Emollient: Soothes, calms and relaxes tissues.

Balsam, chamomile, chickweed, common elder, mallow, mullein, St. John's wort, pansy, plantain, violet.

Expectorant: Provokes the expulsion of phlegm or mucus obstructing the respiratory tract.

Balsam, chokecherry, coltsfoot, comfrey, elecampane, ground ivy, horseradish, maidenhair fern, mullein, plantain, violet, watercress.

Febrifuge: Fights fever symptoms.

Avens, catnip, chamomile, chickweed, dandelion, ground ivy, Joe-pye weed, linden, pansy, rosehip, valerian, yarrow.

Fungicide: Destroys fungi and yeasts (internal and external).

Balsam, celandine, elecampane, figwort, ground ivy, mugwort, pennyroyal, tansy, valerian, walnut, yarrow.

Galactagogue or galactogen: Increases milk secretion.

alfalfa, clover, grape, mallow, raspberry, wild carrot.

Hemostatic: Stops hemorrhaging.

Avens, coltsfoot, comfrey, common speedwell, loosestrife, plantain, shepherd's purse, yarrow.

Hypertensive: Increases blood pressure.

Angelica, Indian tobacco, mint, mugwort, tansy, wild thyme.

Hypnotic: Promotes sleep.

Catnip, hawthorn, hop, Indian tobacco, Labrador tea, lettuce, linden, valerian.

Hypoglycemic: Lowers blood sugar.

Agrimony, barberry, burdock, chamomile, dandelion, elecampane, hawthorn, nettle, rosehip, walnut.

Hypotensive: Reduces blood pressure.

Catnip, chamomile, hawthorn, inden, St. John's wort, lvalerian.

Immunostimulant: Activates the immune system.

Ash, balsam, barberry, bedstraw, burdock, catnip, common elder, clover, curled dock, dandelion, elecampane, goldenrod, ground ivy, horseradish, Indian tobacco, Joe-pye weed, juniper, maidenhair fern, mint, mugwort, nettle, oak, plantain, quitch grass, rosehip, St. John's wort, violet, watercress, yarrow.

Laxative: Aids the elimination of waste through the intestines.
Balsam, barberry, bearbind, chamomile, chicory, curled dock, dandelion, Joe-pye weed, mallow, mint, plantain, quitch grass, tansy, violet.

Lipotropic: Emulsifies and aids elimination of fatty waste from the blood and tissues.
Barberry, burdock, celandine, chamomile, chickweed, clover, curled dock, goldenrod, mint, mugwort, mouse-eared hawkweed, pansy, wild ginger, wild thyme, yarrow.

Mucilaginous: Has the property of swelling in water and of repairing the mucous membranes.
Balsam, kelp, mallow, slippery elm.

Mucolytic: Dissolves mucus, especially that of the mucous membranes in the digestive and respiratory tracts.
Angelica, balsam, bedstraw, chamomile, celandine, clover, comfrey, common elder, elecampane, ground ivy, horseradish, Indian tobacco, Joe-pye weed, linden, maidenhair fern, mallow, mint, mullein, nettle, rosehip, wild thyme, violet.

Narcotic: Promotes sleep.
Catnip, hop, linden, St. John's wort, valerian.

Ophthalmic: Cures and cleanses the eyes.
Agrimony, avens, blueberry, celandine, chamomile, cinquefoil, common speedwell, eyebright, fern, ground ivy, linden, loosestrife, mallow, mugwort, pansy, plantain, raspberry, St. John's wort, violet, watercress.

Parasiticide: Eliminates parasites (external or internal).
Balsam, celandine, elecampane, figwort, mugwort, pennyroyal, tansy, valerian, walnut, wild thyme.

Pectoral: Soothes problems of the respiratory system.
Balsam, coltsfoot, comfrey, common elder, elecampane, horseradish, kelp, mallow, mullein, plantain, slippery elm, violet, woundwort.

Pro-estrogenic: Contributes to the production of estrogen.
Alfalfa, angelica, clover, hop, motherwort, mugwort, pennyroyal, wild thyme.

Pro-progesteronic: Contributes to the production of progesterone.
Evening primrose, meadowsweet, pansy, walnut, yarrow.

Regenerating or vulnerary: Aids in the repair of tissues in the case of lesions.
Agrimony, avens, birch, cinquefoil, coltsfoot, comfrey, figwort, horsetail, Joe-pye weed, loosestrife, mallow, mugwort, mullein, oak, pansy, plantain, strawberry, violet, woundwort, yarrow.

Resolvent: Helps get rid of engorgement or inflammatory swelling without suppuration.
Agrimony, balsam, burdock, chickweed, coltsfoot, comfrey, figwort, ground ivy, plantain, quitch grass, violet, woundwort.

Rubefacient: Produces temporary congestion (by topical application on the skin) which helps expel toxins, e.g., in the case of a boil.
Chickweed, comfrey, elecampane, horseradish, Indian tobacco, watercress, wood sorrel, wild ginger.

Sedative: Soothes pain and moderates the exaggerated functional activity of an organ.
Catnip, Indian tobacco, valerian, willow.

Sternutatory: Provokes sneezing (if breathed in through the nose) and thereby releases mucus.
Elecampane, ground ivy, horseradish, Indian tobacco, wild ginger.

Stomachic: Stimulates the appetite, fortifies the stomach and helps with gastric digestion.
Alfalfa, angelica, catnip, celandine, chamomile, comfrey, juniper, kelp, mint, pansy, walnut, wild carrot, wild ginger, wild thyme.

Sudorific: Provokes sweating in the case of fever or water retention.
Ash, birch, chamomile, common elder, hop, horseradish, Joe-pye weed, linden, meadowsweet, mouse-eared hawkweed, red clover, rosehip, violet, wild thyme.

Thyroid tonic: Stimulates the functioning of the thyroid.
Celandine, elecampane, ground ivy, horseradish, kelp, nettle, oak, wild thyme.

Tonic: Fortifies the organs and tissues, renews energy over the long term.
Balsam, clover, dandelion, ground ivy, horseradish, kelp, mint, mugwort, nettle, watercress, wild thyme, yarrow.

Vasodilator: Promotes the dilation of blood vessels.
Chickweed, hawthorn, horseradish, Indian tobacco, motherwort, pansy, raspberry, rosehip, watercress, wild thyme.

Vermifuge: Destroys and expels intestinal worms.
Elecampane, male fern, mugwort, valerian, walnut, figwort, wild thyme.

Vulnerary: Cures wounds.
Agrimony, balsam, bedstraw, chamomile, comfrey, common speedwell, evening primrose, figwort, Joe-pye weed, loosestrife, mallow, mullein, plantain, St. John's wort, violet, wild thyme, yarrow.

CHAPTER 7

Toxic Plants

Each substance can be a poison or medicine.
It all depends on the amount administered.
—PARACELSUS, *DE MODO PHARMACANDI*

he subject of the toxicity of medicinal plants is very topical and at the center of passionate debate. Because of this concern, many healers have been treated like poisoners or witches. Today, to protect its citizens, governments have prepared a list, sometimes arbitrary, of the plants they consider to be dangerous, prohibiting their cultivation, processing and sale.

It is certainly useful to clearly identify the most dangerous plants and to avoid contact with them or to avoid using them, but it is important to remember that they merit our respect and the right to live. Indeed, they often contain highly concentrated active principles that are sometimes useful in small doses for an expert in pharmacognosy (science of plants and their medicinal uses).

If you are not qualified, be content to admire them, to greet them when passing, and to warn your children of the potential danger they represent.

After you receive a little practical advice on how to treat poisoning, you will find a description of the 10 most toxic plants common to both Europe and Canada.

First aid in the case of plant poisoning

If a poisonous plant has been ingested, call the Poison Center. If urgent, induce vomiting using one of the following plants: wild ginger, chamomile, oak or violet roots.

Prepare an infusion: 2 T in 1 cup (250 ml) water. Drink the hot and concentrated liquid.

Following are 10 of the most toxic wild plants that are common to northern Europe and North America.

ic Plants • Toxic Plants • Toxic Plants • Toxic Plants • Toxic Plants • Toxic Plants • Toxic Plants • Toxic Plants • Toxic Plants • Toxic Plants • Toxic
ic Plants • Toxic Plants • Toxic Plants • Toxic Plants • Toxic Plants • Toxic Plants • Toxic Plants • Toxic Plants • Toxic Plants • Toxic Plants • Toxic
ic Plants • Toxic Plants • Toxic Plants • Toxic Plants • Toxic Plants • Toxic Plants • Toxic Plants • Toxic Plants • Toxic Plants • Toxic Plants • Toxic
ic Plants • Toxic Plants • Toxic Plants • Toxic Plants • Toxic Plants • Toxic Plants • Toxic Plants • Toxic Plants • Toxic Plants • Toxic Plants • Toxic
ic Plants • Toxic Plants • Toxic Plants • Toxic Plants • Toxic Plants • Toxic Plants • Toxic Plants • Toxic Plants • Toxic Plants • Toxic Plants • Toxic
ic Plants • Toxic Plants • Toxic Plants • Toxic P

CLIMBING NIGHTSHADE

SOLANACEAE FAMILY

Latin name: *Solanum dulcamara*

Common name: bittersweet

This climbing perennial can be found in moist areas, on the edge of forests and alongside running water. The leaves are oval; the mauve, star-shaped flowers with the prominent yellow center grow beside the red ovoid berries. Nightshade contains numbing alkaloids. The fruit is very purgative. In the past, small doses of nightshade were taken to combat asthma, skin disorders and rheumatism. Today, it is used solely for homeopathic purposes.

279

ic Plants • Toxic Plants • Toxic Plants • Toxic Plants • Toxic Plants • Toxic Plants • Toxic Plants • Toxic Plants • Toxic Plants • Toxic Plants • Toxic
ic Plants • Toxic Plants • Toxic Plants • Toxic Plants • Toxic Plants • Toxic Plants • Toxic Plants • Toxic Plants • Toxic Plants • Toxic Plants • Toxic
ic Plants • Toxic Plants • Toxic Plants • Toxic Plants • Toxic Plants • Toxic Plants • Toxic Plants • Toxic Plants • Toxic Plants • Toxic Plants • Toxic
ic Plants • Toxic Plants • Toxic Plants • Toxic Plants • Toxic Plants • Toxic Plants • Toxic Plants • Toxic Plants • Toxic Plants • Toxic Plants • Toxic
ic Plants • Toxic Plants • Toxic Plants • Toxic Plants • Toxic Plants • Toxic Plants • Toxic Plants • Toxic Plants • Toxic Plants • Toxic Plants • Toxic
ic Plants • Toxic Plants • Toxic Plants • Toxic Plants • Toxic Plants • Toxic Plants • Toxic Plants • Toxic Plants • Toxic Plants • Toxic Plants • Toxic

DATURA

SOLANACEAE FAMILY

Latin name: *Datura stramonium*

Common name: thornapple

*O*riginally from South America, datura now grows around the world. It prefers rubble and embankments, and escapes from gardens where it is grown as an ornamental plant. A hardy annual 20 in to 3.3 ft (50 cm to 1 m) high, it emits an acrid and sulphurous scent. The leaves are large, oval and roughly dentated. The large white trumpet-shaped flowers eventually become the ovoid and thorny fruit. The seeds are the most dangerous part of the plant: they are saturated in hypnotic and stupefying substances. They are used in homeopathy to treat asthma and Parkinson's disease, in particular because of the high concentration of active principles.

280

Plants • Toxic Plants • Toxic Plants • Toxic Plants • Toxic Plants • Toxic Plants • Toxic Plants • Toxic Plants • Toxic Plants • Toxic Plants • Toxic Plants • Toxic P
Plants • Toxic Plants • Toxic Plants • Toxic Plants • Toxic Plants • Toxic Plants • Toxic Plants • Toxic Plants • Toxic Plants • Toxic Plants • Toxic Plants • Toxic P
Plants • Toxic Plants • Toxic Plants • Toxic Plants • Toxic Plants • Toxic Plants • Toxic Plants • Toxic Plants • Toxic Plants • Toxic Plants • Toxic Plants • Toxic P
Plants • Toxic Plants • Toxic Plants • Toxic Plants • Toxic Plants • Toxic Plants • Toxic Plants • Toxic Plants • Toxic Plants • Toxic Plants • Toxic Plants • Toxic P
Plants • Toxic Plants • Toxic Plants • Toxic Plants • Toxic Plants • Toxic Plants • Toxic Plants • Toxic Plants • Toxic Plants • Toxic Plants • Toxic Plants • Toxic P
Plants • Toxic Plants • To

HEMLOCK OR SPOTTED WATER HEMLOCK

APIACEAE FAMILY

Latin name: *Cicuta maculata*

Common names: poison hemlock, water hemlock

*H*emlock can be found in moist areas. It resembles wild carrot: the leaves are divided into 3 leaflets and its beige-colored umbels, into umbellets. The stem is stained with purple lines. The entire plant is saturated in cicutoxins. This substance is deadly, even in small doses. It leads to horrible convulsions, and paralyzes the sensory nerves and respiratory muscles slowly but surely, as Plato mentions in his description of the death of Socrates. Condemned to death by the popular Athenian court in 399 B.C., he quietly continued philosophizing even after having drunk the poison, requesting that smiling faces surround him. Once his legs became paralyzed, he was forced to lie down, and then his arms swelled. Once his heart and respiratory muscles were affected, he perished.

281

ic Plants • Toxic Plants • Toxic Plants • Toxic Plants • Toxic Plants • Toxic Plants • Toxic Plants • Toxic Plants • Toxic Plants • Toxic Plants • Toxic Plants • Toxic
ic Plants • Toxic Plants • Toxic Plants • Toxic Plants • Toxic Plants • Toxic Plants • Toxic Plants • Toxic Plants • Toxic Plants • Toxic Plants • Toxic Plants • Toxic
ic Plants • Toxic Plants • Toxic Plants • Toxic Plants • Toxic Plants • Toxic Plants • Toxic Plants • Toxic Plants • Toxic Plants • Toxic Plants • Toxic Plants • Toxic
ic Plants • Toxic Plants • Toxic Plants • Toxic Plants • Toxic Plants • Toxic Plants • Toxic Plants • Toxic Plants • Toxic Plants • Toxic Plants • Toxic Plants • Toxic
ic Plants • Toxic Plants • Toxic Plants • Toxic Plants • Toxic Plants • Toxic Plants • Toxic Plants • Toxic Plants • Toxic Plants • Toxic Plants • Toxic

IRIS

IRIDACEAE FAMILY

Latin name: *Iris versicolor*

Common name: blue flag

𝒥ris grows in moist areas and swamps, and, of course, in our gardens. Emblem of the French royal family since King Clovis, it became the heraldic symbol of Quebec. This pretty royal blue flower, variegated with yellow, black and white, consists of 3 stylized and curved petals. The leaves are long, basal and pointy. The whitish and fleshy roots irritate the liver, pancreas and intestines. Its powder long served as a cosmetic, combined with rice powder and cicatrizing powder.

282

Plants • Toxic Plants • Toxic Plants • Toxic Plants • Toxic Plants • Toxic Plants • Toxic Plants • Toxic Plants • Toxic Plants • Toxic Plants • Toxic
Plants • Toxic Plants • Toxic Plants • Toxic Plants • Toxic Plants • Toxic Plants • Toxic Plants • Toxic Plants • Toxic Plants • Toxic Plants • Toxic P
Plants • Toxic Plants • Toxic Plants • Toxic Plants • Toxic Plants • Toxic Plants • Toxic Plants • Toxic Plants • Toxic Plants • Toxic Plants • Toxic P
Plants • Toxic Plants • Toxic Plants • Toxic Plants • Toxic Plants • Toxic Plants • Toxic Plants • Toxic Plants • Toxic Plants • Toxic Plants • Toxic P
Plants • Toxic Plants • Toxic Plants • Toxic Plants • Toxic Plants • Toxic Plants • Toxic Plants • Toxic Plants • Toxic Plants • Toxic P

JACK-IN-THE-PULPIT

ARACEAE FAMILY

Latin name: *Arum trifolium*

Common names: Devil's ear, dragon root, memory root

$\mathcal{J}$ack-in-the-pulpit prefers deciduous forests. Its dark red floral spike with white stripes blooms in May and acts as a shelter for large insects and a tomb for small ones. All the parts of the plant (flowers, leaves, fruit and root) contain thick crystals of highly toxic calcium oxalate. In the past, it was used to treat asthma, syphilis and ringworm.

283

Toxic Plants • Toxic Plants • Toxic Plants • Toxic Plants • Toxic Plants • Toxic Plants • Toxic Plants • Toxic Plants • Toxic Plants • Toxic Plants • Toxic
Plants • Toxic Plants • Toxic Plants • Toxic Plants • Toxic Plants • Toxic Plants • Toxic Plants • Toxic Plants • Toxic Plants • Toxic Plants • Toxic
Plants • Toxic Plants • Toxic Plants • Toxic Plants • Toxic Plants • Toxic Plants • Toxic Plants • Toxic Plants • Toxic Plants • Toxic Plants • Toxic
Plants • Toxic Plants • Toxic Plants • Toxic Plants • Toxic Plants • Toxic Plants • Toxic Plants • Toxic Plants • Toxic Plants • Toxic Plants • Toxic
Plants • Toxic Plants • Toxic Plants • Toxic Plants • Toxic Plan Toxic Plants • Toxic Plants • Toxic Plants • Toxic Plants • Toxic

PARSNIP

APIACEAE FAMILY

Latin name: *Pastinacca sativa*

Common name: wild parsnip

Parsnip lives in ditches, on the banks of rivers and streams. This plant is the only yellow northern umbelliferous biennial. It can be seen from afar when it blooms, around the time of the feast of St. John, with its high, strong and ridged stems, and its great yellow umbels. The entire plant contains photosensitive psoralens that provoke brown spots on the skin: exposed to the sun, the spots become permanent.

284

c Plants • Toxic Plants • Toxic Plants • Toxic Plants • Toxic Plants • Toxic Plants • Toxic Plants • Toxic Plants • Toxic Plants • Toxic Plants • Toxic F
c Plants • Toxic Plants • Toxic Plants • Toxic Plants • Toxic Plants • Toxic Plants • Toxic Plants • Toxic Plants • Toxic Plants • Toxic Plants • Toxic F
c Plants • Toxic Plants • Toxic Plants • Toxic Plants • Toxic Plants • Toxic Plants • Toxic Plants • Toxic Plants • Toxic Plants • Toxic Plants • Toxic F
c Plants • Toxic Plants • Toxic Plants • Toxic Plants • Toxic Plants • Toxic Plants • Toxic Plants • Toxic Plants • Toxic Plants • Toxic Plants • Toxic F
c Plants • Toxic Plants • Toxic Plants • Toxic Plants • Toxic P   ic Plants • Toxic Plants • Toxic Plants • Toxic Plants • Toxic F

POISON IVY

ANACARDIACEAE FAMILY

Latin name: *Toxicendron radicans*

$\mathcal{P}$oison ivy lives along paths, on vacant lots and along embankments. It is a shrub or climbing plant, characterized by the 3 leaves affixed to a long petiole. In August, it produces well-hidden whitish flowers, and then berries. Simple contact with this plant provokes an invasive suppurating dermatitis. Absorbing the plant leads to asphyxia by edema. The irritants that cause this reaction also, paradoxically, treat chronic dermatitis, as demonstrated in homeopathy.

285

c Plants • Toxic Plants • Toxic Plants • Toxic Plants • Toxic Plants • Toxic Plants • Toxic Plants • Toxic Plants • Toxic Plants • Toxic Plants • Toxic
c Plants • Toxic Plants • Toxic Plants • Toxic Plants • Toxic Plants • Toxic Plants • Toxic Plants • Toxic Plants • Toxic Plants • Toxic Plants • Toxic
c Plants • Toxic Plants • Toxic Plants • Toxic Plants • Toxic Plants • Toxic Plants • Toxic Plants • Toxic Plants • Toxic Plants • Toxic Plants • Toxic
c Plants • Toxic Plants • Toxic Plants • Toxic Plants • Toxic Plants • Toxic Plants • Toxic Plants • Toxic Plants • Toxic Plants • Toxic Plants • Toxic
c Plants • Toxic Plants • Toxic Plants • Toxic Plants • Toxic Plants • Toxic Plants • Toxic Plants • Toxic Plants • Toxic Plants • Toxic Plants • Toxic
c Plants • Toxic Plants • Toxic Plants • Toxic Plants • Toxic Plants • Toxic Plants • Toxic Plants • Toxic Plants • Toxic Plants • Toxic Plants • Toxic

TALL BUTTERCUP

RANUNCULACEAE FAMILY

Latin name: *Ranunculus sceleratus*

Common names: bachelor button, blisterwood, yellow weed

The tall buttercup loves moist, poorly drained grasslands. There are more than 275 kinds of buttercup. However, they all share deeply divided leaves and yellow, shiny flowers with 5 petals. In Sardinia, there is even a similar buttercup called sardonic and which provokes a laughing fit … among people who have eaten too much mutton from sheep that have grazed on this buttercup. The tall buttercup is light sensitive and irritating to the touch because of a substance called anemonin. North American Indians treated skin cancer (malignant wounds that would not heal) with a poultice made from this plant.

ic Plants • Toxic Plants • Toxic Plants • Toxic Plants • Toxic Plants • Toxic Plants • Toxic Plants • Toxic Plants • Toxic Plants • Toxic Plants • Toxic
ic Plants • Toxic Plants • Toxic Plants • Toxic Plants • Toxic Plants • Toxic Plants • Toxic Plants • Toxic Plants • Toxic Plants • Toxic Plants • Toxic
ic Plants • Toxic Plants • Toxic Plants • Toxic Plants • Toxic Plants • Toxic Plants • Toxic Plants • Toxic Plants • Toxic Plants • Toxic Plants • Toxic
ic Plants • Toxic Plants • Toxic Plants • Toxic Plants • Toxic Plants • Toxic Plants • Toxic Plants • Toxic Plants • Toxic Plants • Toxic Plants • Toxic
ic Plants • Toxic Plants • Toxic Plants • Toxic Plants • Toxic Plants • Toxic Plants • Toxic Plants • Toxic Plants • Toxic Plants • Toxic Plants • Toxic

TRAVELER'S JOY

RANUNCULACEAE FAMILY

Latin name: *Clematis vitalba*

Common name: virgin bower

Traveler's joy lives among hedges, along walls and on trellises. It is a perennial liana; its bark can be peeled in strips. It has creamy white flowers that grow in racemoses that flower in July. The strange fruit is shaped like a hairy spider with long, feathery styles. It used to be called the "beggar's herb," for beggars would rub their skin with this plant to provoke pustules and inspire pity. Used internally, traveler's joy induces convulsions, bloody diarrhea or vomiting because of its high alkaloid and saponin content.

287

Plants • Toxic Plants • Toxic Plants • Toxic Plants • Toxic Plants • Toxic Plants • Toxic Plants • Toxic Plants • Toxic Plants • Toxic Plants • Toxic P
Plants • Toxic Plants • Toxic Plants • Toxic Plants • Toxic Plants • Toxic Plants • Toxic Plants • Toxic Plants • Toxic Plants • Toxic Plants • Toxic P
Plants • Toxic Plants • Toxic Plants • Toxic Plants • Toxic Plants • Toxic Plants • Toxic Plants • Toxic Plants • Toxic Plants • Toxic Plants • Toxic P
Plants • Toxic Plants • Toxic Plants • Toxic Plants • Toxic Plants • Toxic Plants • Toxic Plants • Toxic Plants • Toxic Plants • Toxic Plants • Toxic P
Plants • Toxic Plants • Toxic Plants • Toxic Plants • Toxic Plants • Toxic Plants • Toxic Plants • Toxic Plants • Toxic Plants • Toxic Plants • Toxic P
Plants • Toxic Plants • Toxic Plants • Toxic Plants • Toxic Plants • Toxic Plants • Toxic Plants • Toxic Plants • Toxic Plants • Toxic Plants • Toxic P

WHITE FALSE HELLEBORE

LILIACEAE FAMILY

Latin name: *Veratrum album*

Common name: white ellebore

*H*ellebore appears in early spring on the edge of forests. Its immense, veined light green leaves are hairy underneath. The greenish-white flowers grow in panicles. The plant is saturated in irritating alkaloids that provoke a localized numbing, intense burning and severe hypotension, which can lead to coma after a dose of only 2 grams.

288

Conclusion

Everywhere tranquil nature offers its help and advice,
Sow the good grain, my child,
God will provide the sun!
—Victor de la Prade

I prepared this book while following the changing of the seasons, paying careful attention to the birth of my friends, the plants. By observing them with a telephoto lens, I was stunned and fascinated by their simple perfection. This year, as never before, I let my body and my spirit absorb the magic of the simples, the popular name given to wild medicinal plants in God's pharmacy.

Of course, I could have revealed 10 times the number of secrets told here about each plant, but this work is not directed at botanists, chemists or other specialists. I simply wrote it to teach you how to discover and recognize wild plants during your walks.

Many plant lovers will thus learn to observe a living plant in its environment and, in renewing the signatures theory, will be able to make the connection between its appearance and its virtues. They will also learn that plants can treat the spirit as well as the body.

In the expectation that you will one day attain this knowledge, I hope you will fall in love with the fabulous world of medicinal plants.

Helpful Addresses in Quebec

Académie de phytothérapie du Canada
" The only school not connected to any
business!"
5811 Christophe-Colomb Avenue
Montréal QC H2S 2G3
(514) 270-7529

Association Flora Québéca
80, Route 116
Ulverton QC J0B 2B0
Tel.: (819) 623-1729
Fax: (819) 826-3314
E-mail: floraquébéca@ireseau.com
Association established by specialists in wild
plants to protect species threatened by
human ignorance.

**École d'enseignement supérieur de
naturopathie du Québec**
1250 Rodolphe-Forget Avenue
Suite 300
Sillery QC G1S 3Y7
(418) 682-2446

Guilde des herboristes du Québec
P.O. Box 47555
Station Plateau Mont-Royal
Montréal QC H2H 2S8
(514) 990-7168
Association of Quebec herbalists: work-
shops, newspaper, conferences, directory,
references, etc.

Jardins du Grand Portage
800 Portage Road
Saint-Didace QC J0K 2G0
(450) 835-5813
Workshops on organic market,
horticultural and herb gardening.
Guided tours in the summer.

Jardin des Tournesols
22A, Les Plateaux
L'Anse-Saint-Jean QC G0V 1J0
(418) 272-3115 and 372-3115
Produces medicinal and derived plants.
Courses and training. Accommodation and
guided tours in the summer of the gardens
located on top of mountain in the magnificent Saguenay region.

Jardin O'Kelly
213 Rocheleau Road
Sutton QC J0E 2K0
(450) 538-5587
Cultivation and production of medicinal
perennial plants: a product list is available
upon request. Visit the gardens in the
summer.

La Bottine aux herbes
3778 Saint-Denis Street
Montréal QC H2W 2M1
(514) 845-1225
Shop specializing in all herbal products:
accessories, books, Quebec and organic
herbs.

291

La Clé des champs

2278 2nd Rang
Val-David QC J0T 2N0
(450) 368-9114 or 937-3900
E-mail: jardin@polyinter.com
Weekend seminars. Cultivation and
production of high-quality herbal remedies.
Workshops and guided tours of the gardens
in the summer.

L'Apothicaire

817 25th Avenue
Saint-Eustache QC J7R 4K3
(450) 491-1942 and 491-5813
Visit the medicinal plant gardens.
Production of child-care products.

Les Herbes Enchantées

2105 Roxton Road South
Roxton Pond QC J0E 1Z0
(450) 375-7678
E-mail: jfontaine@endirect.qc.ca
Small garden of varied medicinal plants
grouped according to therapeutic themes.
Workshops and guided tours arranged by
appointment.

L'Armoire aux herbes

375 Rang des Chutes
Ham-Nord QC G0P 1A0
(819) 344-2080 or 344-2002
E-mail: herbothèque@ivic.qc.ca
The most beautiful and biggest medicinal
herb garden in Quebec. High-quality correspondence courses offered. Theme workshops and guided tours offered in the
summer. Organic* medicinal plant products
available.

Librairie Biosfaire

4571 Saint-Denis Street
Montréal QC
1-800-613-3262
Fax: (514) 483-8288
Alternative bookstore with large stock of
works on holistic medicines, practical living
and spirituality.

Mikaël Zayat

121 Châteauguay Street
Bromont QC J2L 1A9
(450) 534-1671 or 534-4376
Master aromatherapist, importer and dis-
tiller of indigenous essences. Workshops
upon request; high-quality essential oils
available.

Anny Schneider, herbalist and nomadic naturopath

(450) 375-0970
E-mail: annyschneider@moncourrier.com
Nature walks arranged upon request, conferences, and consultations by appointment
in my office in Granby.

*Agricultural technique based on the philos-
ophy of Rudolf Steiner, originally from
Switzerland, which consists of adding
homeopathic concentrates, for example, to
compost. Remarkable results are achieved
(as demonstrated by the magnificent gardens grown according to the rules of this
technique). This technique is identified by
the internationally recognized acronym
"Demeter."

Helpful Addresses in France

Associations, societies, institutes

Association des consommateurs de plantes
médicinales
19, rue Milton
75000 Paris

Association Gaïa—Institut de recherche et
de formation sur les élixirs floraux
11, route Sablée
92370 Chaville
Tel : 01.43.79.90.24

Conservatoire national des plantes médici-
nales aromatiques et industrielles
Route de Nemours
Milly la Forêt
Tel : 64.98.83.77

F.N.C.P.M.A.
(Fédération nationale des coopératives de
plantes médicinales aromatiques)
Vielle route de Salon
13330 Pelisanne

Institut de recherche sur les propriétés de la
flore
Haut Ourgeas
04330 Barrime

Institut Kepler
6, avenue Georges-Clémenceau
69230 Saint-Genis Laval
Tel : 0.78.56.19.41 (magazine *Weleda 96*)

O.N.I.P.P.A.M.
(Office national Inter professionnel des
plantes à parfum, médicinales et aromatiques)
B.P. 8
04130 Voux
Tel : 92.79.34.46

Nature et progrès
Association simples (Branch focusing on
everything related to herbalism)
Céo Dubigon, Bel-air
42660 Jonzieux

L'œil ouvert
(Association of consumers of organically
grown products)
9, rue Cels
75014 Paris
Tel : 43.35.18.33

Société française de phyto-aromathérapie
19, boulevard Beauséjour
75016 Paris
Tel : 01.45.24.65.92

Société française d'ethnopharmacologie
(Traditional medicinal plants and pharmacopeia)
1, rue Récollets
57000 Metz
Tel : 03.87.76.22.00

Syndicat national de l'herboristerie
2, quai Jules-Courmont
62002 Lyons
Tel : 04.78.49.66

Groups of producers or businesses that offer organically grown plants

Biotope des Montagnes
Soudorgues
30460 Lasalle

Body Nature
79250 Les Aubiers
Flore de Saintonge
La Villedieu
17470 Aulnay

L'Herbier du Diiois
Ets Touret
26150 Die
Plantes d'Auvergne
Le Canivet
03250 Le Mayet De Montagne

Schools that offer herbalism courses

Association pour le Renouveau
De l'herboristerie
6, rue Jongkind
75015 Paris

BTS de Biotechnicien phytologue
Lycée Simone-Weil
Boulevard du Maréchal-Joffre
43000 Le Puy

L'école des plantes
5, rue du Petit-pont
75015 Paris

L'école lyonnaise des plantes médicinales
69006 Lyons

Newspapers

Médicine Naturelle et longévité
26 bis, rue Kléber
93017 Montreuil Cedex
Tel: 01.48.70.40.75
Fax: 01.48.70.40.74

Phytotherapy
Éditions Galiéna
158, rue du Dessous-des-berges
75013 Paris
Tel: 01.45.84.97.66

HELPFUL ADDRESSES IN BELGIUM

Agro-Biologie Info Conseils
Rue Wast
5974 Opprebais

Mathilde Lomed Herboriste
Aambachtenlaan 29
3030 Leuven

Denolin Herboriste
Rue de Château 47
1420 Braine l'Alleud

Pharmaflore
Rue de l'Herboristerie 40
7860 Lessines

Établissements Mercennier
Rue de la Crête 24
7880 Flobecq

Planteurs Réunis
Grand-Rue 55
7872 Acrem

Distributor of herbal products

Biover
Monnikenwerve 109B
8000 Bruges

HELPFUL ADDRESSES IN SWITZERLAND

Biomedica
18, boulevard des Philosophes
1200 Geneva, Switzerland
Tel: (22) 29.44.88
Clinic that focuses on natural therapies

J.P. Martin called Dumont
6, avenue des Communes réunies
1212 Grand Lancy, Switzerland
Tel: (022) 17.94.29.19
Fax: (022) 79.42.344
E-mail: mar-di-dum@vtx.ch
Certified herbalists, suppliers

Fondation Soleil
Dr. Christian Tal Schaller
38, chemin du Bois des Arts
1225 Switzerland
Tel: 19.41.22.48.96.76
Slogan: "Good health is learned!"
Publishes excellent books on health

Pharmacie Conod
11, rue Pichau
Lausanne, Switzerland
Tel: (021) 22.75.04

Helpful Addresses in Canada

Herbs related Associations:

Ontario Herbalists Association
RR1, Port Burwell, Ontario N0J 1T0
www.herbalists.on.ca
cjh@herbalists.on.ca

Canadian Association of Herbal
Practitioners
West 4th Avenue, Vancouver, BC V6J 1M2

Canadian Herb Society
5251 Oak Street, Vancouver, BC V6M 4H1
www.herbsociety.ca

La Guilde des Herboristes du Québec
CP 47555 Comptoir postal Plateau Mont-
Royal Montréal Québec H2H 2S8
Tel: 514 990-7168
e-mail: guildherboriste@hotmail.com
www.iquebec.com /guildedesherboristes

Saskatchewan Herb and Spice Association
Box 124, Sintaluta,
Saskatchewan, S0G 4N0
Fax: 1-306 727-226
e-mail: g.Musings@dlcwest.com
www.saskherbspice.org/

Schools:

Dominion Herbal College
7527 Kingsway, Burnaby, BC V3N 3C1
www.dominionherbal.com
e-mail: herbal@uniserve.com

Mohawk-Macmaster Institute for Applied
Health Sciences
1400 Main Street West, Hamilton ON
L8S 1C7
www.mohawk.on.ca

Wild Rose College of Natural Healing
1220 Kensington Road, Calgary T2N 3P5
www.wrc.net

Douglas College
PO Box 2503,
New Westminster, BC V3L 5B2

University of Saskatchewan Herb Research
Program
51 Campus Drive,
Saskatoon, SK S7N 5A8

West Coast College of Complementary
Health Care 6th floor, Spencer Building,
Harbour Center,
555 West Hastings Street
Vancouver BC V6B 4N6

Canadian College of Naturopathic Medicine
1255 Sheppard Avenue East,
Toronto ON M2K 1E2
Tel: 416 498-1255
e-mail: info@ccnm.edu

Herbalism related research sites in North America

American Botanical Council:
www.herbalgram.org

Herb Research Foundation:
www.herbs .org

US Food and Drug Administration
www.fda.org

National Institute of Health office of
Alternative Medicine: altmed.od.nih.gov

Health Canada Natural Health Products:
www.hc-sc.gc.ca/healthcare/cahc/
index.htlm

Richters Herb specialist:
httpp; //www.richters.com

The alternative Medicine Home Page :
http;/www.pitt.edu/-cbw/alt.html

Ethno medicinals http//.walden.mo.net/-
tonytork/

Healthweb; http :
//www.healthweb.com/linksherbs.htlm

Herbal Hall:
http;//www.herb.com/herbal.htm :Herb
Net http //: wwwherbnet.com
Dr Dukes Phytochemical and
Ethnobotanical Database : http://www.ars-
grin.gov/duke/

Michael Tierra 's Planet Herbs site:
http// :www.planetherbs .com

Michael Moore's herbal treasure house:
http / www.rt66.com/hbmoore.com.
homepage.htlm

University of Washington medicinal herb
garden; http://www.nnlm.nlm.nih.gov/
pnr/uwnhg/

**American Herb Producers and
Distributors :**

Avena Botanicals, Box 365,
West Rockport, ME 04865

Frontier Cooperative Herbs 3021
78th Street, PO Box 299,
Norway IA 52 318
www.frontierherb.com

Gaia Herbs: 62, Littleton Road
Harvard MASS 01 451

Jeanne Rose's Herbal Products
219 Carl Street, San Francisco CA 94117

Sage Mountain Herb Products
P.O. Box 240, East Barre, Vermont 05 649

Bibliography

French titles

Azoulay, David. *Guide de santé pour les plantes*. [Health Guide to Plants]. Montreal: Quebec-Livres, 1996.

Boudreault, Michel. *Guide pratique des plantes médicinales du Québec*. [Practical Guide to the Medicinal Plants of Quebec]. La Prairie: Éditions Broquet, 1983.

Braine, Arlette. *Des plantes pour tous les jours*. [Plants for Everyday]. London: Presse Pocket, 1993.

Chevalier, Andrew. *Encyclopédie des plantes médicinales*. Encyclopedia of Medicinal Plants. Montreal: Sélection du Reader's Digest, 1997.

Chiej, Roberto. *Les plantes médicinales*. [Medicinal Plants]. Paris: Solar, 1982.

Debuigne, Gérard. *Dictionnaire des plantes qui guérissent*. Larousse Book of Plants That Heal. Paris: Larousse, 1972.

Golbert, Guy. *Guide des plantes remèdes*. [Guide to Plant Remedies]. Paris: Éditions du Jour, 1973.

Gurudas. *Élixir floraux et médecine vibratoire*. [Floral Elixirs and Vibration Medicine]. Grenoble: Le Souffle d'or, 1987.

Hilaire, Christiane. *Les Plantes qui guérissent de A à Z*. [Plants That Heal from A to Z]. Lyons: L'Ami des Jardins, vol. 1, 1973, vol. 2, 1975.

Howard, A.B. *Les Extraits d'herbes*. [Herbal Extracts]. Saint-Félicien: Éditions La bécassine bleue, 1984.

Laberge, Danièle. *Le Guide santé de votre armoire aux herbes*. [The Health Guide to Your Herb Medicine Cabinet]. Ham-Nord: L'Armoire aux herbes, 1994.

Laberge, Danièle et al. *Le Cours par correspondance Herbart*. [The Herbart Correspondence Course]. Ham-Nord: L'Herbothèque, 1995.

Lacoursière, Estelle, Julie Therrien and Michel Sokolyk. *Fleurs sauvages du Québec*. [Wild Flowers of Quebec]. Montreal: Les Éditions de l'Homme, 1998.

Lanthier, Aldéi. *Les Plantes curatives*. [Curative Plants]. Montreal: Éditions de mon pays, 1981.

Lequenne, Fernand. *Le Jardin de santé*. [The Garden of Health]. Les Hautes Plaines de Mane: Marabout Service, 1972.

Les Guides Fleurbec: Groupe Fleurbec.
- Plantes sauvages comestibles. [Edible Wild Plants]. 1981.
- Plantes sauvages des villes et des champs. [Wild Plants Around Cities and Fields]. Vol. 1, 1978, vol. 2, 1983.
- Plantes sauvages du bord de la mer. [Coastal Wild Plants]. 1985.
- Plantes sauvages printanières. [Wild Spring Plants]. 1988.

Magrini, Gigliola. *Les Plantes et la santé*. [Plants and Health]. Paris: Éditions Atlas, 1978.

Manta, Daniel and Diego Semolli. *Nos amies les plantes*. [Our Friends, the Plants]. Geneva: Éditions Famot, 1977.

Marie-Victorin, Brother. *La Flore laurentienne*. [Laurentian Flora]. Montreal: Presses de l'Université de Montréal, 1964.

Mességué, Maurice. *Mon herbier de santé*. [My Health Herbal]. Paris: Le Livre de poche, 1975.

Millanvoye, Georges. *Mini-encyclopédie des médicines naturelles*. [Mini-encyclopedia of Natural Medicine]. Paris: France Loisirs, 1986.

Nigelle, Éric. *Joie et santé par les fleurs et le miel*. [Joy and Health Through Flowers and Honey]. Aubenas: La Diffusion nouvelle du livre, 1968.

Palaiseul, Jean. *Nos grands-mères savaient*. [Our Grandmothers Knew]. Paris: Robert Laffont, 1972.

Paschtschenko, Paulia. *La Guérison par les plantes selon les Znakhari*. [Healing with Plants According to the Znakhari]. Saint-Laurent: Éditions du Trécarré, 1991.

Provost, Marie. *Les Plantes qui guérissent*. [Plants That Heal]. Saint-Augustin de Portneuf: Bibliothèque Québécoise, 1991.

Rocher, Yves. *Mieux vivre par les plantes*. [Living Better Through Plants]. Paris: Hachette, 1977.

Schauenberg, Paul. *Guide des plantes médicinales*. [Guide to Medicinal Plants]. Neuchâtel: Delachaux et Niestlé, 1969.

Schneider, Anny. *La Pharmacie verte*. [The Green Pharmacy]. Montréal: Les Éditions de l'Homme, 1997.

Valnet, Jean. *Phytothérapie*. [Phytotherapy]. Paris: Maloine, 1983.

Vigneau, Christiane. *Plantes médicinales*. [Medicinal Plants]. Lyon: Éditions Masson, 1985.

English Titles

Beyerl, Paul. *The Master Book of Herbalism*. Custer: Phoenix Publishing, 1996.

Castleman. Michael. *The Healing Herbs*. New York: Bantam Books, 1995.

Foster, Steven and James A. Duke. *Eastern and Central Medicinal Plants*. New York: Houghton Mifflin, 1990.

Gerard, John. *Gerard's Herbal*. London: Senate, 1994.

Grieve, Maud. *A Modern Herbal*. New York: Dorset Press, 1992.

Hutchens, Alma R. *Handbook of Native American Herbs*. Boston: Shambhala, 1992.

Hutchens, Alma R. *Indian Herbology of North America*. Boston: Shambhala, 1991.

Kloss, Jethro. *Back to Eden*. Loma Linda (USA): [n.p.], 1982.

Lust, John. *The Herb Book*. New York: Bantam Books, 1974.

Millspaugh, Charles F. *American Medicinal Plants*. New York: Dover Publications, 1974.

Murray, Michael T. *The Healing Power of Herbs*. Roklin: Prima Publishing, 1995.

Polunin, Miriam and Christopher Robbins. *The Natural Pharmacy*. Vancouver: Raincoast Books, 1994.

Royal, Penny C. *Herbally Yours*. Payson: Sound Nutrition, 1979.

Tierra, Michael. *The Way of Herbs*. New York: Pocket Books, 1990.

Tyler, Varro E. *A Honest Herbal*. New York: Pharmaceutical Product Press, 1993.

Tyler, Varro E. *Herbs of Choice*. New York: Pharmaceutical Product Press, 1994.

Weed, Susun. *Healing Wise*. New York: Ash Tree Publishing, 1989.

Weiss, Rudolf Fritz. *Herbal Medicine*. Portland: Medicina Biologica, 1988.

German Titles

Kaiser, Josef H. *Das grosse Kneipp Hausbuch*. [The Great Kneipp Book for the Home]. München: Knaur, 1975.

Podlech, Dieter. *Heilpflanzen*. [Healing Plants]. München: Gräfe und Unzer, 1989.

Spanish Titles

Magaña, Rafael Hernandez and Mireya Gally-Jorda. *Plantas Medicinales*. [Medicinal Plants]. Mexico: Arbol Editorial, 1991.

Index

301